Executive Coaching

Executive Coaching

The Essential Guide for Mental Health Professionals

LEN SPERRY, M.D., PH.D.

Published in 2004 by
Brunner-Routledge
270 Madison Avenue
New York, NY 10016
www.brunner-routledge.com

Published in Great Britain by
Brunner-Routledge
27 Church Road
Hove, East Sussex
BN3 2FA
www.brunner-routledge.co.uk

Brunner-Routledge is an imprint of the Taylor & Francis Group.
Printed in the United States of America on acid-free paper.

10 9 8 7 6 5 4 3 2 1

Library of Congress Cataloging-in-Publication Data

Sperry, Len.
Executive coaching: the essential guide for mental health professionals/Len Sperry.
p. cm.
Includes bibliographical references and index.
ISBN 0-415-94613-1 (hardback: alk. paper)
1. Executive coaching. 2. Executives—Training of. 3. Mental health personnel. I. Title.

HD30. 4.S67 2004
658.4'07154 — dc22 2004006674

Contents

Foreword

In 1953, Dr. William C. Menninger, who had been chief of U.S. Army psychiatry during World War II, and was then back in the management of the Menninger Foundation, asked me to take on a novel project. As a psychiatrist he had spent his professional life treating mentally ill people and while in the Army he managed the entire military service for treating soldiers who became mentally ill. He came away from that experience with a feeling that something ought to be done for keeping well people well. For the 3 years prior, I had been heavily involved in the reform of the Kansas State Hospital System, which required work with the public and the Kansas legislature. Presumably, therefore, I knew something about dealing with the public, which few of my clinical colleagues did, and therefore I was the logical candidate to undertake this new project. Neither he nor I knew anything about *prevention* of mental illness, nor did we know where to begin. Nevertheless, the task was in my hands.

If one were to develop a program for keeping well people functioning well, obviously that was a public health task. Obviously also, it could best be accomplished through already organized groups of adults in institutional forums that were central to their lives. Almost by definition, that meant working with organizations where people were employed. Work was central to the lives of most adults, and how organizations were managed had a significant effect on how people felt about themselves, their work, and their lives.

I undertook a 50,000 mile trip around the country, visiting large corporations and university departments of psychology and psychiatry. I interviewed personnel executives, industrial physicians, industrial psychologists, those few psychiatrists who worked in industrial medical departments, labor leaders, and others who I thought could shed some light on problems and practices in organizations that might have some effect on mental health.

I came away from that experience disappointed to learn that what we thought we had to know about people in order to treat them when they became mentally ill was almost totally unknown in management. Even large business organizations that were well respected for their management practices did not seem to have any significant awareness of what went on in people's heads. Something had to be done to help managements develop such an understanding.

With Dr. Menninger's support and that of the Rockefeller Brothers Fund, I created the Division of Industrial Mental Health at the Menninger Foundation. The first project I undertook was a series of seminars for executives and industrial physicians on psychoanalytic theory applied to management problems. Each of the executives who took part in these week-long sessions presented a case problem about somebody with whom he or she worked that was discussed in a small seven-person group, each group led by a psychologist or psychiatrist. In addition to the lectures and small group discussions, each participant had a personal interview with his or her group leader. That interview was devoted to whatever issues the participant wanted to raise. The issues ranged from career problems to family conflicts to managing transitions to making use of local clinical resources. In the seminars for physicians in industry, the participants interviewed patients in local mental health clinics under the guidance of psychiatrists on those staffs. For many, it was the first time they had ever talked with a psychologist or psychiatrist. Some were struggling with problems at work or in their families and they needed professional help and were referred to local sources of that help.

The seminars proved to be helpful and popular. However, in them we were bringing to the participants knowledge developed from clinical practice. We really didn't know very much about what went on within business organizations. To cope with that lack of understanding, with two colleagues, a sociologist and a psychiatrist, I undertook a study in the Kansas Power and Light Company. We interviewed 840 employees over two-thirds of Kansas. We talked with them in their offices, rode with them in their trucks, sat on piles of dirt when they were digging trenches, and once were in a boat in the middle of the Kansas River when a gas pipeline burst. We carried our lunchboxes with us and ate with them in the field. We wore our safety helmets as they did. When it was cold in the field, we shivered with them. In short, we were deeply immersed in the organization and saw firsthand the problems of people at work and the styles of management under which they did their tasks.

That experience gave us firsthand knowledge about the problems of people at work, including their exposure to the elements, to various managerial practices, to the dangers many of them confronted daily, even in the electric generating power plants where turning the wrong valve could blow the place up. We learned much that was not in the books and had firsthand knowledge which we could then transmit in seminars, lectures, and books.

In the seminar cases and in the interviews with the participants, in effect we were executive coaches. It took another 45 years before executive coaching became recognized as a professional practice.

Now executive coaching has become a fad. Almost everybody and his brother and sister have become an executive coach. Although there are many disciplines related to management practice, and experts in those disciplines are legitimate coaches about those specialties, many who hold themselves out to be executive coaches are guided only by their good intentions. Although now there is a rapidly developing psychological literature on executive coaching, and that topic is extensively discussed in professional articles, books, symposia, and lectures, not many of the psychologists who offer themselves as executive coaches are clinically trained. Some have had long experience in organizations. Some have had training in counseling. Some have had no formal psychological training, but have developed a body of insights and experience that are particularly helpful. But those without clinical training will have a more difficult time of trying to coach those who are narcissistic, rigidly overcontrolling, manipulative, depressed, or crippled by feelings of inadequacy.

Clinicians who have the professional skills and competence to deal with character problems usually have had little experience with managements, managerial practices, career trajectories, mergers and acquisitions, downsizing, financial crises, or organizational politics. Although many clinicians should be and could be good executive coaches, to do so they should become knowledgeable about organizational cultures and practices, and the wide range of coaching problems they will encounter. There aren't many guides for that transition.

The need for such guidance is the task that Len Sperry addresses in this book. He brings long clinical experience with the problems of people in organizations to the process of teaching clinicians how to understand and work with the immediate practical problems of managers and executives. In doing so, he focuses on the task I started out with nearly a half century ago, namely, how to keep well people functioning well. Clinicians who assume the executive coaching role will find Sperry's understanding and guidance helpful. They may even find the results of his extensive professional experience invaluable.

In addition to coaching others, clinicians inevitably encounter issues that touch on their own problems and their own career issues. These are rarely dealt with in the coaching literature. Sperry makes the unique contribution of helping the coach consider the intra-personal problems he or she experiences in the coaching process. That contribution is an important step beyond what is in the contemporary coaching literature. Taken together, these insights, experiences, and guides, make *Executive Coaching: The Essential Guide for Mental Health Professionals* an important and indispensable resource for mental health professionals involved in executive coaching.

Harry Levinson, Ph.D.

Acknowledgments

This book is grounded in over 30 years of working with executives. I feel honored and profoundly grateful to have known, worked with, and learned from these leaders and their organizations. Over the years, I have had the good fortune to know Harry Levinson, Ph.D. and Harry Prosen, M.D. as mentors, and I must express my heartfelt admiration and gratitude for their role in my personal and professional development. Lee R. Hess, Ph.D., Peter Brill, M.D., and Jon Carlson, Ed.D., Psy.D. have meant the world to me and words fail to convey my deep appreciation for their friendship. Finally, I would like to recognize my esteemed colleagues, Carl Chan, M.D. and Jon Gudeman, M.D. at the Medical College of Wisconsin, Maureen Duffy, Ph.D. and Scott Gillig, Ph.D. at Barry University, and Bill Nicoll, Ph.D. and Alex Miranda, Ph.D. at Florida Atlantic University.

Publishing a book is a major team endeavor, and I've been blest to work with some of the best and brightest in the publishing world. My heartfelt gratitude to the editorial staff at Brunner-Routledge: George Zimmar, Shannon Vargo, Dana Bliss, Marsha Hecht and Alice Mulhern.

Introduction

Executive coaching has clearly captured the attention of top management, executives who want and need to increase performance, as well as individuals in the mental health profession. The major appeal of coaching among top management and executives rests on the perception that coaching is a powerful and highly effective approach to productivity and leadership excellence, and that it is a relatively brief and cost-effective alternative to psychotherapy and traditional training and development approaches. The main appeal to mental health professionals is that coaching offers a viable as well as lucrative alternative to psychotherapy practice in a managed care environment.

There are probably more than 10,000 coaches in America offering executive coaching. Only about 20% are trained and licensed mental health professionals. The rest are M.B.A.-trained consultants, have athletic coaching or training experience, or are simply entrepreneurs attracted by the $250 to $500 hourly fees that coaches working with corporate clients can command.

It appears that executive coaching can and does achieve its promise of increased performance and/or well-being with certain clients. The fact that executive coaching is not effective with all clients, often because of co-morbid psychological problems, suggests that formal psychological training and experience can be significant assets. Because of their unique training and experience in assessment and diagnosis, mental health professionals have much to offer the emerging field of executive coaching, since these professionals can both select and work with the most appropriate candidates for coaching, as well as competently refer those who are better candidates for psychotherapy. In addition to an alternative to managed care practice, executive coaching appeals to many mental health professionals because it is an alternative to the pathology-oriented, medical model. Instead, executive coaching is based on the developmental model. This means that mental health professionals can focus their efforts beyond merely reducing symptoms and resolving major problems. Instead, they can assist already healthy and productive individuals to increase their personal, relational and spiritual well-being.

Besides the obvious financial benefits, coaching also offers practice flexibility that clinical practice does not: executive coaching sessions can even be conducted by phone or Internet. The "clinical world" differs considerably from the "corporate world" and coaching is not watered-down psychotherapy. Effective coaching requires a realistic understanding of organizational dynamics as well as some measure of training in the methods and professional issues unique to coaching. This book can provide the reader a map of the territory of the "corporate world" and the practice of executive and personal coaching.

Why the need for this particular book when there are already several coaching books in print? First of all, most books on executive coaching are not written expressly for mental health professionals. Second, the few that target mental health professionals either merely restate the content of general coaching books or are primarily collections of "how I became a coach and practice coaching" stories. These books have little or no coverage of topics that concern those with psychotherapeutic training. Simply comparing coaching and psychotherapy in a few pages and offering a summary table or chart of their differences is not useful or sufficient for most mental health professionals.

Based on my experience giving seminars on executive coaching, mental health professionals who are seriously considering executive coaching as a practice option or career change really want and need to understand the ins and outs of executive coaching before they make major decisions to secure additional training and then expand their practices or shift careers. They should consider several issues. What are the practice differences between executive coaching and personal or life coaching? What additional training and experience are required to practice executive coaching ethically and legally compared to the requirements for providing personal or life coaching? Which executives are the best and least suitable candidates for executive coaching? What are the indications and contraindications for executive coaching compared to the indications and contraindications for psychotherapy? What is the relationship between executive coaching and executive consultation, and can mental health professionals trained as executive coaches ethically perform executive consultation? What additional training and experience are needed to function as an executive consultant? How does the process of executive coaching differ from psychotherapy? What are the specific indications for skill-focused executive coaching compared to performance-focused and development-focused executive coaching? What are the strategies and methods of practicing these three different approaches? Can coaching be practiced with a team or is it only a one-to-one intervention?

Executive Coaching: The Essential Guide for Mental Health Professionals is unique in that it addresses the concerns noted above and others. It provides extensive background information that is essential for the practice of executive coaching. It offers the reader a clearly articulated "map" and illustrations of the actual process of executive coaching in its various forms: skill-focused, performance-focused and development-focused executive coaching. Numerous case examples, some of which include transcriptions of coaching sessions, provide the reader with an insider's view of the executive coaching process in several contexts. Included are indications and strategies for utilizing executive coaching with an executive, with an executive and a problematic employee, and with an executive in a team context.

This book will be of primary interest to mental health clinicians who seek alternatives to managed care practices, who have interest in working with higher functioning clients on self-fulfillment and other personal development issues, or who would like to have more flexible practices provided by coaching. This book may also be of interest to non-clinically trained coaches who seek ways to identify clients who are poor candidates for coaching or work with those who are "stuck" in their coaching efforts. Executives who are looking for the insider's view of what effective executive coaching is like may also find the book of interest.

Executive Coaching consists of ten chapters. An overview of the field of executive coaching from the perspective of the mental health professional is provided in chapter 1. This chapter explores executive coaching and distinguishes it from executive consulting, training and development, and counseling and psychotherapy and suggests a number of reasons mental health professionals, i.e., those with psychological training, are well disposed to practice executive coaching. Chapter 2 discusses the client by presenting a portrait of the executive in terms of personality and character, leadership style, skills, and competencies. Chapter 3 portrays the corporate world in which executives live and function as well as their job demands. Following these three rather global and descriptive chapters, chapter 4 begins to focus more directly on executive coaching by addressing the matter of suitability: who is an appropriate candidate for executive coaching and who is not as well as the suitability of those who provide executive coaching. Chapter 5 focuses on the actual process. It describes the models, modes, stages, and types or functions of executive coaching. The three chapters that follow describe and illustrate the actual practice of executive coaching. The three basic types of coaching are described and extensively illustrated with case material. Skill-focused coaching is covered in chapter 6, performance-focused coaching in chapter 7, and development-focused coaching in chapter 8. Other strategies that can be combined with coaching to increase executive productivity and well-being are described in chapter 9, while chapter 10 addresses several professional issues in developing a practice in executive coaching.

1
Executive Coaching as a Practice Option

Coaching has taken center stage in the world of personal change and development. In glowing media reports, high profile CEOs and celebrities in the sports and entertainment world attribute much of their success to their coaches. Recently, a weekly news magazine called coaching the second hottest consulting field behind management consulting. Many see coaching as a panacea for all manner of personal, professional, and corporate problems, while some top executives view coaching as a quick and inexpensive alternative to psychotherapy. Interestingly, a recent study examining media perceptions of executive coaches and their effectiveness as compared to psychologists found that the public had much more favorable views of coaches than psychologists with regard to competence and helpfulness (Garman, Whiston, & Zlatoper, 2000).

In the past few years, presentations on coaching at national conferences and continuing education workshops for therapists have drawn large crowds. Institutes and online programs to train and "certify" coaches have sprung up and, at least according to their entrepreneurial founders, are flourishing. Coaching is pitched to mental health professionals as a viable and profitable alternative to practicing therapy in a managed care environment. By training to become coaches, mental health professionals are promised that they can leave managed care behind and easily earn six-figure incomes (Campbell, 2001). But is executive coaching really a viable practice option for mental health professionals?

This chapter begins by describing and defining coaching. It then distinguishes coaching from a number of related strategies for improving executive performance, such as consulting, training and development, and psychotherapy. Next, it discusses the various similarities and differences between coaching and therapy. This leads to a consideration of the main types of coaching: life coaching, personal coaching, managerial coaching, and, the subject of this book, executive coaching. The effectiveness of executive coaching is then addressed. Finally, the chapter ends with a discussion of the viability of executive coaching as a practice option for mental health professionals.

Descriptions and Definitions of Coaching

What is coaching? At the current time, no consensus on the scope, format, methods, duration, and frequency of sessions exists among the various descriptions and definitions of coaching. The lack of consensus is understandable since this area of professional endeavor is more recent than executive consultation and counseling. Some representative definitions and descriptions of executive coaching are provided in this section.

Witherspoon (2000) insists that coaching is basically a growth-oriented, personal relationship. Accordingly, he describes executive coaching as "an action-learning process to enhance effective action and learning agility. It involves a professional relationship and a deliberate, personalized process to provide an executive with valid information, free and informed choices based on that information, and internal commitment to those choices" (p. 167). Two expected outcomes of coaching should be more effective action and increased ability to learn, i.e., asking for feedback and reflecting before and after making a decision or initiating an action. Similarly, Goldsmith, Lyons, and Freas (2000) describe coaching as a strategic process that adds values to those who are coached as well as to the organization. "Coaching establishes and develops healthy working relationships by surfacing issues (raw data gathering), addressing issues (through feedback), solving problems (action planning), and following through (results)—and so offers a process in which people develop and through which obstacles to obtaining business results are removed" (p. xviii).

Others describe coaching from a more performance-based perspective. For instance, O'Neil (2000) defines coaching as the process of increasing an individual's skill and effectiveness in three areas: (1) communicating the organization's purpose, vision, and goals to key constituencies; (2) building relationships and facilitating interactions that result in outstanding team performance; and (3) producing results and outcomes (pp. 5–6).

Kilburg (1996) defines coaching as "a helping relationship formed between a client with managerial authority and responsibility in an organization and a consultant who uses a wide variety of behavioral techniques and methods to help the client achieve a mutually identified set of goals to improve personal performance and personal satisfaction, and consequently, to improve the effectiveness of the client's organization within a formally defined coaching agreement" (p. 142).

Some believe that coaching is probably a necessary, and perhaps even a sufficient, condition for achieving organizational transformation. Coaching can be transformational which is to say that "through a behavioral change brought about in individuals, a leader may transform the organization and gain commitment.... In coaching, people are offered the chance to align their own behavior with the values and vision of the organization ... and then putting these individuals back in alignment, one person at a time—coaching can make real impact and build healthy organizations—top-down, and from the grass roots up" (Goldsmith, Lyons, & Freas, 2000, p. xviii).

Performance or Personal Development?

While there are differences in these various definitions, they nevertheless seem to reflect only two basic viewpoints. In one, the primary purpose of coaching is performance enhancement and the secondary purpose is personal development; in the other, the primary purpose of coaching is personal development and performance enhancement is secondary. Those who advocate for the personal development view point out that the original meaning of the word *coaching*—derived from the word *carriage* in the English language—was "to convey a valued person from where he or she is to where he or she wants to be."

Not surprisingly, these advocates insist that the basic purpose of coaching is to bring out the best in individuals, and that focusing primarily on an individual's overall development usually leads to increased professional effectiveness and job performance. As will be noted in a subsequent section of this chapter, advocates of this view of coaching tend to practice personal coaching or life coaching. On the other hand, those who view the purpose of coaching primarily as performance enhancement and secondarily as personal development are more likely to practice executive coaching.

Executive Coaching, Consulting, Training, and Psychotherapy

In the business world, several strategies and methods have been found to be effective in increasing an individual's job performance. In the executive suite, four different strategies are commonly utilized: executive coaching, executive consulting, executive training and development, and executive counseling or psychotherapy. This section describes and differentiates each of these in terms of professions and then as functions. We begin by discussing these four strategies in terms of professions.

Strategies as Professions

The four strategies are described as they are embodied within four separate professions. The case can be made, organizationally and legally, that the four professions are autonomous.

Executive Consultation—This is an organizational consultation strategy in which a consultant forms a collaborative relationship with an individual executive to address a broad range of professional and personal issues of concern to the executive. Because these discussions can range from complex financial and personnel decisions to delicate personal health issues, this type of consultation is not for a beginner. Rather it requires a seasoned consultant with an encyclopedic knowledge and broad experience base. The signature characteristic of this form of consultation is that the consultant serves as a sounding board and expert adviser who can quickly and effective assess the personal and organizational dynamics influencing the executive's concerns. Chapter 9 describes and illustrates this strategy in more detail.

Executive Psychotherapy—This form of psychotherapy is a strategy and process in which a therapist and executive establish a close, collaborative relationship and utilize psychotherapeutic methods to achieve greater self-understanding and resolution of the executive's work-related problems and/or symptoms. Usually briefer, less intense, and more focused on work-related issues than traditional counseling or psychotherapy. work-focused psychotherapy is a form of executive counseling that focuses on work-related issues. It is described and illustrated in chapter 9.

Executive Training and Development—With this approach, training and development specialists endeavor to assist executives, as well as other employees, to learn and master knowledge, skills, and competencies. From a training and development perspective, learning results from instructional input, practice and reinforcement. Learning is believed to be optimized when it is individualized to a learner's unique needs and learning style. Accordingly, learning modes that are interactive, individualized, and easily accessed are preferred over traditional classroom didactic instructions and seminars. Most training and development today takes place via interactive electronic and other computer-based modalities. While training and development methods are useful in achieving various learning outcomes, they seem to excel at learning that involves technical and analytic skills.

There are probably two main differences between coaching and training and development. First, as noted, is that while training is very effective for teaching technical and analytic skills, coaching can achieve learning outcomes in relational and strategic skills as well as technical ones. Second, while both coaching and training consider individualization unlike important, coaching emphasizes learning within a respectful, trusting, and collaborative relationship unlike training and development.

Executive Coaching—This is a specialized type of executive consultation. A coach works collaboratively with an executive to improve the executive's overall professional productivity and personal well-being. The focus of such coaching can be on increasing skills, performance, or development. It is usually directed at communicating vision and acting strategically, understanding individual and organizational dynamics, building relationships and mobilizing commitment, facilitating team performance, or improving specific corporate results. Unless it is part of an ongoing leadership development program, executive coaching tends to be fairly focused and of short duration.

Table 1.1 summarizes this discussion.

Strategies as Functions

The various strategies for improving executive performance and development such as coaching, therapy, consultation, and training and development can be thought of either as professions (coach, therapist, consultant, trainer) or as functions. When we consider discrete professions, we like to think that trainers

TABLE 1.1 Comparison of Four Strategies of Executive Development

Strategy	Distinctive Features
Executive Coaching	A *coach* works collaboratively with an executive to accomplish specific goals and objectives involving the executive's productivity and well-being; typically focuses on increasing skills and performance or on personal and professional development; usually of short duration
Executive Consultation	A *consultant,* functioning as a sounding board, expert adviser and/or evaluator, forms a collaborative relationship with an individual executive to address a *broad range* of professional and personal issues of concern to the executive; often an ongoing process of longer duration
Executive Psychotherapy	A *therapist* and an executive establish a close, collaborative relationship and utilize psychotherapeutic methods to achieve greater *self-understanding and resolution* of work-related problems and/or symptoms; usually briefer, less intense, and more focused on work-related issues than traditional counseling or psychotherapy; often weekly meetings of short to medium duration, depending on need
Executive Training and Development	A *training and development specialist* focuses on developing the requisite leadership skills and competencies of individuals targeted for advancement to executive positions or on enhancing the skills and competencies of those already in executive positions; usually of short duration; longer in the context of a formal leadership development program

only train, consultants only consult, therapists only provide therapy, and coaches only provide coaching. The reality is that the various strategies for improving executive performance and development are discrete but overlapping functions that can conceivably be provided by one professional. Figure 1.1 portrays these four functions as separate and autonomous strategies of the same value and importance—as noted by their similar size.

Figure 1.2 portrays these four functions wherein coaching is largely informed by a training and development perspective. Coaches who come from training and development backgrounds often are quite comfortable viewing coaching as a variant of training and development. Thus, it should not be too surprising that they typically define coaching in terms of skill deficits and specific targets and tend to "specialize" in skill-focused executive coaching.

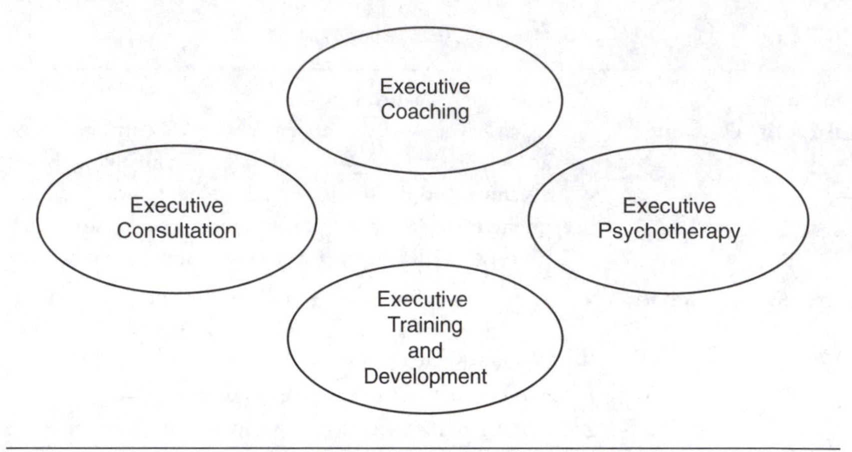

Fig. 1.1 Coaching, consulting, training, and therapy as separate functions.

The increased sizes of the circles representing the coaching and training and development functions reflect their perceived superior value and importance in comparison to the consultation and psychotherapy functions.

Figure 1.3 portrays these four functions wherein coaching is largely informed by a consultation perspective. Coaches who come from business or management consulting backgrounds often are quite comfortable viewing coaching as a variant of consultation. Thus, it should not be too surprising that they typically define coaching in terms of team, organizational, and professional development outcomes or are likely to "specialize" in performance-focused executive coaching.

Figure 1.4 portrays these four functions wherein coaching is largely informed by a counseling or therapy perspective. Coaches who come from mental health backgrounds often are quite comfortable viewing coaching as a variant of counseling therapy. Thus, it should not be too surprising that they typically define coaching in terms of relational and personal and professional

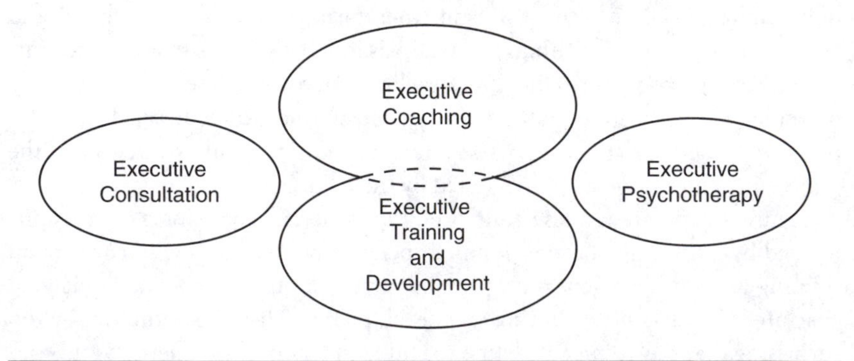

Fig. 1.2 Coaching viewed from a training and development perspective.

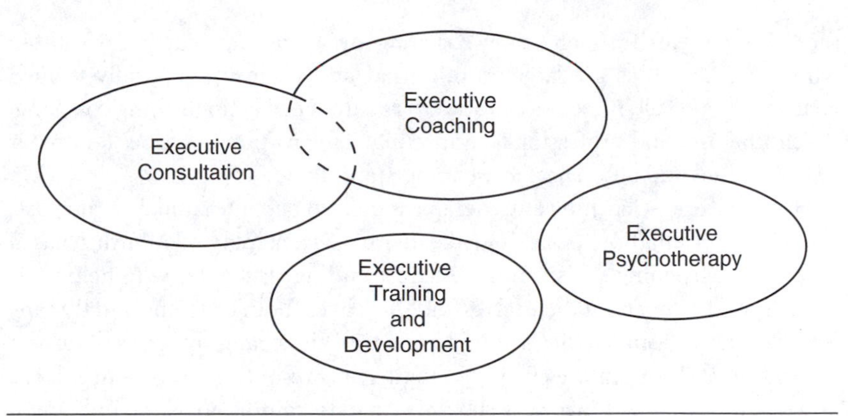

Fig. 1.3 Coaching viewed from a consulting perspective.

development outcomes or are likely to "specialize" in development-focused executive coaching.

Coaching and Therapy: Similarities and Differences

There is mounting interest in defining and clarifying how the practice of coaching is unique and different from the practice of professional counseling and psychotherapy. Not only is the public interested in this distinction, but so are a number of professional organizations and licensure and certification bodies. Justifiably, these groups are concerned that some coaches appear to be practicing psychotherapy without licensure. Recently, a proposal was made to a Colorado licensing board that anyone practicing coaching in the state who did not possess a license in one of the mental health disciplines would be required to register with that board as a nonlicensed therapist. This proposal

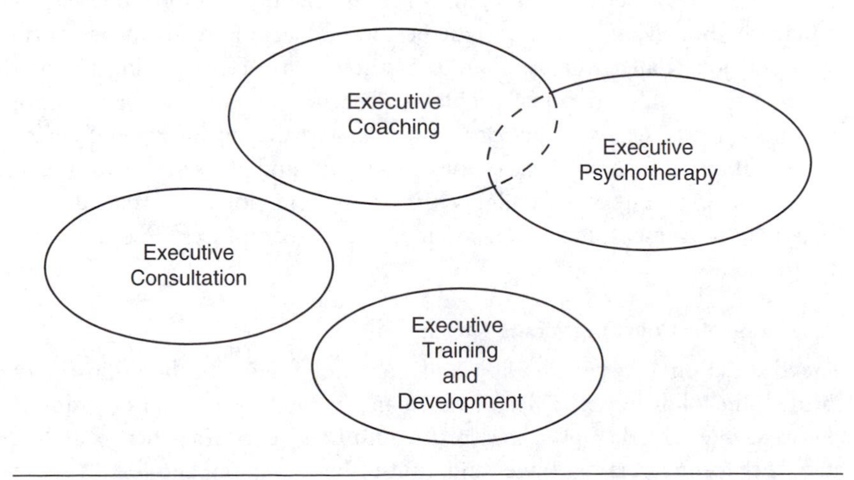

Fig. 1.4 Coaching viewed from a therapy perspective.

sent shock waves through many coaching organizations, particularly those whose memberships are largely unlicensed and nonpsychologically trained coaches. As a result, these organizations are intent on distinguishing coaching, psychotherapy, and professional counseling. This section describes a number of similarities and differences as we understand them.

Similarities—Coaching and therapy appear to be quite similar in purpose, intent, and orientation. Coaching, like therapy, is a helping relationship based on effective listening skills, empathetic responding, and a desire to help individuals feel better about themselves and their lives. Both coaching and therapy are grounded on similar views of human nature and change in terms of respect for the client, belief in the client's strengths and resources to solve problems, and the importance of involving the client in determining goals and outcomes. Finally, both apply a variety of intervention strategies, tools, and techniques to facilitate change in the client.

Differences—Coaching differs from therapy in a number of ways. Coaches work with healthy individuals who are ready and willing to change, self-confident, able to form close personal relationships, able to hear corrective feedback, and willing to commit substantial time, energy, and resources (money) to life changes. In fact, as we point out in chapter 4, coaches are advised to avoid working with resistant, damaged, needy, dependent, emotionally disabled, or addicted people, and those who are not ready for change. Confidentiality is more complex than it is with therapy. Boundaries in coaching are often less rigid. Sessions usually take place at the client's site, and the coach might also interact with the client in various social and business settings. While such relating would be considered appropriate and perhaps even necessary, such relating outside scheduled sessions would be considered inappropriate for therapy. A key point of difference is that coaching is more focused on the future and a person's strengths whereas therapy is more focused on deficits, pathology, and the past. Furthermore, coaching tends to be short-term and job-related whereas therapy is more remedial, attacking motivational, attitudinal, or personal problems. Coaching is not about processing emotional hurts, healing emotional wounds, and diagnosing mental health issues, but rather focuses on the client's present life and plans for the future. In short, coaching is intended for highly functioning individuals; it is data driven, focused in the present, and action-oriented. Table 1.2 captures these and other differences.

Case Example: Coaching versus Therapy

The distinction between therapy and coaching might be best illustrated through the following example. A harried and hassled mother seeks therapy. If she were to go for therapy, a therapist would likely encourage her to understand her feelings, express anger and guilt at her situation, and learn to take time for herself. If she were to go for coaching, a coach would be more likely to

TABLE 1.2 Comparison of Coaching and Therapy

Coaching	**Therapy**
Present and future focus	Focus on the past
Action-oriented	Reflective-oriented
Data from client and 360 degree evaluation by others	Data primarily from client
Growth- or skills development-oriented	Pathology-oriented
Problem is primarily person–environment "fit"	Problem is primarily intrapsychic
"Client" is less clear (may be organization paying coaching fee)	Client is clearly the person in therapy
Confidentiality is complex	Confidentiality is clear and absolute
Meetings of variable length	Fifty-minute sessions
Flexible boundaries, including social setting	Rigid boundaries
Work around personality issues	Work through and resolve personality issues
Meet on client's turf, at neutral site, or even via Internet	Meet in therapist's office
Organization may choose coach	Client or HMO chooses therapist
Organization feels enhanced by intervention	Client feels enhanced
Information may be (carefully) shared	Information is not shared

Source: Based on Sperry, *Corporate Therapy and Consulting*, 1996, p. 184.

focus on the goal of reducing stress and suggest specific strategies to accomplish that goal. However, the coach would be less likely to process the mother's feelings about the stress or its causes. Modeling action-oriented problem-solving, the coach would probably provide the mother with a list of names of maid services, baby-sitters, gyms, or personal trainers and suggest she call them. A schedule would be established for making the calls, and then the client would confirm to the coach by phone, e-mail, or fax that she made these calls (Campbell, 2001).

Different Types of Coaching

Various types of coaching are practiced today. Although they have obvious similarities, they have many differences as well. This section describes the three common types of coaching: life coaching (also called personal coaching), executive coaching, and managerial coaching.

Life (or Personal) Coaching

Coaches who are involved with providing professional coaching services to executives and professionals distinguish two broad kinds of coaching: executive coaching and personal coaching (also referred to as life coaching). The distinction is worth noting.

Life coaching has been defined as "a powerful human relationship where trained coaches assist people to design their future rather than get over their past. Through a typically long-term relationship, coaches aid clients in creating vision and goals for ALL aspects of their lives and creating multiple strategies to support achieving those goals" (Williams & Davis, 2002, pp. xiv–xv). Similarly, personal coaching has been described as a process which "involves helping generally well-functioning people create and achieve goals, maximize personal development, and navigate transitions on the path to realizing their ideal vision for current and emerging chapters of their lives. Most personal coaching clients are focused on the development of an ideal future self, an ideal career, or an improved family life" (Auerbach, 2002, p. 10).

Executive Coaching

As noted earlier in this chapter, executive coaching is a form of executive consultation in which a coach works collaboratively with an executive to improve the executive's skills and performance as well as for professional and personal development. While executive coaching has many definitions, the composite definition developed by the Center for Creative Leadership (Douglas & Morley, 2000, p. 40) characterizes it well:

> Reduced to its essence, executive coaching is the process of equipping people with the tools, knowledge, and opportunities they need to develop themselves and become more effective (Peterson, 1996). Executive coaching involves the teaching of skills in the context of a personal relationship with the learner, and providing feedback on the executive's interpersonal relations and skills (Sperry, 1993). An ongoing series of activities tailored to the individual's current issues or relevant problems is designed by the coach to assist the executive in maintaining a consistent, confident focus as he or she tunes strengths and manages shortcomings. (Tobias, 1996)

Executive Coaching versus Life or Personal Coaching

How exactly is executive coaching different from life or personal coaching? Auerbach (2002) begins to distinguish executive coaching from personal coaching by noting that executive coaching "focuses especially on issues related to effectiveness and fulfillment at work. Common themes in executive coaching are developing key executive and managerial skills, enhancing team-building and leadership qualities, identifying and optimizing the use of key strengths, and building the competencies of emotional intelligence" (p. 14). The key distinction, for Auerbach, is that while personal coaching has a general focus on an individual's overall personal development and well-being, executive coaching has a specific focus on effectiveness and fulfillment at work. In other words, the specific focus on work effectiveness is what distinguishes between personal and executive coaching for Auerbach.

While generally agreeing with Auerbach's definition, the view of executive coaching espoused in this book is more nuanced. We would contend that the key factor is not simply a focus on work itself, but rather a focus on work-related considerations *within* an organizational or corporate context. We would add that to be effective, executive coaches must be ever mindful of the corporate context and organizational dynamics in aiding their clients in planning and achieving developmental goals. Generally speaking, personal and life coaches are less mindful, if at all, of such organizational dynamics.

Consider the example of two acquaintances who have similar training and backgrounds in marketing. One is a freelance marketing consultant who has "no stomach for the corporate world" and enjoys the entrepreneurial life. The other is a marketing director working for a Fortune 100 company who has been immersed in corporate life for 14 years. The influence and impact of corporate context will be very different for each. Thus, while corporate context is likely to significantly impact the full-time employee and her career, health, and well-being, the corporate context and organizational dynamics of the places she consults with will have little or no influence on the freelancer. Freedom from the perceived negative influence and impact of contextual dynamics is a reason professionals choose to work outside the corporate world.

In our way of thinking, the marketing consultant would be a candidate for personal or life coaching and would conceivably find such coaching quite useful and beneficial in achieving personal and career goals. On the other hand, the marketing director would be a candidate for executive coaching. She would most likely be better served working with an executive coach with expertise in organizational dynamics in achieving both her performance goals as well as her personal and professional development goals.

In subsequent chapters, we go on to describe three different types or functions of executive coaching: skill-focused, performance-focused, and developmental or development-focused executive coaching. All three are concerned with effectiveness and fulfillment, but primarily within an organizational or corporate context.

Managerial Coaching

Coaching of employees by their manager or supervisor is called managerial coaching. Eitington (1997) aptly describes managerial coaching as "the ongoing, day-to-day efforts by the manager/supervisor to upgrade performance and develop people more fully. The objective is to empower people—tap their potential and unleash their creativity—to secure their fullest possible commitment to organizational objectives and their own jobs" (p. 280). This definition emphasizes that there are two targets or goals of managerial coaching: improving performance and developing employees.

Like managerial coaching, executive coaching is mindful of organizational dynamics and takes place in a corporate environment. It should not be too surprising that these targets are essentially the same for executive coaching, wherein coaches work with executives to increase their performance and develop their potential. It might be said that there is a circular relationship between both types of coaching. Presumably, executives who have been coached are expected to coach the employees who report to them.

Is Executive Coaching Effective?

Earlier we differentiated coaching and therapy in terms of several factors. Another factor on which the two can be distinguished is with regard to scholarship and research. In this section we briefly review the matter of scholarship and research in executive coaching. A reasonable question is whether executive coaching has been demonstrated to be an effective method of change.

In her review of books and articles on coaching, Campbell (2001) reports that coaching practice appears to be based on the writings of a few business gurus about their coaching experience. Furthermore, she notes that many writers and workshop presenters "present their ideas and suggestions for change as their own. Yet, page after page, coaching books and workshop materials contain philosophies, assumptions, and techniques borrowed from therapy and psychotherapy as well as communications theory and organizational development" (p. 4). Her implication is that plagiarism is not uncommon in the coaching literature. However, the situation is quite different for articles and books published in the literature on executive coaching, particularly when authored by executive coaches and consultants with professional training and credentials in organizational psychology and consulting psychology.

Currently, little, if any, empirical research reported supports coaching theory. However, some empirical research studies on the outcomes of executive coaching have been performed. In a review of seven recent empirical studies, it was concluded that executive coaching is effective. More specifically, the studies reviewed indicated that (1) executives viewed their coaching positively; (2) executive coaching did increase executive performance; and (3) executive coaching did facilitate developmental changes in executives (Kampa-Kokesch & Anderson, 2001).

Another study found that psychologically trained executive coaches who were able to rapidly and authentically connect with executives and were guided by professional ethical principles were perceived as highly effective coaches (Wasylyshyn, 2003). In short, it appears that executive coaching has been demonstrated to be effective.

Mental Health Professionals as Executive Coaches

When it comes to giving advice on concerns about daily living, general career issues, or balancing family and work, mental health professionals are likely to have sufficient knowledge and experience to coach others on such issues, without the need for much additional specialized coaching training or knowledge and experience with organizational dynamics. Generally speaking, mental health professionals can more easily transition into personal or life coaching than into executive coaching because their psychological training and experience readily transfer to the practice of personal or life coaching. With some additional formal training, many should be able to provide competent personal or life coaching. This training can be helpful in utilizing various coaching interventions and "certification" might be useful in advertising their new practice styles.

However, most mental health professionals will need considerable training and supervised experience to effectively provide formal executive coaching. As we will show in subsequent chapters, working knowledge and experience dealing with executives in a corporate context and organizational dynamics are parts of the requisite training and supervised experience necessary to provide effective and ethical executive coaching. Chapter 10 extends this discussion in terms of the ethical and legal matters of competency and scope of practice.

A strong case can be made that mental health professionals are the optimal providers of executive coaching. In fact, in chapter 4 we contend that all candidates for executive coaching should be evaluated for their suitability for coaching. Clearly, mental health professionals who have the psychological expertise to evaluate psychiatric conditions and personality disorders—both counter-indications for executive coaching—should perform such assessments and make appropriate referrals when indicated. Expecting executive coaches who have only training and experience in business or sports to evaluate an executive's suitability for coaching is foolhardy and ethically problematic.

Several conclusions can be drawn from this discussion. First, there are many similarities between coaching and therapy. Second, mental health professionals have the kind of training and experience that can be extremely valuable in providing effective coaching. Third, coaching is a growing profession that offers career mobility and a wide range of opportunities for those who are willing to strike out in a new direction and acquire additional training and experience. The question is: should mental health professionals make the transition into coaching practice? The answer, of course, depends on a number of factors, not the least of which are the mental health professional's aspirations and mind-set.

Lynn Grodzki, a psychotherapist who also practices coaching with business people, suggests that some therapists can make the transition more easily than others (2002). She believes it depends largely on mind-set. As noted in Table 1.3, the mind-sets of a therapist and a coach differ considerably: proactive, pragmatic and energetically optimistic versus supportive, interpretive, and serious. Grodzki also describes the mind-set of the "coach–therapist"—a blend of both functions. The more the coach and coach–therapist role is compatible with the mental health professional's own personal disposition and values, the more

TABLE 1.3 Mind-Sets of Coach, Therapist, and Coach–Therapist

Coach	Therapist	Coach–Therapist
Proactive, practical, energetic and optimistic, strategic; nonpsychologically-minded	Supportive, interpretive, serious, reparative; directly and intentionally psychologically minded	Active and facilitative, listens without interpretation, strategic; indirectly psychologically minded

that individual is likely to feel challenged and fulfilled by coaching. Thus, if the therapist mind-set suits your values, interests and temperament, coaching may not be a good "fit" for you. The coach–therapist mind-set and role are further described in chapter 10.

Concluding Note

Today coaching is a well regarded new profession that holds considerable potential. The demands for both personal or life coaching and executive coaching are quite high, and the demands are expected to continue for the foreseeable future. Many see coaching as an effective way to improve their lives or work performance, while others mistakenly see it as a quick and inexpensive alternative to psychotherapy.

The fact is that coaching is in some ways similar to psychotherapy and the training and experience that most mental health professionals have acquired can be invaluable in providing effective coaching to a wide range of individuals. That does not mean that mental health professionals have either the disposition or mind-set to be effective coaches, nor does it mean that they can successfully—and ethically and legally—practice the various types of coaching without the requisite training and experience. However, if you are willing to get such training and have the disposition and the desire to work professionally with highly intelligent, creative, and energetic executives, executive coaching may be for you, and this book can guide you on the journey to becoming an executive coach.

References

Auerbach, J. (2002). *Personal and executive coaching: The complete guide for mental health professionals.* Ventura, CA: Executive College Press.

Campbell, J. (2001). Coaching: A new field for counselors? *Counseling and Human Development, 34*(3), 1–14

Douglas, C. & Morley, W. (2000). *Executive coaching: An annotated bibliography.* Greensboro, NC: Center for Creative Leadership.

Eitington, J. (1997). *Winning manager: Leadership skills for greater innovation, quality and employee commitment.* Houston, TX: Gulf Publishing.

Garman, A., Whiston, D., & Zlatoper, K. (2000). Media perceptions of executive coaching and the formal preparation of coaches. *Consulting Psychology Journal: Practice and Research, 52*(3), 201–205.

Goldsmith, M., Lyons, L., & Freas, A. (2000). Preface. In M. Goldsmith, L. Lyons, & A. Freas (Eds.), *Coaching for leadership: How the world's greatest coaches help leaders learn.* San Francisco: Jossey-Bass/Pfeiffer, pp. xv–xx.

Grodzki, L. (2002). The new private practice. In L. Grodzki (Ed.). *The new private practice: Therapist-coaches share stories, strategies and advice.* New York: Norton, pp. 1–21.

Kampa-Kokesch, S. & Anderson, M. (2001). Executive coaching: A comprehensive review of the literature. *Consulting Psychology Journal, 53*(4), 205–228.

Kilburg, R. (1996). Toward a conceptual understanding and definition of executive coaching. *Counseling Psychology Journal, 48*(2), 134–144.

O'Neil, M. (2000). *Executive coaching with backbone and heart: A systems approach to engaging leaders with their challenges.* San Francisco: Jossey-Bass.

Peterson, D. (1996). Executive coaching at work: The art of one-on-one change. *Consulting Psychology Journal: Practice and Research, 48*(2), 78–86.

Sperry, L. (1993). Working with executives: Consulting, counseling and coaching. *Individual Psychology, 49*(2), 257–266.

Sperry, L. (1996). *Corporate therapy and consulting.* New York: Brunner-Mazel.

Tobias, L. (1996). Coaching executives. *Consulting Psychology Journal: Practice and Research, 48*(2), 87–95.

Wasylyshyn, K. (2003). Executive coaching: An outcome study. *Consulting Psychology Journal: Practice and Research, 55*(2), 94–106.

Williams & Davis (2002). *Therapist as life coach: Transforming your practice.* New York: Norton.

Witherspoon, R. (2000). Starting smart: Clarifying coaching goals and roles. In M. Goldsmith, L. Lyons, & A. Freas (Eds.). *Coaching for leadership: How the world's greatest coaches help leaders learn.* San Francisco: Jossey-Bass/Pfeiffer, pp. 165–185.

2
Executives and Executive Coaching

Executive coaches have unique opportunities to collaborate and work with some of the brightest, most talented, creative and interesting individuals on the face of the earth. Mental health professionals who intend to or have just begun to coach executives would do well to learn as much as they can about these clients who are, in many ways, quite different from clientele seeking mental health services.

This chapter profiles the senior executive. It overviews information about his or her lifestyle, job demands, personality dynamics, and management style. It begins by distinguishing management and leadership and then describes effective leadership and various ranges of leadership effectiveness. It describes the effective executive in terms of leadership effectiveness and its component dimensions: leadership style, leadership skills and leadership competencies. Then it discusses leadership talents, skills and competencies as they relate to the leadership style that reflects the executive's personality and management style. Each of these dimensions provides a target for planning and implementing executive coaching processes and interventions on which subsequent chapters elaborate.

Leadership and Management

Leadership and management are the coins of the realm in executive coaching. Since these terms are used synonymously by some and differently by others, we offer operational definitions of both. Management can be thought of as the capacity to complete assigned organizational responsibilities on time with the help of employees, while leadership is the capacity to develop and galvanize the commitment of others to make an organization effective and successful. Which is more important? While in the recent past this was a theoretical and academic question of some concern, today many are increasingly convinced that both characteristics are important and essential. In fact, it appears that effective executives have well developed competencies and skills in both management and leadership. In this and subsequent chapters, the designation *effective leadership* refers to both an executive's management *and* leadership functions.

Executive Levels, Functions, and Roles

What are executives like and what do they do in a typical day? This section briefly describes the titles, functions, and roles of executives; their typical days and demands on their time; their motivational styles, and the organizational barriers and predictable career crises that they face.

Levels

Executives and managers exist at all levels of an organization. Senior executives or top managers are those at the upper levels of an organization. Usually this upper level includes the chief executive officer (CEO), the chief operating officer (COO), and the vice presidents of various divisions or subsidiaries or of specific areas like human resources or personnel, operations, marketing, and finance. These are "line" positions, and persons in these positions have actual decision-making responsibilities for subordinates. This is in contrast to "staff" positions; persons holding staff positions have primarily supportive rather than decision-making functions. Often the president of the organization is the CEO, although sometimes the chairman of the corporation's board of directors may serve as CEO, with the president functioning as COO. Top management's primary role is to set broad organizational policies, goals, and strategies.

Junior executive is an imprecise designation for persons in staff positions supporting senior executives. Middle managers have titles like plant manager, general manager, operations manager, or department manager. They function to implement the strategies and policies set by top management. They also coordinate the work of first-line managers. First-line managers have titles like section manager, foreman, or supervisor, and their function is to supervise employees. Over the past decade, the ranks of middle management have been greatly diminished through mergers and downsizing to make corporations "leaner and meaner."

Functions

Generally speaking, managers at all levels perform five general functions: leading, planning, decision making, organizing, and controlling. As noted earlier, the leading or leadership function has been emphasized over the other four administrative or management functions. The emphasis of each of these five functions varies with the different levels of management. Specifically, the organizing and controlling functions are emphasized for supervisors, with the leading and planning functions emphasized at the senior executive level (Kelly, 1980).

Roles

All managers fulfill three roles—interpersonal, decisional, and informational—and require three different types of skills to function effectively—technical, relational, and strategic. Interpersonal roles include those of leader, figurehead, and liaison. Decisional roles include negotiator, resource allocator, entrepreneur, and conflict manager. Informational roles include monitor, disseminator, and spokesperson. Executive skills are described in a subsequent section of this chapter and in chapter 6.

Typical Executive Day and Demands on Time

Senior executives typically work 55- to 70-hour weeks. A classic study by Mintzberg (1973) showed that effective executives work at a relatively relentless pace, with few if any breaks during their work days. Approximately 60% of their time is occupied with formal, scheduled meetings. The rest of their time is filled with less formal face-to-face encounters that tend to be brief, lasting less than 9 minutes per encounter, and are often focused on managing crises. Approximately one-third of their time is spent with subordinates, whereas only 10% involves their superiors. Between 22 and 33% of their time is spent outside their offices, primarily in contact with clients, colleagues, or peers. These executives were noted to be preoccupied with scheduling, showed disdain for written communications such as their mail, and skimmed professional articles at a rate of two per minute. It should be noted that Mintzberg's research involved only male executives.

Executives and Leadership Effectiveness

Effectiveness can be defined as a function of both productivity and health. The effective manager can be thought of as simultaneously functioning on two tracks: the *performance track* for which the end point is productivity and the *people track* for which the end point is health. Productivity is defined here as a measure of task and people outcomes, while performance is defined as a more inclusive term that includes both process—i.e., how an executive relates to others—and outcome, i.e., productivity (Sperry, 2002a). Health reflects the people dimension and includes factors such as job satisfaction, commitment, morale, and personal well-being. Thus, a manager may manifest high levels of productivity in the short run but still not be an effective leader. A productive manager may exhibit only one or two of the seven competencies that characterize the effective leader.

Leadership Effectiveness Continuum

Efforts to study leadership effectiveness have provided important clues about the requisite attributes and competencies associated with effective leader functioning. One of the first and most interesting sets of studies of leader effectiveness was described by Luthans and colleagues (1985; 1988). Their initial efforts to isolate the attributes of successful leaders led them to operationally define different types of effectiveness. In their 1985 study, they reported their findings on attributes of successful managers at various levels of an organization. They found that "success," operationally defined as salary increases and promotions, did not appear to be associated with traditional leadership attributes or functions such as greater involvement with strategic planning and coordinating activities associated with top management. Rather, success was associated with networking activity, particularly with outside constituencies.

In a subsequent study, Luthans (1988) further differentiated successful managers from what he called "effective" and "average" or traditional managers.

Fig. 2.1 Continuum of leadership effectiveness.

Effective managers were defined as those who achieved the highest levels of productivity and quality through motivating workers. Successful managers were defined as those who achieved rapid career outcomes in addition to above average levels of productivity in their units. By contrast, average managers were defined as those who achieved low to average productivity, quality, and career advancement.

Interestingly, those designated as effective managers spent more time interacting with their own employees than networking with colleagues outside the corporation, while those designated as successful managers spent more time networking with individuals outside the organization. Luthans' research is important for several reasons, not the least of which was his attempt to operationally define leadership effectiveness. This section delineates a continuum consisting of four ranges of leadership effectiveness based on my executive consulting and coaching experience (Sperry, 2002a). This continuum has three ranges: minimal, moderate, and maximal. Based on subsequent research, the continuum was expanded to four ranges. Figure 2.1 illustrates the continuum and four ranges. Each of four ranges is subsequently described.

Of the four descriptions that follow, only minimally effective leadership will be discussed in detail. In many instances, executives functioning at this end of the continuum are unlikely to remain in their positions for long, as they are forced to leave or derail. Occasionally, these individuals may be offered coaching or another executive development strategy. Usually, however, coaching is provided to executives who function at the average to moderate range of effectiveness. They are more likely to be responsive to interventions aimed at maximizing their productivity and health than executives with lower levels of effectiveness.

Minimal Effectiveness

Approaching the far left end of the leadership effectiveness continuum is minimally effective leadership. Minimally effective leadership is characterized by productivity and/or health and relational behaviors that are well below average functioning. Derailment reflects a form of minimally effective leadership. As noted earlier, derailment means "getting off track" because of disappointing performance. The derailed executive is someone who "either leaves the organization nonvoluntarily (through resignation, being fired, or retiring early) or is plateaued as a result of a perceived lack of fit between personal characteristic and skills and demands of the job" (Leslie & Van Velsor, 1996).

What are the chances of an executive derailing? Someone assuming a new or different executive position today has a 40% chance of derailment within

12 to 18 months (Betof & Harrison, 1996). An American Management Association study reported that 22% of employers surveyed had fired executives from positions that they occupied for less than 3 months (Johnson, 2000). Johnson contended that underdeveloped "emotional intelligence" (Goleman, 1998) is a major reason for derailment.

Leslie and Van Velsor's research describes some factors contributing to derailment. These include poor working relations, excessive ambition, and excessive authoritarianism (1996). A British survey indicated these reasons for executives' derailment: 82% failed to build partnering relationships with subordinates or peers; 58% were confused or unclear about job expectations; and 50% lacked the necessary internal political savvy (Manchester Consulting, 1997). Finally, a recent article in *Fortune* argued that executive failure or derailment is not a matter of having the ability and vision to succeed, but is rather a problem of execution. Derailed executives were characterized as indecisive, missing deadlines, and failing to keep commitments. Typically, the reason for derailment is a failure of the selection process, i.e., a poor match or fit between executive and position, or not recognizing and addressing the problem soon enough.

Derailment and other forms of poor productivity and health are very costly to corporations. At the present time, accurate data on the total costs to corporations are not yet established. However, it is possible to provide some estimates based on the cost of replacing a derailed executive. Assuming that a senior executive earned a salary of $250,000, the direct costs for a severance package including pay and benefits, outplacement assistance, as well as recruitment costs to refill the position, including search firm fees, candidate travel expenses, and moving expenses might range from $700,000 to over $1,000,000.

However, this figure does not include the indirect costs associated with termination. Indirect costs include a number of factors such as productivity lost while the terminated executive was employed, productivity lost while awaiting replacement, training costs and productivity lost during the training period, lower morale and productivity of subordinates, increased difficulty and expense of recruiting others, higher unemployment insurance rates, lost credibility of the management function, and possibly litigation costs associated with wrongful discharge.

Beatty (1994) notes that many consider the indirect costs to be at least five to ten times the direct cost. For a senior level executive below the level of CEO, with salary and benefits in the range of $400,000 to $500,000 per year, the combined indirect *and* direct replacement cost would be considerably higher. Given the golden parachute clauses that are common in executive employment agreements, the replacement costs often exceed $5 million for executives below the level of CEO and often exceed $10 million for low profile CEOs.

Moderate Effectiveness

Moderately effective leadership is characterized by productivity and profitability in the average range of functioning. As noted earlier, managers at this level of functioning are the main targets of executive initiatives aimed at maximizing their productivity. Such initiatives include executive coaching and leadership development programs. Executives in this range tend to be much more responsive to interventions aimed at maximizing their productivity and health than executives in the lowest range of effectiveness.

High Effectiveness

Leadership in this range is characterized by high levels of productivity, quality, and profitability. Highly effective executives are sometimes referred to as "peak performers" (Lark & Richards, 2000). Corporate leaders like Jack Welch, Lee Iacocca, and Bill Gates are high visibility examples of executives functioning in this range.

While it is true that corporations whose leadership is primarily in the moderate to effective range can be quite successful in terms of productivity, quality, and profitability, at least in the short run, growing and sustaining those outcomes in the long run is difficult to achieve and maintain. Sustained success and viability seem to require something more than merely approaching the highly effective range of leadership.

Optimal Effectiveness

Executives who possess that "something more" are likely to be optimally effective executives. This range of leadership effectiveness is the ultimate goal of strategies for maximizing productivity and health. In my opinion, a high, sustained level of organizational effectiveness cannot be achieved unless a critical mass of executives approaches optimal effectiveness. To the extent this critical mass is reached and exceeded, the organization's culture will shift more in the direction of a culture of effectiveness that will further shape and facilitate effectiveness. This range of leadership effectiveness is also referred to as *Level 5 leadership* (Collins, 2001) and *transforming leadership.*

Transforming leadership is a term that has acquired two different meanings. In the first instance, it refers to the leader of good character and virtue who manifests integrity and concern and exercises the capacity to foster and achieve transformation in workers and the organization. In the second instance, it refers to a way of thinking about leadership above and beyond its customary focus on increasing performance and productivity. Both meanings are reflected in our view of transforming leadership.

Transformation is at the heart of transforming leadership. Transformation is defined as the act or process of transforming or changing the form, nature, or character of something—whether that something is an object, a work process, or an individual. Recent studies suggest that transforming leaders foster basic change or transformation in not only work processes but in the characters and personalities of the individuals in their organizations (Collins, 2001). This transformation seems to come about slowly and imperceptibly, largely due to the presence and passionate commitment of a transforming leader or leadership team. At the present, a profile of the competencies, attributes, and skills of these kinds of leaders is emerging. However, much less is known about the process of developing this optimal level of leadership. Nevertheless, subsequent chapters describe coaching strategies that can be useful in enhancing this level of executive functioning.

Level 5 Leadership

Level 5 leadership is another designation for what can be called transforming leadership. Level 5 was first described by Jim Collins, a leading leadership researcher who studied apparently effective corporations (2001). In 1995, he embarked on a 5-year research study to answer that question. Collins and his research team looked for corporations that shifted from good performance to great performance and were able to sustain the pattern for at least 15 years. The researchers then compared them to corporations that failed to make sustained shifts from good to great. They looked for a specific pattern: cumulative stock returns at or below the general stock market for 15 years, punctuated by a transition point, then cumulative returns at least three times the market over the next 15 years.

They began with 1,435 corporations listed among the *Fortune* 500 from 1965 to 1995 and found only 11 corporations that sustained this good-to-great pattern. The main finding of this 5-year study was that Level 5 leadership is a critical factor for corporate transformation. While Level 5 leadership is not the only requirement among factors such as finding and keeping the right personnel, using selective technology accelerators, and creating a culture of discipline to transform a good organization into a great one, it is essential. In other words, good-to-great transformations cannot occur without Level 5 leaders at the helm. Interestingly, the absence of Level 5 leadership was notable among the comparison organizations. Leaders at the other four levels in the hierarchy could and did produce high degrees of success, but not at levels sufficient to elevate their organizations from mediocrity to sustained excellence. These findings not only contradict most of the conventional wisdom of leadership, i.e., highly successful corporations require larger-than-life leaders, but much of leadership and management theory.

What is Level 5 leadership? Collins (2001) devised a hierarchy of five levels of leadership. A person at Level 1 is called a *Highly Capable Individual.* This executive makes productive contributions through talent, knowledge, skills, and good work habits. The Level 2 leader is designated a *Contributing Team Member* who contributes to the achievement of group objectives and works effectively with others in a group setting. Level 3 is achieved by the *Competent Manager* who organizes individuals and resources toward the effective and efficient pursuit of predetermined objectives. The *Effective Leader* is at Level 4. This executive is recognized for the capacity to catalyze commitment to and vigorous pursuit of a clear and compelling vision and stimulates his or her group to achieve high performance standards. Finally, the *Level 5 Leader* is the executive who builds enduring greatness through a paradoxical combination of personal humility plus professional will. According to research, the Level 5 executive requires the capabilities of all the lower levels, plus the special characteristics pertaining to Level 5.

Two other study findings are worth mentioning. First, in more than two-thirds of the comparison corporations, Collins identified a narcissistic pattern that either contributed to the demise or continued mediocrity of the company. This pattern was common in corporations led by talented yet egocentric Level 4 executives. The corporations achieved a steep level of growth followed by noticeable decline in later years. Lee Iacocca, the former CEO of Chrysler Corporation, characterizes this pattern. Because of Iacocca's initial heroic measures, Chrysler's stock rose 2.9 times higher than the general market about halfway through his tenure. Unfortunately, Iacocca then diverted his attention to becoming a celebrity. He appeared regularly on national talk shows, made more than 80 TV commercials, promoted his best selling autobiography, and even considered a candidacy for the U.S. presidency. As Iacocca's personal wealth soared, Chrysler's stock fell 31% below the market in the second half of his tenure.

A second noticeable difference relates to succession planning. Because Level 5 leaders have ambition for their organizations and not for themselves, they routinely select superb successors. That is because Level 5 leaders want to see their organizations become even more successful in the next generation. By contrast, Level 4 leaders often fail to set up their companies for enduring success after they leave. In more than three-quarters of the comparison corporations, Collins found executives who set up their successors for failure, chose weak successors, or used both tactics. How do Level 5 and the other four levels of leadership relate to the continuum of leadership effectiveness? Figure 2.2 maps the relationship.

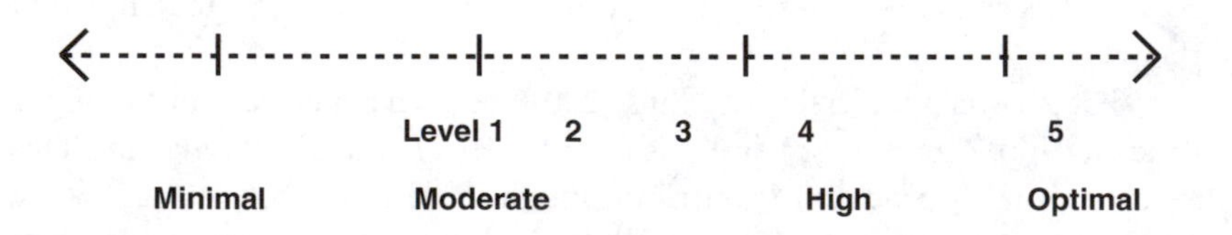

Fig. 2.2 Leadership levels and the continuum of leadership effectiveness.

Executive Leadership Styles

Leadership style is a rather broad and imprecise designation commonly used by executives and other managers. Leadership style is variously defined but typically refers to a leader or manager's personal style of approaching job-related tasks and relating to others in the work setting. Style reflects an individual's unique pattern of behaviors, values, and personality dynamics. Personal dynamics are different from organizational dynamics, and while they influence each other, a leader's personal dynamics or personal style can significantly impact the culture and dynamics of an organization. Two dimensions of leadership style will be described in this section: personality styles and management styles. Six common personality styles of executives are described along with three current views of management styles. Finally, a case example illustrates these styles.

Personality Styles

There is considerable interest in the personality dynamics of executives. Kets de Vries (1989; Kets de Vries & Miller, 1987) has written widely about the personality dynamics of senior managers. He believes that individuals with certain personality styles tend to gravitate toward senior management positions, whereas individuals with other styles do not. While Kets de Vries' characterizations of a manager's personality in clinical terms, i.e., narcissistic, paranoid, histrionic, etc., accurately portray the functioning of leaders, many executives are uncomfortable with the use of such diagnostic designations to describe professional managers and their job functioning. Therefore, the following descriptions of six personality styles utilize the nonclinical designations suggested by Sperry (1996, 2002b). While some executives will find that a single personality style sufficiently captures their unique style, other executives will find that their personalities include two or more styles. The case example later in this chapter illustrates this point.

Three ranges of personal, relational and work functioning can be delineated: minimal, adequate, and optimal. What constitutes adequate functioning and what differentiates it from minimal and optimal functioning? The Global Assessment of Functioning (GAF) Scale–Axis V of the *Diagnostic and Statistical Manual (DSM)*-IV-TR provides a useful metric (APA, 2000). Adequate functioning is represented with a GAF of 65 to 84. Generally speaking, individuals may experience some transient reactions to psychosocial stressors, yet they function reasonably well socially and at work and have the capacity to engage in some meaningful interpersonal relationships. Optimal functioning is represented with a GAF of 85 to 100. Generally speaking, such individuals have very good to excellent functioning in a wide range of activities, are satisfied with their lives, and are socially effective. Their problems never seem to get out of hand, and they are sought out by others because of their many positive qualities.

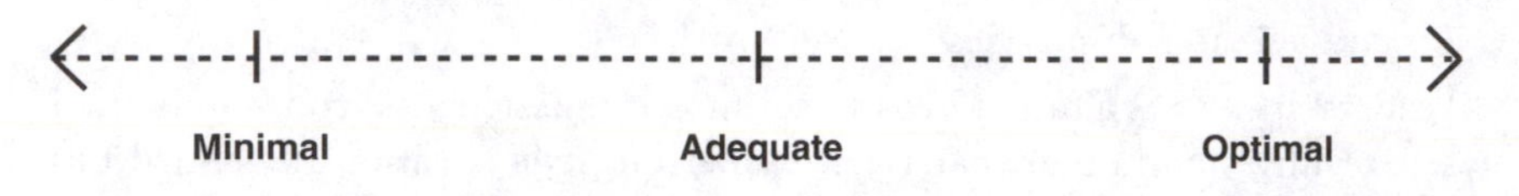

Fig. 2.3 Continuum of personality style functioning.

On the other hand, minimal functioning is represented by a GAF score below 65. These individuals tend to experience moderate to severe distress or symptoms and have considerable difficulty with work, social, and interpersonal relationships to the point of impairment.

Figure 2.3 illustrates a continuum of personality style functioning (Sperry, 2002b) indicating three ranges: minimal functioning, adequate functioning, and optimal functioning. The balance of this section describes these three ranges of functioning for each of the common personality styles of executives; cf. Sperry (2002a) for a more detailed discussion of these personality styles.

Self-Confident Personality Style

Optimal Functioning—Individuals with optimal functioning are energetic and self-assured. They believe in themselves and their own values without expecting special treatment or privileges. They tend to be attractive and charming individuals who become outstanding in a profession or in an avocation. Because they embody widely admired qualities, others want to model their achievements. Highly competent, adaptable and focused, they are very likely to achieve challenging goals. They can expertly present and advocate for an idea or proposal in ways that are both acceptable and compelling. They easily enlist the support and commitment of others to worthy projects that serve the common good. At their best, they are genuine and authentic individuals who fully accept themselves. Worth as a person is not based on success or fame or the appearance of either. Accordingly, these individuals can live modestly and relate to others with heartfelt simplicity and grace.

Adequate Functioning—Although emotionally vulnerable to negative assessments and feelings of others, adequately functioning individuals can surmount them with style and grace. They are shrewd in dealing with others and utilize the strengths and advantages of others to achieve their own goals. Usually, they are quite effective in selling themselves, their ideas, and their projects. They believe in themselves, their abilities, and their uniqueness, yet favor special treatment and privilege. Also, they tend to be able competitors who love getting to the top and enjoy staying there. These individuals can visualize themselves as the best or most accomplished in their fields. They readily accept accomplishments, praise, and admiration gracefully and with self-possession. They possess a keen awareness of their thoughts and feelings and have some awareness of the thoughts and feelings of others. Finally, they expect others to treat them well at all times.

Minimal Functioning—Individuals at this level of functioning tend to react to criticism with feelings of rage, stress, or humiliation. They are interpersonally exploitive and take advantage of others to achieve their own ends. They possess grandiose senses of self-importance, and believe that their problems are unique and understood only by other special people. Preoccupied by fantasies of unlimited success, power, brilliance, beauty, or ideal love, they have a sense of entitlement and unreasonable expectations of especially favorable treatment. Not surprisingly, they require almost constant attention and admiration. They lack empathy and are unable to recognize and experience how others feel; they are preoccupied with feelings of envy. The DSM-IV-TR counterpart is the narcissistic personality disorder.

Adventurous Personality Style

Optimal Functioning—These individuals are confident, assertive, and effective at getting what they need and want. Disposed to taking initiatives and making things happen, they value independence and foster it in others. By nature they are strong-willed, impassioned individuals who are natural leaders that others respect and turn to for direction. They earn respect by acting honorably, by using power constructively, by championing and protecting others, and by promoting worthwhile causes. They seek justice and fair play, and have positive visions for their world. At their best, they become compassionate, merciful, and forbearing individuals who achieve great degrees of self-control and protect and support the rights of others with their strength and the courage of their convictions.

Adequate Functioning—Executives who function at this level prefer to follow their own drummers and typically live by their own internal codes of values. Although they are seldom influenced by others or society's norms, they can respect others' values. As adolescents they were usually high-spirited hell raisers and mischief makers. Most of the time, they are generous with money believing that as it is spent, more will turn up somewhere and somehow. While they often have wanderlust, they are able to make plans and sustain commitments, albeit for limited time spans. They have a gift for communicating and easily befriend others, although they may not offer much depth to these relationships. Typically, courageous, physically bold and tough, they will stand up to those who take advantage of them. They seldom worry about others, but rather expect others to be responsible for themselves. They often have strong libidos and while they may desire others, they can remain monogamous for long periods. They usually focus on living in the present and seldom experience guilt feelings.

Minimal Functioning—Individuals who function at this level are unable to sustain consistent work by using their talents, skills, ingenuity, and wits. They fail to conform to social norms with regard to lawful behavior. They may perform antisocial acts that constitute grounds for arrest. They break rules and are irritable and aggressive as indicated by involvement in fights or assaults. They may repeatedly fail to honor financial obligations or plan ahead; they tend to be impulsive. They seem to have little regard for the truth and may lie and "con" others for personal profit or pleasure. Furthermore, they can be reckless regarding their own safety and the safety of others. Thus, they may drive while intoxicated or engage in high risk driving behavior such as speeding in school zones. As parents or guardians, they lack the ability to function responsibly. Showing remorse and sustaining long-term monogamous relationships are difficult. While the DSM-IV clinical counterpart to this personality style is the antisocial personality disorder, few executives would fully meet criteria for this diagnosis. Nevertheless, some will manifest a few of these or behavioral indicators. This less extreme form is known as antisocial trait disturbance.

Dramatic Personality Style

Optimal Functioning—These individuals are deeply empathetic and compassionate. They put themselves in the place of others and are caring and concerned. They see the potential and goodness in those around them and readily respond with appreciation and encouragement. Because serving others is their basic priority, they are extraordinarily generous, giving, and helpful. Even if it requires personal sacrifice, they go out of their way to meet others' needs. In the course of doing so, they are able to maintain healthy boundaries and attend to their own needs as well. Since they have found the love they seek within themselves, they can be altruistic and unconditionally giving without any expectation of reciprocity. At their best, they are deeply humble, gracious, and patient individuals who have mastered the art of nurturing themselves and others.

Adequate Functioning—Individuals at this level of functioning typically enjoy compliments and praise. They are charming, engaging, and appropriately seductive in appearance and behavior. Usually, they are very attentive to their appearance and grooming and enjoy colorful clothes, style and fashion. While they are lively, fun loving, sensation-oriented, and often impulsive, they can delay gratification. They enjoy being the center of attention and rise to the occasion when all eyes are on them. Others enjoy being around adequately functioning individuals because they are interesting, emotionally demonstrative, and physically affectionate. They react emotionally but appropriately most of the time. Furthermore, they display a style of speech that is appropriately global and specific at the same time.

Minimal Functioning—These individuals seem to continually seek or demand reassurance, approval, or praise from others. Physical attractiveness is often very important and they may spend inordinate amounts of time and money on their appearance. At times, they may be inappropriately sexually seductive in appearance and behavior. They express emotion with inappropriate exaggeration and are often self-centered and express little tolerance for delaying gratification. Most notable is their level of discomfort in situations where they cannot be the centers of attention. They may display rapidly shifting and shallow expressions of emotion and utilize a style of speech that is excessively impressionistic and lacking in detail. The DSM-IV-TR counterpart is the histrionic personality disorder.

Leisurely Personality Style

Optimal Functioning—Individuals who function optimally are emotionally stable and have refreshingly positive outlooks on life. While coming across as easygoing, patient, and gentle, they remain firm in their convictions and are not easily misled. Their steadiness, common sense, and quiet demeanor exert a calming and healing influence on others. While usually laid back, they can act decisively and courageously when a situation demands it. They exhibit unhurried attitude and pace and will conscientiously set and meet realistic deadlines. Since they easily can appreciate others' points of view, they make effective negotiators and counselors. At their best, they are autonomous and fulfilled individuals who exude genuine contentment, optimism, and equanimity. Because they maintain high degrees of centeredness and composure, they achieve unparalleled levels of balance in their lives.

Adequate Functioning—Individuals in this category can be somewhat pessimistic about the present and the future, and when tired or stressed will typically complain about the demands in their lives. Although they can usually fulfill their given responsibilities, they seldom function at or above their levels of ability. Although they are not likely to be exploited, they effectively resist unreasonable demands. Relaxed about time, they typically display Type B personalities. They can cooperate with others and are usually comfortable with groups and family members. They are not overawed or impressed by authority.

Minimal Functioning—These individuals resist fulfilling their given responsibilities by procrastinating, "forgetting," sulking, or being argumentative. An underlying pessimism pervades their thoughts, attitudes, feelings, and actions. They protest, without justification, that unreasonable demands are placed on them. They intentionally work slowly or perform badly on tasks they do not want to do. They may obstruct the efforts of others and fail to do their share; they can be uncooperative. They resent useful suggestions made by others concerning how they could be more productive or effective. The DSM-IV-TR counterpart is the passive–aggressive or negativistic personality disorder.

Conscientious Personality Style

Optimal Functioning—These individuals are highly principled and conscientious; they constantly strive to be impartial, fair, and objective. Truth and justice are their primary values and such individuals are models of the highest levels of personal and professional integrity. They are willing to make personal sacrifices and delay gratification for the greater good, and utilize their time, energy, and passion to fulfill their callings in life. Because of their moral sensitivity and articulateness, they make excellent teachers and role models. Furthermore, because they can maintain centeredness and composure even under pressure, they are likely to achieve unparalleled levels of excellence and balance in their lives. At their best, they become extraordinarily wise and humane, with superb senses of vision and discernment. As a result, they tend to make realistic choices and provide wise counsel to others. Because of their acceptance of shortcomings in themselves and others, they serve as inspirations to many. They are life-affirming, hopeful, and kind while balancing personal integrity with generosity. They experience a deep sense of serenity and peace that comes from acceptance of their lives and life circumstances.

Adequate Functioning—Individuals at this level of functioning desire to complete tasks and projects without flaws or errors. They take pride in doing all jobs and tasks well, including the smallest details. They want work to be done "just right" and in a specific manner, yet they have some tolerance. They are dedicated to work and are capable of intense, single-minded effort. They carefully consider alternatives and their consequences in making decisions, and have strong moral principles and strong desires to do the right thing. They are no-nonsense individuals who do their work without much emotional expenditure. Generally speaking, they are careful, thrifty, and cautious, and able to share from their abundance. Furthermore, they tend to save and collect objects and are reluctant to discard objects that have, formerly had, or someday may have value for them.

Minimal Functioning—Individuals at this level are characterized by perfectionism that interferes with task completion. They tend to be preoccupied with organization, details, rules, lists, orders, and schedules to the extent that the major point of the activity is lost. They unreasonably insist that others submit exactly to their way of doing things and may exhibit unreasonable reluctance to allow others to perform tasks because of the conviction that others will not do them correctly. They exhibit excessive devotion to work to the exclusion of leisure activities and friendships. Most of the time, they are indecisive. Decision making is avoided or postponed. Overconscientiousness, scrupulosity, and inflexibility about matters of morality, ethics, and values are common traits. Restricted expression of affection is characteristic, as is lack of generosity in giving time, money, or gifts when no personal gain is likely to result. Furthermore, these individuals may be unable to discard worn-out or worthless items even when they have no sentimental value. The DSM-IV-TR counterpart is the obsessive–compulsive personality disorder.

Vigilant Personality Style

Optimal Functioning—These individuals are self-assured and confident in their ability to make decisions and take care of themselves. They tend to be intuitive, sensitive, and perceptive. Superior listeners, observers, and interviewers, they are keenly aware of subtleties, tones, and multiple levels of meaning. They excel at sizing up situations and people and discerning motives and intentions. Accordingly, they are highly proficient scientific investigators, security analysts, detectives, document examiners, and trial attorneys. They are assertive and can defend themselves without losing control and becoming aggressive. At their best, they are loyal and faithful colleagues and friends who take criticism rather seriously without becoming intimidated.

Adequate Functioning—Individuals who function adequately are keenly aware of environmental and interpersonal cues and subscribe to the belief that "it is better to be safe than sorry." Because they are thin-skinned, they can be rather sensitive to criticism, even positive criticism. They question persons and circumstances as part of their vigilant outlook; careful foresight and discernment are other traits. They are keenly observant of others and are particularly sensitive to how others react to them. Not surprisingly, they are careful in their dealings with other people and maintain a certain level of detachment while sizing up potential threats that others may pose.

Minimal Functioning—These individuals are reluctant to confide in others because of unwarranted fears that the information will be used against them. They regularly read hidden meanings or threats into benign remarks or events, for example, suspecting that a neighbor puts out trash early to annoy them. They bear grudges and are unforgiving of insults or slights. They may routinely question, without justification, the fidelity of spouses, sexual partners, friends, and associates. They also expect, without sufficient basis, to be exploited or harmed by others. Finally, they are easily slighted, quick to take the offense, and often react with anger or counterattack. The DSM-IV-TR counterpart is the paranoid personality disorder.

Management Styles

Just as unique personality features, i.e., personality styles, form a large part of an individual's personal style, so too does an individual's management style. While there has been considerable interest in topic of management styles for more than 50 years, there is no consensus among researchers as to what constitutes this stylistic dimension, nor is there a commonly accepted typology of management styles as there is with personality styles. Nevertheless, many managers endorse the Managerial Grid as a useful approach to understanding and assessing management styles. Accordingly, the Managerial Grid and a variant of it are briefly described in this section.

Managerial Grid

The Managerial Grid (Blake & Mouton, 1964) is a well recognized and widely used classification of leadership styles. It relates the two main tracks or concerns of leadership: productivity and people. Management style is classified in terms of emphasis on people and/or productivity. According to the theory underlying this approach, the ideal leadership style has an equal emphasis on people and productivity. Leaders with this style endeavor to develop their employees in such a way as to achieve high productivity, high job satisfaction, commitment, health, and well-being. These five leadership styles are briefly described.

1. *Laissez-Faire Leadership Style:* This leadership style is characterized by minimal concern for people and for production. Such managers pass along orders and lack initiative.
2. *Country Club Leadership Style:* This style is characterized by high concern for people and less attention to production.
3. *Task-Oriented Leadership Style:* This leadership style is characterized by high concern for production and low concern for people.
4. *Middle-of-the-Road Leadership Style:* This style is characterized by adequate concerns for both people and production and attempts to balance the two concerns.
5. *Democratic Leadership Style:* This leadership style is characterized by a high concern for both people and production.

Dual Dimensional Approach

An interesting variant of the Managerial Grid was described by Stephenson (2000). To the dimension of people orientation versus productivity orientation, Stephenson added the dimension of control versus creativity. This dimension accounts for the extent to which some leaders seek to be in control or impose control on others, as compared to leaders who foster divergent thinking, i.e., "thinking outside the box" and favor hands-off, creative environments. Four leadership styles can be derived from comparing the polar opposites of each dimension.

1. *Production Controller:* The leadership style with a high emphasis on productivity and control
2. *Benevolent Autocrat:* The leadership style with a high emphasis on control and people
3. *Inspirational Leader:* The leadership style with a high emphasis on people and creativity
4. *Visionary Strategist:* The leadership style with a high emphasis on creativity and productivity

Case Example

Larry Kimble has the reputation as a leader who makes things happen. He is the 59-year-old CEO of a high-tech corporation that he founded 21 years ago. Before that, Larry had been president of a tool and die company, succeeding his father who created the company after the Depression. In the early 1970s, anticipating that the future for tool and die making would be eclipsed by more sophisticated technology, Larry skillfully began reinventing the company and made it into one of the most successful family-owned businesses in the high-tech sector. While much about the operation of his company changed, Larry was careful to maintain the worker-friendly culture his father had nurtured over a 30-year period.

A humble man who attributes his success to his employees, Larry is proud of the fact that there are still a few employees on the payroll hired by his father. Annual turnover is only about 4% and that is primarily attributed to retirement. In comparison, turnover among his competitors was closer to 30%. Like his father, Larry is passionate about his work and the corporation and has created and maintained a family atmosphere and a culture of trust, respect, and commitment to the corporation, to its customers, and to its 700-plus employees.

Kimble, now in his 60s, keeps hours that few of his younger executive staff can match. He attends early breakfast and dinner meetings and receptions with stakeholders nearly every day of the week. On weekends, when he is not out of town on business or attending trade group meetings, he manages to get away from it all to spend time with his family that includes several grandchildren.

Although he is amazingly active, productive, and energetic, he never gives the impression that he is rushed or in a hurry. His unmistakable sense of harmony and centeredness permeated the rest of his top management team. No one could remember his taking any sick time in all the years he had been CEO. Not surprisingly, employees, the board of directors, and shareholders are hoping Kimble will remain in his position indefinitely.

In terms of personality styles, Kimble manifests both the self-confident personality style shown by his confident, outgoing, energetic, and self-assured manner, and the conscientious personality style as shown by his dedication and single-mindedness to completing tasks, his abiding desire to achieve goals in a conscientious, effective, and efficient manner, and treatment of staff members in an equitable, fair, and caring manner. His management style is characterized by equal and high levels of concern for both people and productivity. Kimble is fair and caring—and even fun to be around—yet holds his staff to mutually agreed-upon performance standards that are reviewed monthly. This is the *democratic style* described by Blake and Mouton (1964). In terms of Stephenson's categories of management styles (2000), Kimble's style appears to have elements of both the Inspirational Leader and the Visionary Strategist.

Leadership and Character

Leadership was discussed in detail earlier in this chapter. Character is the dimension of personality that describes how individuals conduct themselves in interpersonal and organizational situations; it is shaped through the simultaneous development of self-identity and self-regulation. It represents a habitual pattern of thinking, responding, and acting reflective of an individual's moral, social, and spiritual attitudes, and bespeaks "emotional" rather than cognitive intelligence (Goleman, 1998). Accordingly, character has been aptly described as how a person acts when no one is watching.

Unlike temperament which reflects the biological influence on personality, character reflects the influence of socialization and learning on personality. When this socialization process is reasonably adequate and without significant developmental arrests, adaptive, creative, and socially responsible or virtuous behavior—called "good character"—can be expected. Most would consider individuals with good character to be responsible, trustworthy, respectful, caring and dependable friends, colleagues, or team players.

Dimensions of Character

Extensive research bears out this common understanding. Research across cultures indicates that individuals with good or mature character structures tend to be self-reliant or responsible, cooperative, and self-transcendent (Cloninger, Svrakic, & Przybeck, 1993). In contrast, those with immature character structures had difficulty with self-acceptance, were intolerant and revengeful toward others, and felt self-conscious and unfulfilled. Parenthetically, the research indicated that those with immature character structures also met DSM criteria for personality disorders. These three dimensions of character (self-responsibility, cooperativeness, and self-transcendence) are measured by the Temperament Character Inventory (TCI) devised by Cloninger, Svrakic, and Przybeck (1993), wherein a healthy personality or matured character reflects positive or elevated scores on these three character dimensions, while negative or low scores reflect the presence of character or personality disorders. Each of these three dimensions will be briefly described.

Self-Responsibility

Self-responsibility (or self-directedness) refers to self-determination—an individual's ability to control, regulate, and adapt behavior in accord with his or her chosen goals and values. Individuals differ in their capacity for self-determination. Individuals with moderate to high levels of self-determination are considered mature, effective, and well-organized. They exhibit self-esteem, are able to admit faults and accept themselves as they are, feel their lives have meaning and purpose, can delay gratification in order to achieve their goals, and take initiative in overcoming challenges. On the other hand, individuals with lower levels of self-determination have low self-esteem, blame others for their problems, feel uncertain of their identity or purpose, and are often reactive, dependent, and resourceless.

Cooperativeness

The character factor of cooperativeness was formulated to account for individual differences in identification with and acceptance of other people.

Cooperative individuals tend to be socially tolerant, empathic, helpful, and compassionate, while uncooperative individuals tend to be socially intolerant, disinterested in other people, unhelpful, and revengeful. In addition, cooperative individuals are likely to show unconditional acceptance of others, empathy with others' feelings, and willingness to help others achieve their goals without selfish domination. It is not surprising that social acceptance, helpfulness, and concerns for the rights of others are correlated with positive self-esteem.

Self-Transcendence

Self-transcendence and character traits associated with spirituality have largely been neglected in systematic research and omitted from personality inventories. Nevertheless, self-transcendence may be the feature of personality that most people associate with the character traits of respect, caring, and good citizenship. Self-transcendence is essentially the polar opposite of self-interest.

When the three components of self-responsibility, cooperativeness, and self-transcendence are reasonably well developed in executives, the executives tend to act with integrity and manifest good judgment in all situations and circumstances, even when under considerable duress, temptation, or when doing the right thing is not in their immediate self-interest.

Relationship of Character and Leadership

The relationship of character and leadership is complex and has been described in various ways. Bennis (1998) describes the connection between leadership and character. He notes that effective leaders manifest vision and a strong sense of purpose, inspire trust, and accomplish change; then he defines leadership as "character in action" (p. 144).

Character reflects an enduring and consistent way of functioning in both private and public spheres, but hidden aspects of character tend to emerge under conditions of stress, fatigue, or temptation. Usually, individuals attempt to hide or disown their "dark sides"—the more unflattering aspects of their character—and instead emphasize the "bright sides" of their personas. This phenomenon is called "impression management," which is the ability to manifest different personas in response to the press of circumstances. Unfortunately, success in the art of impression management is highly regarded by some in corporate America. The trade-offs for this success are diminished or absent personal integrity and difficulty establishing and maintaining the trust of peers and superiors.

Nexus of Leadership Effectiveness and Personality Style

At this point we have described two key dimensions of executive leadership: effectiveness and style. What, if any, is their relationship? From a linear

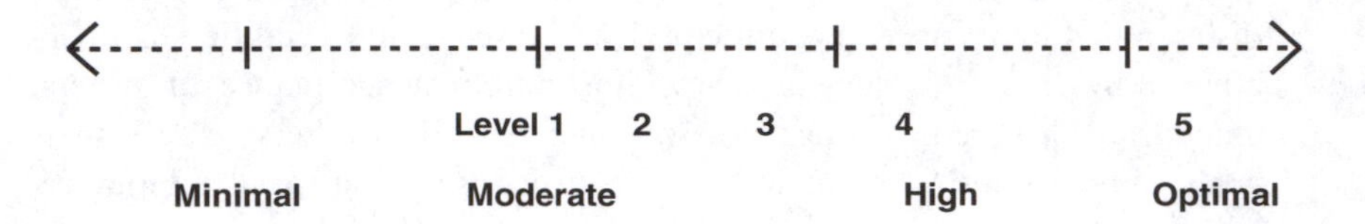

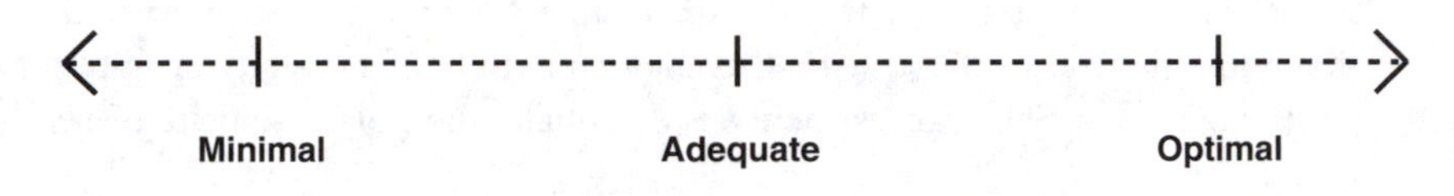

Fig. 2.4 Relationship of leadership effectiveness and personality style functioning.

perspective, it is easy to conceptualize these dimensions as related, but separate, independent, and parallel lines. The fact is that these dimensions are intimately related in a continuous and interdependent fashion. From a spatial perspective, effectiveness and style may be viewed as intersecting lines or closely linked circles, such as in a Venn diagram. Generally speaking, individuals who function at the adequate range of leadership effectiveness are most likely to function in the adequate range of personality style. It also means that their particular personality styles will uniquely flavor their leadership effectiveness. Thus, if you were to observe six executives in the adequate range of effectiveness with six different personality styles in the adequate range, you would note six somewhat different ways in which they act and relate to others.

Figure 2.4 represents the nexus of leadership effectiveness and personality style by juxtapositioning the Continuum of Leadership Effectiveness with the Continuum of Personality Style Functioning. Note that the Levels 1 through 3 of leadership as described by Collins (2001) are situated in the moderate range. Level 4 corresponds to the high range, while Level 5 is situated in the optimal range of leadership effectiveness. Also, note that the moderate range of leadership effectiveness corresponds to the adequate range of personality style functioning.

Skills, Talents, Virtues, and Competencies

Because terms such as skills, talents, and competencies are often used interchangeably, it is helpful to distinguish them. Furthermore, the terms are central to executive coaching in that coaches attempt to refine talents and increase skills and competencies.

Skills

Skills are capabilities that can be transferred from one person to another. In other words, skills are learned behaviors. For example, using software such as Excel can be learned in many ways, such as by direct instruction, watching someone using it, or following a computer tutorial.

Talents

Talents and dispositions are two types of attributes. Talents are natural abilities that influence an individual's recurring patterns of thought, feeling, or behavior. They are in-born traits that cannot be learned. For instance, the talent of good judgment is really an attribute that cannot be easily approximated. Individuals who have good judgment can intuitively make split-second decisions about people or tasks under duress and their decisions turn out to be excellent. Individuals who have been taught problem-solving protocols may be able to follow the protocols and systematically think through a problem reasonably well when they have sufficient time and are under little or no duress. However, these individuals are at a great disadvantage when they are forced to make quick decisions in high demand or emergency situations.

Virtues

Virtues are dispositions or tendencies and habitual patterns of acting in a characteristically positive manner at different times and places. Unlike talents, dispositions must be exercised or practiced in order to be maintained. Virtues such as respect, integrity, honesty, and humility are attributes that reflect good character. As noted earlier, character represents a habitual pattern of thinking, responding, and acting that represents moral, social, and religious attitudes. It reflects a pattern of being in the world that is practiced and perfected over a lifetime rather than learned in a weekend seminar or corporate training program. In other words, character is what a person actually is rather than how a person appears or presents himself or herself to others. It is the opposite of impression management wherein a leader attempts to portray himself or herself in a positive manner to elicit favorable responses from others. As noted earlier, optimal leadership effectiveness reflects good character and virtue.

Competencies

Competencies are capabilities that many use to describe expected behaviors in leaders. Some competencies may actually be talents such as the ability to remain calm when under fire. Other competencies such as ability to implement basic operational systems may actually be skills. Others may be part skills and part talent. "Pure" competencies are those that are primarily skill-based rather than being attribute- or talent-based. Typically, competencies represent one or more skill sets. A skill set, as the name implies, is a set or cluster of related skills. For example, communication is a skill set consisting of several specific skills such as listening, engagement, empathic responding, nonverbal communication, verbal presentation, and written correspondence, to name a few.

Leadership Skills

Several core leadership skills are associated with highly effective executives. The remainder of this section briefly describes eight such skill sets that highly effective leaders have been noted to manifest.

Communication

This skill set provides a manager with several skills and strategies for improving productivity, interpersonal relationships, and job commitment through strategic communication. This set includes core skills such as engagement, active listening, and interpersonal communication as well as advanced skills such as effective writing, ability to make verbal presentations, and conducting effective meetings.

Strategic Thinking and Decision Making

This skill set allows a manager to learn to think strategically, i.e., "outside the box." Two related skills are strategic planning and decision making which, in their best sense, are applications of strategic thinking.

Commitment and Motivation

This skill set prepares a manager with several skills and strategies for assessing the causes of decreased commitment and motivation and skills for increasing employee commitment and trigger their motivation to improve performance.

Stress and Time Management

This skill set enhances a leader's capacity to control and cope with stress on and off the job, with emphasis on several specific skills and strategies for long-term and immediate management of work stress, job strain, and time stressors.

Team Performance

This skill set provides the skills and strategies for influencing the processes of team development and team building to maximize individual and team performance, job satisfaction, and commitment to the organization.

Delegation

This skill set provides a manager with an understanding of empowered delegation—the skills for assigning an employee a task while simultaneously empowering the employee to successfully complete the task.

Conflict Resolution

This skill set provides a manager with the skills to assess and manage conflict and implement measures to prevent it. Also included are skills and strategies for effectively dealing with angry, negative, and uncooperative employees.

Organizational and Individual Assessment

This skill set provides a strategy for assessing various personal and organizational resources and evaluating the impact of these resources—or lack thereof—on the manager in terms of the degree of "fit" among self, job, organization, career, and family.

Those interested in a more detailed discussion of these skills are referred to *Becoming an Effective Health Care Manager: The Essential Skills of Leadership* (Sperry, 2003) for descriptions and strategies for developing or enhancing them.

Leadership Competencies

Effective leadership requires a unique set of core competencies. This section briefly describes the core competencies observed in highly effective and successful leaders and managers (Sperry, 2002a). My observation has been that highly effective or transforming leaders consistently embody all seven of these competencies, not just some of them, and always with the highest levels of behavioral indicators. [cf. Sperry (2002a) for a listing and description of lower levels of behavioral indicators for the various competencies.] By contrast, minimally effective and moderately effective leaders exhibit some but not all of these competencies, and always with much lower levels of behavioral indicators.

Why these particular competencies? Regardless of the types of organizations they lead and manage, transforming leaders seem to embody the following formula: Job expertise + organizational savvy + integrity + energy and passion + strategic visioning and action + team work and employee commitment = high performance and productivity. Table 2.1 describes these competencies along with behavioral markers or indicators that are readily observable in highly effective and transforming leaders.

TABLE 2.1 Leadership Competencies

Possess Requisite Job Capabilities. Highly effective leaders possess requisite job capabilities and a keen understanding of customers, markets, operations, and emerging issues to accomplish the corporate vision. They make and accept decisions based on facts, experience, and warranted assumptions about changes in markets, resources or regulations.

- Draw broadly on resources, knowledge, and expertise to thoroughly and systematically analyze a strategic initiative.
- Work to achieve equitable outcomes in negotiations and are cognizant of relevant facts and data as well as the needs, wants, objectives, and constraints of the involved parties.
- Demonstrate the capacity to make and accept difficult decisions.
- Proactively develop contingency plans in anticipation of changing market, regulations or resources.

TABLE 2.1 (*Continued*)

Exhibit High Energy, Health Status and Passion. Highly effective leaders manifest significant energy reserves to achieve short- and long-range goals despite arduous working conditions. They also maintain high levels of physical and psychological well-being despite adverse circumstances, demands and emotional stress.

- Exude high levels of energy and stamina that insure the capacity to tolerate, when necessary, long work hours, extensive travel, and other arduous job demands and deadlines while also leading active social lives.
- Tolerate exposure to ongoing stressors without compromising their health and well-being and have unlimited ability to socialize where a wide variety of food and drink is a focal point of business entertaining.
- Recover rapidly from minor illnesses, such as a cold or flu in 1–2 days; tolerate injuries, physical exertion, and emotional stress, without undue disruption of their normal schedules; are unlikely to develop chronic health conditions that reduce productivity and work involvement.
- Withstand arduous job demands and deadlines while remaining in excellent health.

Understand Individual and Organizational Dynamics. Highly effective leaders have the capacity to accurately "read" individuals, situations, and the changing dynamics of an organization and can utilize such information to make adjustments in personnel, structure, strategies, and implementation.

- Recognize and are sensitive to the needs and feelings of individuals.
- Appreciate and recognize subtle structural, cultural, strategic, and external dynamics that impact the organization.
- Recognize the importance of the person–organization fit, the person–job fit, the person–family fit, and the person–job–career–organization–family fit.
- Proactively monitor and modify corporate structure, reward systems, and other practices based on individual and organizational dynamics and "fit" considerations.
- Proactively scan the environment and develop long-term approaches that redefine problems or market opportunities in anticipation of changing business conditions or environmental trends and work to enhance community relations.

Act with Integrity, Humility and a Sense of Balance. Highly effective leaders create committed organizations that act with unparalleled integrity, courage, humility, and authenticity. Their employees consider them to be honest and trustworthy. Such leaders serve as role models by acting in a consistent and fair manner. Being around leaders with this competency encourages others to be better workers and persons. Such leaders manifest high degrees of stability and balance among corporate, personal, and family needs and demands. The presence of this competency distinguishes otherwise successful and effective leaders from transforming leaders.

- Genuinely live with integrity and courage; consistently listen to, respond to and serve others.

TABLE 2.1 (*Continued*)

- Consistently keep their egos in check; are humble about their accomplishments; and recognize the efforts of employees and colleagues and the impact of family.
- Lead by example and consistently model fairness, courage, and honesty.
- Effectively maintain a balance among corporate, personal, and family values, needs and demands.

Build Relationships and Mobilize Commitment. Highly effective leaders develop trusting relationships with colleagues and reports and foster highly productive teams. They hire and maintain a strong talent pool by continuously developing individuals' skills, knowledge, and capacities. They also inspire and motivate individuals to achieve and remain loyal to the organization's strategy, vision, and goals.

- Identify and develop organization strengths to match opportunities.
- Anticipate employee and leadership competencies needed within the organization and actively develop others' competencies to meet those needs.
- Expect and are significantly involved in coaching, developing, and supporting staff and effectively model this developmental perspective to others.
- Foster internal and external commitment for the strategy and the organization by involving broad constituencies and multiple perspectives.
- Exude enthusiasm and proactively garner employee commitment to the organization by creating and maintaining a culture of trust, respect, and cooperation.

Communicate a Compelling Vision and Act Strategically. Highly effective leaders create and communicate a compelling vision of the future that reflects corporate values, resources, trends, and opportunities. They regularly solicit ideas, provide honest feedback, share information with staff and others, consistently practice effective listening, and manifest good verbal and written communication skills. Their compelling visions and strategies are then brilliantly executed and implemented.

- Redesign organizational structure and operational systems to support effective corporate communication.
- Create and routinely utilize two-way communication networks to facilitate corporate-wide exchange of best practices.
- Envision the future when developing strategy; anticipate potential obstacles, competitive responses, and alternate scenarios; develop contingency plans.
- Implement strategies throughout their organizations by completely integrating organizational and individual goal planning, assessment, and rewards.
- Build strategic thinking and acting in managerial performance standards and model strategic communication and action in meetings, memos, and other methods.

Produce Extraordinary Results. Highly effective leaders engender high productivity, high morale, and a feeling among workers that they are valued and can grow with the organization—important markers of well-being. These outcomes are the end results

TABLE 2.1 (*Continued*)

of optimal leadership operating with the context of a corporate culture and structure of discipline, optimism, and consistency.

- They possess requisite job expertise and value congruence with the organization.
- They act with integrity, respect and humility.
- They understand individual and organizational dynamics.
- They are energetic and passionate.
- They effectively communicate a compelling vision and act strategically.
- They strive to build and maintain healthy relationships and mobilize commitments to the corporate vision, their team, and the organization.

The skill sets that make up the core competencies are listed in Table 2.2.

Increasing Leadership Effectiveness

The two critical ingredients to becoming an effective executive are competencies and level of fit. The basic premise is that it is easier for an individual to function as an effective manager if he or she is in the right place at the right time and works with the right managers and co-workers. In other words, while skills are necessary for effectiveness, having an adequate fit or match with a job and organization that prizes such skills is sufficient. Highly effective managers are able to develop, enhance, and maintain their leadership skills because their work environment not only permits them to use their skills, but also requires and rewards their utilization.

TABLE 2.2 Core Competencies and Related Skills and Attributes

Core Competency	Corresponding Skills and Attributes
Possess requisite job capabilities	Leaders assumed to have required capabilities
Exhibit high energy, health status, and passion	Stress management
Understand individual and organizational dynamics	Assessment of individual and organizational dynamics
Act with integrity, humility, and a sense of balance	High level of character development
Build relationships and mobilize commitments	Team development; delegation; conflict resolution; commitment and motivation
Communicate compelling visions and act strategically	Communications; strategic thinking, planning, and acting
Produce extraordinary results	Integrate and operationalize all other competencies and skills

The second ingredient is that effective executives are successful at what they do because they possess and manifest all the requisite leadership competencies and corresponding leadership skill sets. Needless to say, executive coaching can be a potent strategy for increasing leadership effectiveness.

Concluding Note

Executives are referred for coaching primarily for the purpose of increasing their productivity and effectiveness. This chapter has profiled the effective executive in terms of levels or ranges of leadership effectiveness and their component dimensions: leadership style, leadership skills, and leadership competencies. It characterized leadership effectiveness in terms of personal experience, energy and integrity, organizational savvy, strategic focus, and the relational capacity for maximizing teamwork and commitment in order to achieve the organization's mission, goals and objectives. Each of these dimensions provides a target for planning and implementing executive coaching processes and interventions on which subsequent chapters elaborate. Before we turn to the actual process of executive coaching, the next chapter describes the context in which executive coaching occurs.

References

American Psychiatric Association. (2000). *Diagnostic and statistical manual of mental disorders, fourth edition, text revision (DSM-IV-TR).* Washington, D.C.

Beatty, R. (1994). *Interviewing and selecting high performers.* New York: Wiley.

Bennis, W. (1998). The character of leadership. In M. Josephson & W. Hanson (Eds.). *The power of character: Prominent Americans talk about life, family, work, values and more.* San Francisco: Jossey-Bass, pp. 142–149.

Betof, E. & Harrison, R. (1996). The newly appointed leader dilemma: A significant change in today's organizational culture. *Manchester Review,* Spring, p. 3.

Blake, R. & Mouton, J. (1964). *The managerial grid.* Houston: Gulf.

Cloninger, R., Svrakic, D., & Przybeck, T. (1993). A psychobiological model of temperament and character. *Archives of General Psychiatry, 50,* 975–990.

Collins, J. (2001). *From good to great: Why some companies make the leap and others don't.* New York: HarperCollins.

Goleman, D. (1998). *Working with emotional intelligence.* New York: Bantam.

Johnson, J. (2000). Learning strategies for newly appointed leaders. In M. Goldsmith, L. Lyons, & A. Freas (Eds.). *Coaching for leadership: How the world's greatest coaches help leaders learn.* San Francisco: Jossey-Bass/Pfeiffer, pp. 209–217.

Kelly, J. (1980). *How managers manage.* Englewood Cliffs: Prentice-Hall.

Kets de Vries, M. & Miller, D. (1987). *Unstable at the top: Inside the troubled organization.* New York: New American Library.

Kets de Vries, M. (1989). *Prisoners of leadership.* New York: Wiley.

Lark, S. & Richards, J. (2000). *The chemistry of success: Six secrets of peak performance.* San Francisco: Bay Books.

Leslie, J. & Van Velsor, E. (1996). *A look at derailment today: North America and Europe.* Greensboro, NC: Center for Creative Leadership.

Luthans, F. (1988). Successful vs. effective real managers. *Academy of Management Executives, 2,* 127–132.

Luthans, F., Rosenkrantz, S., & Nenessey, H. (1985). What do successful managers really do? An observational study of managerial activities. *Journal of Applied Behavioral Science, 21,* 225–270.

Manchester Consulting. (1997). Survey of 826 respondents. Reported in Johnson, J. (2000). Learning strategies for newly appointed leaders. In M. Goldsmith, L. Lyons, & A. Freas (Eds.). *Coaching for leadership: How the world's greatest coaches help leaders learn.* San Francisco: Jossey-Bass/Pfeiffer, pp. 209–217.

Mintzberg, H. (1973). *The nature of managerial work.* New York: Irvington Press.

Sperry, L. (1996). Leadership dynamics: Character and character structure in executives. *Consulting Psychology Journal, 49,* 268–280.

Sperry, L. (2002a). *Effective leadership: Strategies for maximizing executive productivity and health.* New York: Brunner-Routledge.

Sperry, L. (2002b). From psychopathology to transformation: Retrieving the developmental focus in psychotherapy. *Journal of Individual Psychology, 58*: 398–421.

Sperry, L. (2003). *Becoming an effective health care manager: The essential skills of leadership.* Baltimore: Health Professions Press.

Stephenson, P. (2000). *Executive coaching: Lead, develop, retain motivated talented people.* French's Forest, NSW: Pearson Education Australia.

3
The Context of Executive Coaching

So far leadership effectiveness and leadership style, two key elements in executive coaching, have been described. A third key element is the context of coaching. Effective executive coaching does not occur in a vacuum. In addition to establishing a collaborative working relationship and effective intervention strategies, effective executive coaching requires an accurate and thorough understanding of the client's personal and professional style, skills, and competencies, as well as the context giving rise to the request for coaching. Since context can and does significantly impact the executive's productivity and well-being, it must be considered in planning and implementing any coaching intervention. Mental health professionals with little or no training in management and organizational dynamics will find this chapter an overview of certain topics in Organizational Behavior, a basic course in most MBA, organizational psychology, and consulting psychology graduate programs.

Context includes a number of factors including the executive's job, family dynamics, organizational dynamics, and the executive's overall "fit" with job, organization, family, and career. This chapter provides an overview of these contextual factors with an emphasis on organizational dynamics and fit.

Contextual Factors

In this book, *context* refers to organizational and situational factors that influence an executive's functioning on the job and in the organization. This context includes organizational and family dynamics as they impact the executive in his or her position in the organization. This section addresses organizational dynamics and family dynamics. *Organizational dynamics* refers to the composition and functioning of a organization. *Family and social dynamics* refers to the influences that family members and other social support systems have on the executive's values, attitudes, and behaviors (Sperry, 2002).

The section begins with an overview of three contextual factors impacting the executive. This is followed by an extended discussion of organizational dynamics. Five subsystems of corporate organizations will be described along with the stages or processes by which organizations develop, adapt, and decline.

Factor #1—Job

An executive's job may be a source of incredible satisfaction and challenge or a source of dissatisfaction and debilitating distress. Job demand and decisional control are two factors in the job strain model researched by Karasek and Theorell (1990). Job strain is defined as the short-term physiological, psychological, and behavioral manifestations of stress resulting from a job where psychological demands are high and control over the job is low. All job classifications can be thought of in terms of degrees of demand and control. Essentially, the demand/control model articulates a 2 × 2 contingency table of high and low demand on the horizontal axis and high and low control on the vertical axis.

Thus job classifications like telephone lineman and machinist that involve low demand and high control are considered low-strain jobs, while assembly worker and telephone operator are considered high demand, low control jobs. However, even though job demands are high, the extent to which workers can make decisions about how to plan and execute their jobs attenuates the extent of stress and impairment they experience. For example, a study of over 5,000 Swedish and American men found that the lower tenth of workers, measured by their ability to control their own jobs, were five times more likely to develop heart disease then the top tenth of the workplace hierarchy who had the greatest control over their jobs (Karasek & Theorell, 1990). Other job factors that have been related to health problems are shift work and occupational and safety hazards. Shift work, particularly rotating shift work, can significantly impact physical as well as psychological well-being. Workers who chose fixed shift work experienced better health than those on rotating shifts where choice was limited and social and physiological adjustment was difficult (Jamal & Jamal, 1982).

Factor #2—Family Dynamics

Family dynamics can positively or negatively impact executive performance and well-being. Family system dynamics include cohesiveness, boundaries, negotiation and problem-solving capacity, power sharing, communications, and intimacy. Research shows a link between the presence of family support and health maintenance, particularly among married men (Bjorksten & Steward, 1985). The ideal situation is for employees to experience emotional support from both the workplace and their families. McCubbin and Thompson's (1989) extensive study of stock brokers and their families showed that workers' health and well-being could be maintained under great duress when workers experienced nurturing and supportive communications from their spouses, high levels of family hardiness and optimism, and the social support of their job supervisors. On the other hand workers' health deteriorated when they received little or no job supervisor's support, incendiary, harsh, critical, blaming spousal communication patterns, and low levels of family hardiness.

Gottman (1991) reports another type of spousal communication pattern that can greatly impact health. He describes something akin to the "pursuer–distancer" interaction pattern (Guerin et al., 1987) wherein physiological arousal predicated marital dissatisfaction, separation, and divorce. To the extent that the pursuing spouse "attacked" the distancing spouse who experienced high physiological reactivity and engaged in "stonewalling"—avoiding eye contact, limited vocalization, and refraining from other indications of response—researchers were able to predict not only separation or divorce within a 4-year period, but also deterioration of the distancer's physical health (Gottman & Levinson, 1988).

Research data now support the clinical observation that corporate change can greatly impact worker health and well-being, and that job factors, workers' characteristics, and family factors can either exacerbate or buffer the extent of distress and impairment experienced by workers.

Factor #3—Organizational Dynamics

Probably the most obvious contextual factor after an executive's job is the corporate context along with its organizational dynamics. Prevalent forms of organizational change today include downsizing, layoffs, and mergers. To the extent that workers are not active participants in the change process, they experience varying degrees of victimization ranging from stress symptoms, such as insomnia, irritability, and anxiety, to anxiety disorders including post-traumatic stress syndrome. Marks and Mirvis (1998) describe the "merger syndrome" consisting of anxiety, dysphoria, stress reaction, worry and preoccupation, constricted communication, we–theyism, crisis management, and culture clash.

They suggest three strategies to reduce merger syndrome. First, during the initial deliberations for corporate mergers, top management must carefully consider the human implications along with the financial and business aspects. A transition team with members focusing on the people side of the merger is then formed. The second step is emotional preparation of workers accomplished through pre-merger workshops. Third, counseling is made available for workers at all levels who have experienced difficulty coping with the syndrome. McCann and Gilkey (1988) found that establishing effective two-way communications—upward and downwards—was of paramount importance in short-circuiting the merger syndrome.

Organizational Systems and Subsystems

This section extends the discussion of organizational dynamics in terms of an organization's systems and subsystems and its developmental stages. Imagine an organizational system as a set of five overlapping, concentric circles, wherein each circle represents the subsystems of an organization: structure, culture, strategy, leadership, and membership (or "followership") within a larger circle representing the suprasystem or the organization's external environment. Each of these five subsystems will be described in this section [cf. Sperry (1996) for a fuller discussion].

Structure

Structure refers to mechanisms that aid an organization to achieve its intended tasks and goals. The tasks are divided into smaller person-sized jobs or roles and clustered into larger sets assigned to teams, departments, or divisions. Structure specifies the reporting relationships of all roles, their spans of control and scopes of authority, and their locations in a hierarchy of roles—an organizational chart. Structure specifies the expectations of each role along with policies, procedures, and routines for interacting and communicating with others in the performance of the tasks (Miller, 1990).

Roles prescribe the boundaries of acceptable behavior for a particular job, while norms define group behavior. Norms are shared group expectations about what constitutes appropriate behavior. Role ambiguity—the lack of clarity as to how an individual in a role is expected to behave—and role conflict—the inconsistency or contradiction in the messages about a role of an individual in the work context—are often major sources of stress in an organization.

Structure specifies the ways in which a person performs in a role. A formal means of measuring role performance is called performance appraisal. Structure defines decision-making procedures such as which information will be utilized, how routine decisions are made and reviewed, particularly the degree of control and participation of a person in a particular role or job title (Leavitt & Bahrami, 1987). Another basic function of structure is to control and coordinate information among the other subsystems as well as the suprasystem.

An organization's structure might be thought of as a "snap shot" of its work process "frozen" in time so that it can be viewed. That snap shot could show a structure that is orderly or rigid, organic or chaotic, decentralized or overly bureaucratic, or divisionalized or fractured. Because of the interrelated nature of the subsystems, the structure molds culture and strongly influences the decisions of corporate leaders (Miller, 1990). It can greatly account for a worker's job productivity and satisfaction and significantly impact health and well-being.

Culture

Culture is the constellation of shared experiences, beliefs, assumptions, stories, customs, and actions that characterize an organization. The major determinants of culture are the values held by senior executives, the history of the corporation, and the senior executives' vision of the organization. These translate into culture through the shared experiences, memories, stories, and actions of employees. The corporate culture provides a guide to action for new situations and new employees. Culture is to the organization what personality and temperament are to the individual. Thus, culture defines an organization's identity to those inside and outside the organization.

In their classic book, *Corporate Cultures*, Deal and Kennedy (1982) list five aspects of culture: corporate relations or business environment, corporate values, corporate heroes, corporate rules and rituals, and the "secret" network comprised of rumor mongers, spies, cliques, and whispers that form the "hidden hierarchy of power" in the organization. The culture of a corporation may be difficult to describe in words, but everyone senses it. It gives an organization its unique "flavor" and essentially culture is "just the way we do things around here."

This subsystem subtly controls the behaviors of its members. Accordingly, management can influence workers by effectively managing the organization's culture. Stable organizations have strong, clear cultures that are consistent with other subsystems. The general character of a corporation's culture tends to remain the same, but its manifestations may be healthy or dysfunctional.

Strategy

Strategy is an organization's overall plan or course of action for achieving its identified goals (Pfeiffer, Goodstein, & Nolan, 1989). Corporate strategy is based on an organization's vision and mission statements. The vision statement answers the question, "What can the organization become, and why?" The mission statement answers, "What business are we in, and who is our customer?" Strategy determines, "How do we do it?" An organization has three levels of strategy: the corporate strategy that charts the course for the entire organization; the business strategy charted for each individual business or division within the corporation; and the functional strategy that deals with the basic functional areas—marketing, finance, personnel, etc.—within the firm.

Strategy takes the form of a strategic plan, and the process of developing and implementing the strategy is called strategic planning and management. This process will be described in some detail later in the chapter. An important consideration in strategic planning is achieving a good fit between the strategic and structural subsystems, since a given strategy can best be carried out by a given structure (Miller, 1990).

Most organizations believe strategic planning is essential for corporate success. A key function of strategic planning is helping a corporation achieve its goals by effectively organizing its people. Yet, many firms struggle to achieve their goals, often because of a failure to link their business strategies with the ways in which people are managed. For that reason, a workplace psychiatric consultant can impact an organization by advocating that its corporate strategy include both a business plan and a people plan (Sperry, 1991).

Just as a business plan describes targeted business goals and results in measurable terms, a people plan must also detail people results in measurable terms. It is insufficient to state slogans such as "people are our most important asset" or "our employees make the difference." Targeted people goals must be specified just as targeted business goals are specified. Examples of targeted business goals are:

We will increase our market share by 15%.
We will increase sales by 20%.

Examples of targeted people goals might be;

We will have the highest productivity and cost containment scores in the industry.
Ninety percent of our employees will rate their supervisors as good or excellent on showing respect to subordinates.
Ninety percent of our employees will state that they are proud to work here.

Such people results can be articulated, quantified, and assessed through surveys, interviews, or formal third party observations. These results will also be manifested in job productivity, satisfaction, and morale noted on a daily basis (Busch, 1990).

By attempting to incorporate both a people plan and a business plan in its corporate strategy, leadership may need to change past management practices that resulted in high levels of stress, distrust, or dissatisfaction. The goal of integrating both plans is to achieve a reasonable balance and synergy between people and production (Sperry, 1991). An effective integrative corporate strategy should positively impact all the other subsystems, and probably will require changes in the structural subsystem.

Leadership

Leadership refers to a process of influence whereby a leader persuades, enables, or empowers others to pursue and achieve the intended goals of the organization. *Leadership* and *management* were used synonymously until recently. Today, many authors want to distinguish the two terms. They contend that management involves the five functions of planning, organizing, staffing, directing, and controlling, while leadership involves only one component of the directing function. Rather, an effective leader creates a vision that tells members where the corporation is going and how it will get there. The leader then galvanizes members to obtain commitments to the vision by being ethical, open, empowering, and inspiring (Bennis & Nanus, 1997). Not all agree with this bifurcation. Jaques and Clement (1991) contend that good leaders must be good managers and vice versa.

There are several ways of conceptualizing the leadership process. One way is to assume that effective leaders have the flexibility to shift their style from "boss-centered" (autocratic style) to "employee-centered" (participative style) to accommodate the needs of specific situations (Tannenbaum & Schmidt, 1958). Another way is to think of leadership as combining two orientations simultaneously, but in different proportions. One orientation is task-centered; the other is person-centered. By elaborating the possible combinations of these two orientations, Blake and Mouton (1964) derived five prototypic leadership styles.

A third way of thinking about leadership considers three factors. Called *situational leadership*, the best form of leadership is based on situational needs: the personal characteristics of the leaders, the nature of the organization, and worker characteristics. In contrast, *task-oriented leadership* is most effective when all three of the situational needs or factors are favorable and, conversely, in situations wherein the factors are relatively unfavorable. *Relations-oriented leadership* is most effective when the three factors are only moderately favorable and in situations in which only some factors are favorable (Fiedler, 1967).

The leadership subsystem plays a critical role in shaping themes that harmonize the subsystems of structure, culture and strategy (Kets de Vries & Miller, 1984). In Miller's aforementioned research, leadership style was characterized as craftsman, builder, pioneer, or salesman in the successful firms he studied, and later as tinkerer, imperialist, escapist, or drifter when the same corporations began to decline (Miller, 1990).

Membership or Followership

Organizational researchers have largely neglected the attitudes of those in an organization who are led—the workers. Since an important key to a leader's success is the behavior of his or her subordinates, this is an unfortunate oversight. Uris (1964) studied "followership" style and concluded that subordinates have a preference for either the autocratic, democratic, or "free-rein" (participative) leadership style. He found that workers function best with leadership that corresponds with their followership style. For example, a subordinate with an affinity for the autocratic approach will respond favorably to the autocratic leadership style. The lack of match between leadership and followership styles probably accounts for conflict, stress, decreased worker productivity, and decreased performance.

Individuals do not work in isolation. They form memberships in small groups as a way to increase their adaptability within the organizational system. These groups may be formal parts of the structural subsystem such as work teams or they may be informal. The informal group, also called the informal organization (Leavitt & Bahrami, 1987), is formed by workers, usually around a workplace issue or an outside activity. Actually, these groups accomplish much of an organization's work. Chance meetings at the coffee machine, impromptu lunch meetings, and informal telephone calls go a long way toward defining and achieving the organization's intended goals. The presence of a disaffiliative or hostile informal organization can also seriously undermine an organization's objectives.

External Environment

These five internal subsystems interact with and mutually influence one another. The configuration of these subsystems is also greatly affected by an external subsystem, the environment. The environmental subsystem consists of factors outside an organization's internal subsystems that influence it and interact with it. The environment includes economic, legal, political, and sociocultural factors. It also includes technological factors such as community relations, workforce availability, competitors, shareholders and other stakeholders, market saturation, customer demands and changes, government statutes, environmental policies, other regulatory requirements, and standard industrial practices. In times of turbulence and rapid social and technological changes, the environmental subsystem may exert as much or more influence on organizational direction and functioning as other subsystems. This is particularly evident during economic recessions, war or even the threat of war, drought, and other natural disasters.

Organizational Stages

Just as an organism develops and declines, so do organizations. Six stages of organizational growth and decline are described here: new venture, expansion, professionalization, consolidation, early bureaucratization, and late bureaucratization. These stages are adapted from Sperry (1990) and are based on the work of Greiner (1972), Adizes (2000), and Miller (1990).

Stage I: New Venture

Stage I of an organization involves the conception of a new venture. The critical tasks at this stage include defining a target group (e.g., hospital patients, high school seniors, middle managers) and developing a service that targets such a group. Accomplishing these tasks requires the ability to extend or create a market need; the willingness to make risky investments of time, energy, and money to create an organization that satisfies the unmet need; and the ability to create an embryonic organizational structure that can provide that service to the target group. These abilities are characteristic of the entrepreneurial leader, and the entrepreneurial leadership style is most compatible with this stage.

Adizes (2000) noted three distinct leadership roles and patterns: entrepreneur, performer, and administrator. Gerber (1986) similarly referred to these roles as entrepreneur, technician, and manager. The *entrepreneur* is the visionary and risk taker who is creative and innovative. The entrepreneur craves change and control over people and events. The entrepreneur can easily transform an idea into reality and can singlehandedly give birth to an organization. The *performer* is the doer or task-focused leader. The performer is diligent, dedicated, and loyal to the assigned task. The performer focuses exclusively on what needs to be done. The *administrator* focuses on how things should be done. The administrator craves order and the status quo. The administrator manages operating systems better than either the entrepreneur or the performer and is comfortable with bureaucratic matters. The more a leader is able to adapt his or her leadership style to the needs of the organization, the more valuable and effective the leader is.

At first, an organization is likely to be quite small in terms of members and clientele, and thus its structure can be flexible and informal. Thus, Stage I involves developing a basic system for day-to-day operations and finding individuals to staff the organization. Often there is little role differentiation among leaders and followers. The planning and development functions do not need to be formalized at first and on-the-job training is prevalent. Entrepreneurial leadership, especially when combined with performance-style leadership, is particularly effective in keeping the vision and embryonic organizational structure viable (Flambolz & Randle, 2000). The entrepreneurial leadership pattern lends itself to the autocratic or benevolent organizational style. Because of their visionary and risk-taking stances and their hard-won successes, entrepreneur–performer leaders easily become objects of admiration. They tend to attract members who are in awe of the founder's success (Sperry, 1990). These members readily accept a dependent stance and easily acquiesce to the demands of the entrepreneur-performer leader.

Stage II: Expansion

Stage II involves rapid growth. Stage II commences very quickly or after an organization has been in Stage I for a number of years. The major problems that occur in Stage II involve growth rather than survival. Organizational resources are stretched to their limits as a new wave of members joins the organization, as demands for services increase, and as the organization's rather primitive day-to-day operating system becomes overwhelmed. Organizational "growing pains" are painfully present. They signal that changes are needed and cannot be ignored; they imply that the organization has not been fully successful in developing the internal system it needs at a given stage of growth.

If the founder of the organization is unable to cope with the management problems that arise in Stage II, the organization is likely to flounder and even fail (Flambolz & Randle, 2000). Not surprisingly, the critical task at this stage is to develop an infrastructure of operating systems that results in efficiency and effectiveness. As this more complex operating system develops, the organizational structure becomes more differentiated. Basic human resources and management training become necessities at this stage. Whereas little formal management structure beyond "doing what the owner said" was needed in Stage I, more managerial structure is needed in Stage II, particularly with delegation of authority. Entrepreneurs tend to be less interested in the nonglamorous challenges provided by Stage II, as compared with Stage I. Thus, a need arises at Stage II for the administration dimensions of leadership to blend with the entrepreneurial. The entrepreneur–administrator style and the turmoil wrought by growing pains at this stage almost guarantee that members will begin to become disenchanted with leadership and dissatisfied with the organization itself. Member turnover and rebelliousness are manifestations of counter-dependency, particularly when leaders are slow to decentralize and share power or when they vacillate by proposing and then rejecting initiatives to delegate and decentralize the process (Sperry, 1996).

Stage III: Professionalization

Stages I and II represent the entrepreneurial organization. Even though it may have lacked well-defined goals, policies, plans, and controls, the organization prospered. However, as critical size is achieved, the organization begins experiencing "growing pains" related to its initial structure and operating systems (Flambolz & Randle, 2000). New structures and operating systems must be implemented. Another wave of new members requires more formal planning, defined roles and responsibilities, performance standards, and control systems. Developing a strategic planning and management system then becomes the critical task at Stage III. This in turn requires organizational development efforts that provide the concurrent levels of skill training needed to implement this management system.

Those in leadership must change and increase their skills and capabilities. The challenge for the founder and/or entrepreneurial leader is to transition from an entrepreneurial style of operation to a more professional style of management (Flambolz & Randle, 2000). Optimal leadership at Stage III involves an integration of administrative expertise with a sensitivity toward employee needs and development. Not surprisingly, an organizational climate that encourages consultative and participative management suits those who are able to function relatively interdependently.

Stage IV: Consolidation

After transitioning to a professionally managed system, an organization can focus its efforts on consolidation—maintaining a reasonable increase in growth while developing an organizational culture. In Stage I, the organization's culture was transmitted by contact between the founders and members. In Stages II and III, the first wave of members transmitted the culture to the next wave or generation, but this informal mode of socialization became much less effective and adequate with the subsequent waves of members. Culture becomes a critical concern in Stage IV.

Thus, in Stage IV, a more conscious and formal method of transmission is needed. Otherwise members may no longer share a vision of what the organization is or where it is going. As a result, members begin interpreting culture in ways that meet their own needs but not those of the organization. First in Stage IV, the organization's culture must be assessed. The underlying beliefs and norms of the particular organization must be elicited. Examples of unhealthy beliefs and norms include avoiding conflict, setting unrealistic performance expectations, avoiding accountability, and tolerating poor performance. The organization must then decide on more appropriate and healthy cultural forms, for example, treating two-way communications and conflict resolution as high priorities, setting realistic performance expectations, showing concern for quality, encouraging innovation, and refusal to tolerate poor performance.

The organizational structural of Stage IV represents a further enhancement and articulation of the organizational structure of Stage III. Knowledge of and commitment to the organization's mission statement and implementation strategies must be widespread throughout the organization. The mission statement must be reflected in both the orientations of new members and newsletters to existing members. Members are respected and prized, and thus human resources development and employee assistance programs will become integrated parts of the organization. Members' horizons, knowledge base, and skills are regularly upgraded. Leadership that combines entrepreneurship and integration is most compatible with Stage IV functioning. Note that while administrative leadership professionalized the organization in Stage III, entrepreneurial leadership is needed to rekindle and augment the original dream and to motivate and challenge the organization, especially the fourth wave of new members. At Stage IV, individual members who are able to function interdependently with superiors, coworkers, and subordinates are most compatible with the organization's collaborative or participative styles.

The challenge of effective leadership is to assist the organization to arrive at Stage IV and remain there. This requires considerable effort to grow and adapt to the constantly changing external environment—the suprasystem—in which the organization finds itself. Self-renewal becomes the organization's basic strategy. Failure to strategically plan for and manage the corporation can result in a downward trend and decline. Stages V and VI describe this downward trend that can lead to the eventual death of the organization.

Stage V: Early Bureaucratization

As an organization transitions to Stage V, it experiences a subtle but clear shift from substance to form. Status seeking, "business as usual," and appearances characterize the behavior of members. The organization is usually well endowed at this stage and may be cash-rich for the first time in its history.

Later in Stage V, the focus shifts to internal turf wars. Backbiting, coalition building, and paranoia are common. Growing pains are particularly intense as members' dissatisfactions mount. In some organizations, negativity threatens to poison the climate. Leadership at first was content to rest on the organization's laurels, but now shifts to a self-protective mode. Cliques become the usual mode of communication. The best and brightest start leaving the organization. The emphasis has clearly shifted from growth and maintenance to decline. The structures and the planning and development functions are much less responsive than in previous stages. Leadership is marked by administration and, in the later part of this stage, by inefficient administration. Decentralization and delegation become increasingly threatening to leadership, and efforts to re-centralize power are expected behaviors. Counter-dependency behavior, including passive aggressivity, becomes commonplace, reflecting demoralization among workers as well as among managers.

Stage VI: Late Bureaucratization

Many of the subunits and subsystems of the organization become clearly dysfunctional during Stage VI. Miscommunication is commonplace, and two-way communication is limited or nonexistent. Coordination and follow through are the exceptions rather than the rules. The right hand is seldom aware that a left hand exists and certainly does not know what it is doing. New members are no longer informed of the mission statement and strategy. For all members, the organizational culture reflects a sense of helplessness and a lack of common direction. "Come late, leave early," "do as little as you have to," "don't try to change anything," and "protect job security at all costs" are the attitudes that reflect the organizational culture in Stage VI. The critical function is to forestall and avoid extinction because the organization is figuratively in intensive care and is maintained by external life-support systems. The corporate subsystems are conflictive and nonresponsive to the needs of both members and clientele. Little if any training and development occur. Administrators struggle to buy time and prolong the organization's life. Inefficiency and ineffectiveness are to be expected. Clients find access to responsive subsystems the exception rather than the rule. Not surprisingly, the re-emergence of dependency among members complements the autocratic style of leaders. The eventual demise of the organization seems inevitable and consultants report that the prognosis for organizations in Stage VI even after heroic interventions is poor (Adizes, 2000).

As noted earlier, organizational decline and poor person–organization fit are not inevitable. A strategically managed corporation is able to adapt to changing times and circumstances and is able to renew itself and achieve a new level of homeostasis.

Executive Coaching and Fit

The various dimensions of an organizational system are interrelated and influence one another. For example, while external environment shapes strategy, corporate strategy is shaped also by its environment. An organization's structure and culture affect executive behaviors, i.e., productivity, satisfaction, and health, and executive behaviors impact structure and culture. A reasonable degree of fit should exist between the stage of an organization's development and its subsystems.

An organization's success and viability depend largely on the fits of various organizational dimensions, including the fit with executives' skills. The better the fit, the greater will be productivity, job satisfaction, and overall health. Decreased productivity, satisfaction, and greater job stress are associated with poor fit (Beer, 1980). However important the degree of fit of organization subsystems and dimensions, four types of fit are particularly important for executive coaches in understanding their executive clients: executive–job fit, executive–organization fit, executive–family–career fit, and executive–job–organization–family fit.

Executive–Job Fit

The presence of high executive–organization fit is no guarantee of a high level of executive–job fit and vice versa. However, generally speaking, the better the match between employee talents, competencies, skills, and experience with job requirements, the more likely the executive will be productive and satisfied (Lowman, 1993). The poorer the fit, the greater the likelihood of distress, role ambiguity, role conflicts, and derailment. Several job-related factors can negatively or positively impact the degree of fit.

Work schedules can impact job productivity, commitment, and job satisfaction as well as employee health. For some employees, flexible work hours offer an alternative to the traditional fixed working schedule and provide some choices in arrival and departure times. For other employees, work scheduling might require second shift, night shift, or rotating shift schedules. Research indicates that many shift workers experience problems with health and social adjustment. Because of interruptions in circadian rhythm, shift workers often complain of lack of sleep, fatigue, appetite loss, and constipation. They also experience family and marital difficulties (Muchinsky, 1993). In short, such job-related factors can not only affect employee productivity, health, and interpersonal relationships; they can also impact family relations.

Executive–Organization Fit

Levinson (1980) considers executive–organization fit critical to an executive's professional effectiveness and personal well-being. Essentially, the better the fit between the executive's values and beliefs and the organization's values and mission, the greater the likelihood of high job performance, commitment, satisfaction, and personal self-esteem. On the other hand, the poorer the fit, the higher the likelihood of disillusion, distress, and derailment (Muchinsky, 1993).

Executive–Family–Career Fit

This type of fit focuses both on the relationship of the executive to his or her family—both nuclear family and family of origin—and the executive's career path as it impacts and is impacted by the family. Individuals choose specific career paths based on many factors including personal reasons and family influences. Pleasing a parent or carrying on a family tradition may significantly impact a career path as witnessed by the number of physicians who are the sons or daughters of physicians or represent one of several generations of physicians in a family.

Salary, benefits, and status can significantly influence career choice as when an individual foregoes his or her passion for painting or sculpting in favor of a high salary position in order to send a child to a private school or maintain a certain lifestyle. The converse is also true as was noted when managed care was perceived as reducing physician income levels. As a result some individuals with aptitudes for medicine chose to pursue careers in finance or computers instead. The price one pays for a poor fit—appeasing family rather than following a dream—can be high, for example, unhappiness, a lack of fulfillment, etc.

The fit may be low or poor when job demands interfere with family life or an intimate relationship, or stress spills over from job to family or spouse. Organizations that strive to be family-friendly by allowing flex-time schedules and promoting work-life programs can increase self–job–family fit.

Executive–Family–Job–Organization Fit

Despite the potential for a good fit of an executive, job and organization, family dynamics or social support networks can negatively or positively impact job performance, satisfaction, and overall sense of well-being. For this reason, the degree of fit with family dynamics and social support networks needs to be considered. McCubbin et al. (1992) presented convincing data that family factors, i.e., illness, conflicts, and other problems, can significantly impact an employee's productivity and health. These outcomes are more likely with female employees. Similarly, this research and other studies confirm that high levels of satisfaction with a marriage, a relationship with a significant other, family members, or social networks can effectively buffer job-related stress. In short, this dimension of fit should be assessed or evaluated.

Highly Effective Organizations

Much of the discussion in chapter 2 focused on describing the skills, competencies, and styles of effective and highly effective executives. Not surprisingly, effective executives tend to be attracted to and remain in effective organizations. This section will describe some of the characteristic features of effective organizations. Several important studies on effective organizations have recently been published. In addition to Collins' (2001) monumental study of good to great corporations (briefly mentioned in chapter 2), the findings of O'Reilly and Pfeffer (2000) may be of particular interest to those engaged in executive coaching. As a result of their extensive analysis of corporations such as Southwest Airlines, Cisco Systems, Men's Wearhouse, and Cypress Semiconductors, O'Reilly and Pfeffer noted three common themes and several common strategies.

The three common themes shared by all these corporations are: (1) a clear, well articulated set of shared values that serves as the foundation for "management practices that build the core capabilities that in turn provide a basis for the company's competitive success" (p. 232); (2) a high degree of alignment and consistency in corporate practices that express its core values; and (3) in addition to founders and CEOs, senior executives "ensure that corporate values are maintained and constantly made real to all of the people who work in the organization" (p. 232).

Here are the common corporate strategies they noted: (1) a strong culture that aligns norms, attitudes and behaviors to core corporate values; (2) a screening process that identifies and hires only individuals who share corporate values; (3) a major commitment and investment in employee health by providing opportunities for development and career; (4) absolute consistency between corporate values and all corporate practices that express these values; (5) widespread information sharing, including corporate operational and financial data, throughout the organization; (6) team-based systems that promote a sense of purpose and belonging among all employees; and (7) the conviction that the primary role of senior executives is to set and reinforce the vision, values, and culture of the organization, while strategic planning, decision making and operational oversight are secondary roles (pp. 238–245).

Organizational Barriers and Crises Facing Executives

Based on extensive consultation with executives, Bramson (1989) noted a number of barriers or predictable hazards that executives faced as they moved up the corporate ladder. These include job overload, a nonsupportive work environment, competition for the small number of top executive positions, power pathologies manifested in the executive suite, and unethical or illegal organizational practices.

Based on 25 years of research with 5,000 male and female executives, Blotnick (1985) delineated five predictable crises in an executive's career. Interestingly, these inevitable obstacles correspond to the current decade of life. For individuals in their 20s, the crisis involves finding the right corporate stance, that is, managing appropriate and balanced impressions of themselves and avoiding destructive behavior patterns. The crisis for individuals in their 30s involves developing the ability to work with others and to function maturely as a team member. When in their 40s, their challenge is to become indispensable rather than obsolete. Reluctance to keep current about new technical demands and advances in methodology is an ever-present danger for executives in their fourth decade. A major temptation for executives in their 50s is to stagnate and become self-absorbed rather than impart wisdom to subordinates. Erickson used the term "generativity" to describe this mentoring task for late middle adulthood. Mentoring comes naturally to executives during this period if they do not succumb to replaying negative authority transference. Finally, the crisis of executives in their 60s involves the questions of succession and choosing the right heir.

These predictable crises seem "commonsensical," at least to individuals with some basic understanding of human development. However, this is apparently not the case among most individuals in business, Blotnick reported that few business people—only 3% of the 5,000 persons studied—had accurate ideas of the kinds of developments and crises that could make or break their careers.

Concluding Note

The successful practice of executive coaching assumes a working knowledge of the context of coaching, i.e., organizational dynamics, job and career factors, family dynamics, and how they impact personal dynamics. Because of their expertise in assessing personal dynamics, mental health professionals have advantages over others practicing executive coaching, yet they still must acquire a familiarity with the various contextual factors. This chapter has introduced several such factors: job, family dynamics, organizational dynamics, and the concept of fit. The effective executive coach will be mindful of these factors in the assessment, planning, and implementation processes of their coaching.

References

Adizes, I. (2000). *Managing corporate lifecycles.* Englewood Cliffs, NJ: Prentice-Hall.

Beer, M. (1980). *Organization change and development: A systems view.* Glenview, IL: Scott Foresman.

Bennis, W. & Nanus, B. (1997). *Leaders: Strategies for taking charge.* 2nd ed. New York: Harper Business.

Blake, R. & Mouton, J. (1964). *The managerial grid.* Houston: Gulf.

Blotnick, S. (1985). *The corporate steeplechase: Predictable crisis in a business career.* New York: Penguin Books.

Bramson, R. (1989). *Coping with the fast track blues.* New York: Doubleday.

Bjorksten, O. & Steward, T. (1985). Marital status and health. In O. Bjorksten (Ed.). *New clinical concepts in marital therapy.* Washington, D.C.: American Psychiatric Press.

Busch, M. (1990). Linking strategic planning to the management of people. In J. Pfeiffer & J. Jones (Eds.). *1990 Annual: Developing Human Resources.* San Diego: University Associates, pp. 265–270.

Collins, J. (2001). *From good to great: Why some companies make the leap and others don't.* New York: HarperCollins.

Deal, J. & Kennedy, A. (1982). *Corporate cultures: The rites and rituals of corporate life.* Reading, MA: Addison Wesley.

Fiedler, F. (1967). *A Theory of leadership effectiveness.* New York: McGraw Hill.

Flambolz, E. & Randle, Y. (2000). *Growing pains: Transitioning from an entrepreneurship to professionally managed firm.* San Francisco: Jossey-Bass.

Gerber, M. (1986). *The e-myth: Why most businesses don't work and what to do about it.* San Francisco: Harper Business.

Gottman, J. (1991). Predicting the longitudinal course of marriage. *Journal of Marital and Family Therapy, 17,* 3–7.

Gottman, J. & Levinson, R. (1988). The social psychology of marriage. In P. Noler & M. Fitzpatrick (Eds.). *Perspectives on marital interaction.* Philadelphia: Multilingual Matters.

Greiner, L. (1972). Evolution and revolution. *Harvard Business Review, 50,* 37–46.

Guerin, P., Fay, L., Burden, S. & Kautto, J. (1987). *The evaluation and treatment of marital conflict.* New York: Basic Books.

Jamal, M. & Jamal, S. (1982). Work and non-work experiences of employees on fixed and rotating shifts: An empirical assessment. *Journal of Vocational Behavior, 20,* 282–293.

Jaques, E. & Clement, S. (1991). *Executive leadership: A practical guide to managing complexity.* Cambridge, MA: Blackwell Business.

Karasek, R. & Theorell, T. (1990). *Healthy work: Stress, productivity and the reconstruction of working life.* New York: Basic Books.

Kets de Vries, M. & Miller, D. (1984). *The neurotic organization: Diagnosing and changing counterproductive styles of management.* San Francisco: Jossey-Bass.

Leavitt, H. & Bahrami, H. (1987). *Managerial psychology: Managing behavior in organizations,* 5th. ed. Chicago: University of Chicago Press.

Levinson, H. (1980). *Executive.* Cambridge, MA: Harvard University Press.

Lowman, R. (1993). *Counseling and psychotherapy of work dysfunctions.* Washington, D.C.: American Psychological Association.

Marks, M. & Mirvis. (1998). *Joining forces: Making one plus one equal three in mergers, acquisitions, and alliances.* San Francisco: Jossey-Bass.

McCann, J. & Gilkey, R. (1988). *Joining forces: Creating and managing successful mergers and acquisitions.* Englewood Cliffs, NJ: Prentice-Hall.

McCubbin, H. & Thompson, A. (1989). *Balancing work and family life: Wall Street.* Edina, MN: Burgess International Group.

McCubbin, H., Thompson, A., Kretzschmar, H., Smith, F., Snow, P., McEwen, M. et al. (1992). Family system and work environment predictors of employee health risk: A discriminant function analysis. *American Journal of Family Therapy, 20,* 123–144.

Miller, D. (1990). *The Icarus paradox: How exceptional companies bring about their own downfall.* San Francisco Harper Business.

Muchinsky, P. (1993) *Psychology applied to work,* 4th ed. Pacific Grove, CA: Brooks/Cole.

O'Reilly, C. & Pfeffer, J. (2000). *Hidden value: How great companies achieve extraordinary results with ordinary people.* Boston: Harvard Business School Press.

Pfeiffer, J., Goodstein, L., & Nolan, J. (1989). *Understanding applied strategic planning: A manager's guide.* Glenview, IL: Scott Foresman.

Sperry, L. (1990). Development of organizations. *Human Development, 10,* 26–31.

Sperry, L. (1991). Enhancing corporate health, mental health, and productivity. *Individual Psychology, 47,* 247–254.

Sperry, L. (1996). *Corporate therapy and consulting.* New York: Brunner/Mazel.

Sperry, L. (2002). *Effective leadership: Strategies for maximizing executive productivity and health.* New York: Brunner-Routledge.

Tannenbaum, R. & Schmidt, W. (1958). How to choose a leadership pattern. *Harvard Business Review, 36,* 95–101.

Uris, A. (1964). *Techniques of leadership.* New York: McGraw Hill.

4
Selecting Appropriate Clients and Coaches for Executive Coaching

The title of this chapter may strike some as odd. It may not seem unreasonable to assess an executive's suitability for coaching. After all, not every executive who asks for or is assigned to executive coaching will profit from it. While some executives are good candidates for executive coaching, others are not. Certain executives do not profit from coaching for many reasons such as insufficient motivation or reluctance to change. However, it may not be intuitively obvious why coaches should likewise be evaluated as to their suitability for coaching specific executive clients. The fact is that some coaches not only do not help but can actually harm some clients. There is growing sentiment that assessing the suitability of both clients and coaches appears essential for achieving successful outcomes in executive coaching.

This chapter addresses the matter of suitability for executive coaching. It begins by discussing the value of assessing client suitability and describes and illustrates several indicators or criteria of suitability and nonsuitability. Next, it describes and compares the backgrounds and training of executive coaches and the limitations of those without psychological training. The chapter ends with a brief discussion of the requisite psychological skills for effective executive coaching.

Why Assess Client Suitability for Executive Coaching?

Today, the corporate world expects executives to be both highly productive and relationally competent on the job. Many, but certainly not all, executives meet this high standard. In fact, wide variability among executives is apparent and executive coaching holds the promise of increasing both productivity and relational competence where needed. The following case examples illustrate this variability of productivity and relational competence and suggest the potential need for executive coaching

Case 1

Julian Estrada is a 37-year-old associate vice president of customer services for a commercial insurance company. The organization is attempting to implement a major change initiative it hopes will increase profitability and meet customers' increasing expectations for quality and service. However, to achieve both of these goals, the company must reduce high turnover rates (approximately 11% of professional staff and 18% of hourly employees for each of the past 3 years). The CEO and chairman of the board believe that this can only be achieved by directly targeting employee commitment to the organization. Estrada and other senior managers are charged with accomplishing this major change initiative. Estrada has been with the company for 9 years. He was promoted twice during that time and his performance was rated as adequate. However, in preparation for implementing the new initiative, top management conducted a full review of all senior managers. While they were largely satisfied with Estrada's performance in the past, they became increasingly disappointed that he seemed far from reaching his full potential. His last performance appraisal noted, "At times, he doesn't seem to make the obvious connection. It is as if he is in a 'rut' and just going through the motions of being a manager. I wish there was some way that I could light a fire under him and release more of his potential. I'm going to recommend him for executive coaching."

Case 2

Jerry Flynn, is a 34-year-old senior manager at a medium size accounting firm. Two years he left a much larger firm to join this firm with the belief that he would become a partner sooner. When promotions were recently announced, Flynn was not offered a senior partnership even though his work was more than satisfactory and he was considered a "rainmaker" for the firm. In addition, his customers could not be more pleased. Nevertheless, the senior partners were increasingly concerned about the way Flynn treated—and mistreated—support staff and colleagues. People talked about how Flynn viciously humiliated an associate during a staff meeting. That he appeared to be oblivious to the inappropriateness of his behavior was troubling. While a few partners thought it would be best to let Flynn go, others noted he was too valuable because of all the business he brought to the firm. These partners prevailed and an executive coach was assigned to work with Flynn.

Case 3

Valerie Buscemi, was hired as a vice president of sales and marketing. She was incredibly impressive when interviewed, so much so that some on the senior management team thought she was almost too good to be true. The passage of time proved them right. From the moment she started with the company, she exhibited more style than substance. She delegated most of her responsibilities to staff, and while it appeared that she was very busy out in the field meeting with her sales managers and key accounts, no one seemed to ever see her. Not showing up for a key top management team retreat was the last straw. The CEO was under pressure to terminate her immediately.

Case 4

Harold Whitney has been the vice president of product development for a large corporation in the manufacturing sector for about 12 months. One of the CEO's unstated goals of the search that ultimately netted Whitney, was that the new vice president might succeed the current COO when he retired in a year or so. Unfortunately, although Whitney's unit reached and even exceeded its quotas, high turnover rates and low morale were very troubling, particularly since the availability of engineers and other skilled workers in the region was limited and employee performance coaching was not a priority for Whitney. The CEO noted these observations as he prepared for Whitney's first annual performance appraisal. When they met, the CEO expressed his concerns. Whitney simply replied that he expected everyone to give 100% or else. The CEO's other concern was that Whitney took more sick time and personal days than any other executive. Whitney dismissed these concerns as "the price for being a Type A personality." It probably didn't help Whitney's situation that his younger daughter's asthma had been difficult to control since he relocated and his family found it difficult to establish roots in the community. The CEO was uncertain about how he would handle these concerns, but knew he needed to take action soon, particularly since he might need to look elsewhere in his succession planning for the COO position.

Case 5

Cindy Kim is the 31-year-old director of development for a national arthritis foundation. She has been in her present position for nearly 2 years, significantly increased the foundation's endowment, and believes she is ready for greater opportunities and responsibilities. Her dream is to launch and lead her own public relations firm. She reports directly to Ronald Davison, the organization's executive director. During their annual performance appraisal review, they discussed her performance and the challenges of the upcoming fiscal year. Kim was not surprised that her superior rated her as meeting or exceeding performance standards in some areas, but marginal in others, particularly in team leadership. She admits that her staff meetings may not be particularly focused and productive, but she attributes this to her style of wanting to hear all points of view before making decisions. Cindy recognizes that becoming more proficient in team leadership is not only important for her present job but critical to her long term career plans, and she is willing to work with an executive coach to improve it.

Case 6

Jillian Jefferson is a 42-year-old African American regional vice president in a large savings bank where she oversees 12 branch managers. She noted that one of her managers, Albert Jacqui, had been constantly underperforming. He regularly failed to meet deadlines and occasionally seemed to let employee issues "settle themselves" rather than quickly and decisively deal with them. Jefferson has become increasingly dissatisfied with him, yet his branch's performance was consistently high and its customer satisfaction level is one of the highest in the region. Her boss suggested that the bank's psychological consultant might be able to recommend something to help Jacqui, possibly executive coaching or consultation. After a brief evaluation, the consulting psychologist suggested that Jefferson might consider whether her own management style could conceivably be a factor in Jacqui's performance and recommended a more complete evaluation.

Case 7

Larry Kimble was introduced in chapter 2 as a leader who makes things happen. At age 61, he is the CEO of a high tech corporation that he founded 21 years ago. Before that, Kimble had been president of a tool and die company, succeeding his father who formed the company after the Depression. Anticipating that the future for tool and die making would be eclipsed by more sophisticated technology, Kimble reinvented the company and made it into one of the most successful family-owned businesses in the high tech sector.

Kimble is a humble man who attributes his success to his employees and is proud of the fact that a few employees hired by his father are still on the payroll. Larry is passionate about his work and the corporation and has created and maintained a family atmosphere and a culture of trust, respect, and commitment to the corporation, to its customers, and to its 700-plus employees. Kimble works hours that few of his younger executive staff can match. He conducts early breakfast and dinner meetings and receptions with stakeholders nearly every day of the week. On weekends, he gets away from it all to spend time with his family including several grandchildren. Although he is amazingly active, productive, and energetic, he never gives the impression that he is rushed or in a hurry. An unmistakable sense of harmony and centeredness surrounds him and has permeated the rest of his top management team.

Client Suitability and Nonsuitability for Executive Coaching

Executive coaching has been described as a powerful intervention that is neither a panacea nor is it suitable for everyone. What constitutes suitability and what are the indicators or markers of suitability and nonsuitability for executive coaching? Suitability refers to the fit of the goals and expectations of the coaching process and the client's goals, expectations, readiness, and predisposition to engage in the coaching process. Specifically, suitability refers to the client's capacity and willingness to align his or her efforts and collaborate with a given coach, the goals of coaching, and the coaching process. It also refers to the client's predisposition and previous experience with utilizing feedback and direction from managers, coaches, or other change agents, and subsequent success in achieving specified outcomes.

Consider a continuum from most suitable to least suitable for executive coaching. On the most suitable end of the continuum, the profile would involve a very high degree of fit between the client's current capacity, readiness, and willingness to engage in coaching with past success in change efforts and the goals and expectations of the coaching process itself. Correspondingly, on the least suitable end of the continuum, the client would exhibit a very low degree of fit. Seven rather specific markers of suitability and non-suitability can be described.

1. Performance Issues Due to Skill Deficit or Lack of Experience

Since coaching primarily involves training and development with the goal of improving performance, clients with performance issues due primarily to skill deficits or lack of training or experience are usually well suited for executive coaching. On the other hand, experience suggests that clients with performance issues arising primarily from negative attitudes or personal attributes that are incompatible with high level performance are less suitable for coaching. For example, an executive with an attitude of superiority and contemptuousness whose personal or work group's performance is suffering, is not likely to be responsive to coaching. Thus, executives like Jerry Flynn may not be suitable for executive coaching before they make some changes in those attitudes or predispositions. Such changes may require counseling or psychotherapy.

2. Psychological Maturity

Experience shows that executives who are somewhat psychologically mature and have moderate to high self-esteem and no indications of psychiatric disorders or problems involving substance use tend to be much better candidates for executive coaching than those who are psychologically immature and exhibit poor self-esteem or have diagnosable psychopathologies or past or current substance-related disorders. The business world characterizes psychological maturity in various ways. While referring to psychologically mature workers and executives as good employees or good executives, a variety of designations are given for the psychologically immature: difficult executives, different executives, troubled executives, troubling executives or problem executives. Psychologically trained professionals are likely to use terms such as distressed executives and impaired executives (Sperry, 1993).

Difficult executives are the mirror opposites of good executives in that they are individuals who seem out of step with others in the organization. Also referred to as troubling executives and problem executives, these individuals often have problems relating to and leading others and may or may not have performance problems. They may be inconsistent in attending meetings and keeping appointments; they are usually not considered trustworthy or good team players. While they may be courteous and respectful to their superiors, they may treat peers and their reports with disrespect or disregard. The basic issue tends to be unwillingness rather than inability. While they may have listening, empathy, and other relational skill deficits, they may have highly developed technical and strategic skills that can serve them well.

Unfortunately, their skills and performance records may mark them as invaluable to their organizations, and so their behavior and style may be overlooked even though they are problematic to others. Predictably, these executives do not respond to conventional methods of correction such as warnings, threats, heartfelt discussion, or standard executive coaching. They may or may not accept a referral for psychotherapy unless it is framed with an ultimatum that their jobs are contingent upon making changes in a therapeutic context. It is useful to distinguish difficult executives from good executives, different executives, and troubled executives (Sperry, 2003). Table 4.1 provides a capsule summary of these executive types and their suitability for coaching.

TABLE 4.1 Types of Executives

Type	Description
Good Executive	Ready, willing and able to manage staff; tends to goals and projections; appears for appointments, keeps his or her word; tends to be an adequate to good team player and otherwise acts responsibly; when need exists for additional skills or help with performance issues, he or she is typically a good candidate for executive coaching.
Distressed Executive	Continues working but is unable to consistently function well on the job, at home, or in the community because of varying acute stressors; often meets criteria for minor DSM diagnoses (V codes or adjustment disorders); brief therapy can be helpful.
Impaired Executive	Characterized by decreased or deteriorating job performance and functioning that meets criteria for major DSM-IV-TR Axis I diagnoses and often Axis II personality disorders; problems more chronic and severe than those of distressed executive; usually requires psychotherapy and/or management ultimatum.
Difficult Executive	Because of unwillingness rather than lack of ability has problems relating to and leading others; may or may not have performance problems; when considered invaluable to the organization, his or her behavior and style may be overlooked even though they are problematic to many. If and when the executive has skill deficits or performance issues, he or she is not suitable for standard executive coaching without therapy or other leverage; often meets DSM criteria for a personality disorder.
Troubled Executive	Has personal issues or nonwork-related concerns (marital and family, financial, health, mental health, alcohol- and substance-related, or grief and bereavement issues) that impact job behavior and performance; is either "distressed" or "impaired," and is a candidate for psychotherapy or related interventions rather than coaching.
Different Executive	May talk or act in off-beat, less than conventional manner, but tends to meet performance objectives and attend to designated responsibilities; if executive coaching is indicated, he or she may be a suitable candidate, provided the coaching is tailored to his or her worldview.

Distressed Executives The distressed executive is typically an active member of his or her corporation, family, and community, but is unable to consistently function well on the job, at home, or in the community because of varying stressors. Yet, despite their distresses and occasional crises, they are able to bounce back from setbacks in contrast to impaired executives. Epidemiological data on distress in the executive population are scant. Nevertheless, Smith and Siwolop (1988) estimate that approximately 15% of executives could be considered distressed. Unrealistic deadlines, crushing workloads, and poor communications are cited as major job-induced stressors, as well as a host of competing personal, family, and social stressors. The most frequent reasons distressed executives seek help are marital problems, personality clashes with peers and superiors, suppressed emotional reactions to peers and superiors, problems with control of hostile impulses, difficulty asserting or responding to authority, hidden conflicts over dependency and disappointed ambitions, and unconscious fears of success with associated tendencies toward self-defeat typically triggered by problems related to career choices or relations with superiors (Moss, 1981).

In DSM-IV-TR terms (APA, 2000) these factors constitute V-codes and adjustment disorders. Kiechel (1990) reports another common form of distress for executives: insomnia. Executive insomnia appears to be a function of stress, evening socializing, heavy travel across time zones, and workaholism. Furthermore, aggressive Type A personalties tend to experience anxiety in disproportionate numbers and this further exacerbates their insomnia.

Because their performance is inconsistent, top management needs to attend to distressed executives. However, designating such an executive for executive coaching is typically problematic, unless the coach is psychologically trained and can assess levels of distress, evaluate conditions, and make recommendations for medical or psychological interventions. Often brief and focused therapy can be quite useful in normalizing executive functioning and well-being. Executive coaching, if still indicated, can proceed after that.

Impaired Executives Impairments present most commonly in the executive suite as drug- and substance-related disorders, stress-related disorders, and marital problems (Kiechel, 1988). In a study of 1,870 executives from one major U.S. corporation, major depression and alcohol abuse and dependence were the most common forms of impairment. Among men, the lifetime and 1-year prevalence rates for depression were 23% and 9%, respectively, while the rates were 36% and 17% for women. Lifetime and 1-year prevalence rates of alcohol abuse and dependence were 16% and 4%, respectively, for men and 9% and 4% for women (Bromet et al., 1990).

In his clinical study of senior executives, Speller (1989) found that alcohol- and substance-related disorders, depression, acute psychosis, and bipolar disorder were the most common forms of impairment among executives. There was no indication that sex differences were observed in this study. Pasick (1990) likewise noted that male executives entering therapy most commonly present with depression, anxiety, and substance abuse or dependence disorders. However, further exploration of these presenting problems revealed underlying work-related issues: workaholism; stress-related disorders; success addiction (similar to workaholism except that the craving is specifically for success rather than increased work time), work dissatisfaction, and underemployment.

Kets de Vries (1989) indicates that in some organizations, impairment presents more commonly as personality disordered behavior in executives. While personality disordered executives can wreak corporate havoc, they often are not recognized by others as impaired. The primary reason is that executive impairment has traditionally been construed only in terms of Axis I disorders in the DSM multiaxial system.

It may be helpful to define executive impairment operationally as a dysfunctional pattern of behavior reflected in decreased or deteriorating job performance and functioning that meets criteria for DSM-IV-TR Axis I and/or II diagnosis, excluding V-codes and adjustment disorders. The dysfunctional patterns will be observed as decompensated behaviors in which the impaired executives behave in irresponsible, uncooperative manners and/or in inappropriate, unpredictable, or strange manners. They may become apathetic and pessimistic, indecisive and confused or forgetful. Their insight and judgment may deteriorate and they may lose their business sense and savvy. They may become violent or overreact to relatively insignificant matters; they may become overwhelmed in the face of intense and painful affects. Unlike the distressed executive who is able to bounce back from unexpected setbacks and master challenges, the impaired executive finds it more and more difficult to normalize. In time, his or her level of function both inside and outside the executive suite will be significantly reduced.

Why are DSM-IV-TR criteria included in the operational definition of impairment? These criteria are useful in identifying obvious Axis I forms of executive impairment such as major depression, acute psychosis, substance-related and bipolar disorders and differentiating them from Axis II personality disorders. In some cases, impairment manifests itself in comorbid Axis I and II presentations.

3. Work versus Nonwork-Related Issues

Executives who do not face major nonwork-related issues tend to be better candidates for executive coaching than those who face significant nonwork-related concerns. These include relational, financial, legal, or health matters. Executives whose work performances are complicated by such nonwork-related issues or concerns are not likely to profit fully from executive coaching largely because of their preoccupations with those concerns. Until some resolution is made of some of the family problems faced by Harold Whitney, it will probably be difficult for him to fully focus on his executive coaching agenda.

4. Self-Direction and Responsibility

It is has been observed that those who are self-directed and consistently take responsibility for their behaviors and actions tend to be much better candidates for executive coaching than those who have difficulty being self-directed and taking responsibility for their actions. Considerable research by Robert Cloninger and his associates (1993) suggest that the capacity for self-directedness and self-responsibility and cooperativeness are markers of relatively healthy individuals who are more likely to be productive collaborators and good team players compared to those who have considerable difficulty taking responsibility for their actions and being collaborative and cooperative. Cloninger found that difficulty with self-responsibility and noncooperativeness are characteristic of individuals with DSM-IV personality disorders. Valerie Buscemi's tendencies to over-delegate and utilize other strategies for avoiding responsibility would not make her a good candidate for executive coaching.

5. Cooperation and Collaboration

Similarly, executives who are generally cooperative and collaborative and thus good team players are better candidates for executive coaching than those who have difficulty with cooperation and team efforts. Cloninger's research cited above is relevant here. Not all individuals who dislike working in a team context have personality disorders, but if these individuals are unable to cooperate in other contexts and are likewise irresponsible, they probably are personality disordered. In any event, they are not suitable for executive coaching. The case of Valerie Buscemi again comes to mind.

6. Success in Previous Change Effort

Executives who achieved previous positive responses to management initiatives or change efforts including therapy or coaching are probably better suited to executive coaching than those with negative or inconsistent responses to management efforts such as coaching. The basic point is that past success predicts future success, and experience has shown that those who have been successful at previous change efforts such as smoking cessation are likely to be successful in other change efforts such as executive coaching.

7. Readiness for Change

Since effective coaching is a collaborative venture, both executive client and coach must be ready and willing to become fully involved in the coaching process. Irrespective of the extent of an executive coach's experience and expertise, unless the executive or client is really invested in the coaching process, the expected outcomes will not be achieved. This readiness and willingness to engage in the coaching process, i.e., to change, cannot be taken for granted. In fact, the absence of readiness for change probably accounts for most failures in coaching.

This is also true for other organizational change efforts whether quality, continuous quality improvement, or work teams. Readiness for change and the dynamics of the stage of change were developed by Prochaska, Norcross, and DiClemente (1994). They identified six stages of change. Those practicing executive counseling, consulting, and coaching would do well to have a working knowledge of these stages and the underlying construct of readiness for change. As those being coached cycle through these stages, the executive coach needs to not only understand the stage of readiness, but must know how to respond appropriately so as to facilitate the move of the individual to a higher stage of readiness.

Precontemplation—This is the first stage of change. It involves denial or lack of awareness of the need for change. In terms of coaching, this means that the individual refuses to even talk about coaching. It represents the lowest degree of level of readiness for change. At this stage, the best strategy is to provide information, establish trust, and create doubt. A key question to pose at this stage is: What's wrong with the way things are right now?

Contemplation—Contemplation is the second stage. While an individual may be aware that a problem exists, he or she does not perceive a need to do something about the problem. As with the first stage, insisting that an individual in need of coaching begin a coaching process or appointing a coach to work with that individual is not only premature, it is counterproductive. It is much better to actively listen to the individual and perhaps identify the positive and negatives about making a change. A reasonable question at this stage is: Will making a change be worth it?

Decision—The third stage of readiness for change is decision or determination. The individual recognizes the problem and the need for doing something about it, decides to change, and begins to make plans to change. While it involves a higher level of readiness than the first two stages, there is no guarantee that the individual will actually engage in the coaching process. Nevertheless, helping the individual consider the what and how of coaching, providing information on the types and processes of coaching, or offering to introduce him or her to potential coaches can facilitate movement to the next stage of change.

Action—In this fourth stage, the individual is actually engaged in the change process. In terms of coaching, this stage represents the optimal level of readiness for change. Only at this stage can a client work collaboratively with a coach to assess, plan, and implement coaching. The coach's primary responsibilities are supporting the change efforts and affirming the client's commitment and involvement. A basic question here is: What will you do?

Maintenance—Maintenance is the stage in which the individual's efforts to change are still in process. The expected outcome has not yet been achieved or the change does not feel "natural." It is important for coaches to recognize the client's uncomfortableness at this stage and support him or her, possibly by helping with the so-called soft skills (assertive communication, problem solving, and other relational skills that provide news ways of viewing the job) and the necessary skills to increase the client's sense of empowerment during this uncomfortable stage. A basic question to ask at this stage is: What could help?

Recycling—The sixth and final stage is recycling or relapse which means that the coaching outcome was not sustained because of lack of support from top management, because the coaching ended prematurely, or because the individual relapsed and slipped back to a lower stage, usually contemplation. At this stage individuals are decidedly ambivalent about trying again, and usually use excuses to explain their failures. They need help in resolving this ambivalence, evaluating their commitments to change, and often assistance in identifying and eliminating obstacles to successful change. A basic question to ask at this stage is: What is your intention to change today?

Table 4.2 summarizes these factors and suggests a profile of a client's suitability or nonsuitability for executive coaching.

In short, executives with the highest suitability for executive coaching will exhibit many if not most of the suitability markers noted in Table 4.2. Not

TABLE 4.2 Profile of Client Suitability and Nonsuitability for Executive Coaching

Suitability Markers	Nonsuitability Markers
Performance issues primarily due to skill deficits or lack of experience	Performance issues primarily due to attitude or personal attribute
Absence of significant nonwork-related issues	Presence of significant nonwork-related issues, i.e., relational, legal, health, etc.
Previous success in planned change efforts or response to management initiatives and/or coaching	Uneven or negative response to management initiatives and/or coaching
Sufficient readiness for change	Insufficient readiness for change
Relatively psychological maturity, moderate to high self-esteem, and no psychopathology or substance	Psychological immaturity, poor self-esteem, current psychopathology or substance problems
Usually self-directed problems and willing to take responsibility for actions	Usually has difficulty taking responsibility for actions
Usually cooperative and collaborative	Difficulty with cooperation and team efforts

surprisingly, the more an executive exhibits nonsuitability markers, the less likely he or she is to profit from executive coaching.

To Coach or to Refer?

A closer look at the seven markers suggests that the first three (performance issues, absence of nonwork-related issues, and previous success at change effort—all reflecting situational factors) belong to different genres from the last three (psychological maturity, self-responsibility, and cooperativeness—all reflecting personality dispositions) and the fourth, readiness for change which can be both situational and dispositional. In my opinion, executives who are sufficiently immature and/or have Axis I psychopathologies, have difficulty taking responsibility for their actions *and* are typically noncooperative (markers of Axis II personality disorders) are generally speaking *not* suitable for executive coaching even if they show suitability on the other four markers.

After a course of successful psychotherapy or other psychological intervention, they may be better able to profit from executive coaching, but are not likely to benefit before that. Such executives should be referred for such services. In my opinion, even highly competent and experienced psychologically trained executive coaches should refer such executives and refrain from providing executive "coaching" which is really psychotherapy.

On the other hand, executives who may have one or more of the other four markers of nonsuitability, particularly nonwork-related stressors, may be able to profit from executive coaching at the hands of an experienced psychologically trained coach. The following case example hopefully illustrates this point.

Case Study: Psychotherapy or Executive Coaching?

Cynthia Walker is the 35-year old-assistant vice president of the accounting division of a recently merged financial institution. Her last performance review noted morale problems in the division. Fearful she would be terminated, Walker sought out the advice of an executive coach who was also a member at her country club. He was a counseling psychologist who practiced executive coaching as well as psychotherapy. He reviewed her concerns and tentatively concluded that the primary source of disharmony in the division was an older female accountant, Janice Davis, who was disgruntled with the recent merger and generally difficult to work with because of her almost incessant demands for special privileges. Walker felt intimidated by Davis. Walker believed that her problem managing the division and the difficult employee stemmed from her passive nature and domineering mother, and thought she might need formal psychotherapy. She read an article on the impact of family dynamics and negative transference in the workplace and thought that such an explanation fit her situation. Her boss, the CFO, apparently concurred as he dubbed the situation "a mother–daughter thing." The executive coach was not convinced that negative transference was the primary dynamic. Instead he suggested that because of Walker's underdeveloped skills in assertiveness and negotiation, executive coaching was indicated, and if it proved to be insufficient, they could consider a referral for psychotherapy.

In a one-to-one context, the coach utilized role playing to assess Walker's communication and negotiation skills. The coach modeled both skills in the context of role playing and role reversal. The coach first took on the role of manager and then that of difficult employee. Throughout the remainder of the first 2-hour session, Walker and the coach worked on preparing Walker for a forthcoming 6-month performance review with the difficult employee. Roles were practiced and reversed until Walker was confident she could reasonably handle the performance review. When they met the second time, Walker reported that the review had gone reasonably well as compared to previous reviews. Specific expectations regarding Walker's attitude and productivity had been mutually negotiated. Nevertheless, Walker was still somewhat intimidated by Davis. Skill building continued with role playing focusing on typical encounters between both women. The coaching was also directed at replacing Walker's denigratory self-talk with more positive self-talk when she anticipated dealing with the accountant.

By the time of the third coaching session, morale in the division was better and Walker felt more confidence as a manager. In this example, coaching rather than psychotherapy appeared to be the initial intervention of choice and was effective. Had an adequate course of coaching been only partially successful, formal psychotherapy might then have been offered. Thus, while it appeared that Walker might have at least one marker of nonsuitability for coaching, she responded well to coaching provided by an experienced psychologically trained executive coach.

Client Suitability for Coaching: Reviewing the Seven Cases

We return now to the seven case examples briefly presented earlier in this chapter. By utilizing the markers of client suitability and nonsuitability for executive coaching, we can more objectively predict which executives are likely to be suitable candidates and which are not. Based on available information, Julian Estrada, Harold Whitney, and Cindy Kim appear to be suitable for coaching. The course of executive coaching with Harold Whitney is found in chapter 8. A description of the course of executive coaching with Estrada and also with Kim is found in chapter 7. Valerie Buscemi does not appear to be a suitable candidate. A primary reason for Buscemi's nonsuitability is that individuals who meet criteria for narcissistic personality disorder seldom are able to respond in the long run solely to executive coaching. Similarly, Jerry Flynn may not be suitable for coaching without prior psychotherapy. The case of Jerry Flynn continues in a subsequent section of this chapter. While it may appear that Albert Jacqui may need coaching, it may actually be the case that his manager, Jillian Jefferson, might profit from coaching because it appears that her management style may be disempowering. A fuller consideration and follow-up of this case is included in chapter 7. Finally, while Larry Kimble appears to be a superb candidate for executive coaching, there is little to suggest that he needs it given his high levels of productivity and health.

Coach Suitability: Not All Executive Coaching Is the Same

In the past few years, it has become more and more popular for top management to contract with coaches to work with certain executives. Although some of these coaches are psychologically trained, usually mental health professionals with training and experience in psychotherapy, the majority are likely to be former athletes, lawyers, business school professors, and management consultants. Presumably, nonpsychologically trained coaches can assist executives to improve their performance, but some reports indicate that executive coaches without formal psychological training have actually done more harm than good (Berglas, 2002). Such coaches may downplay or ignore deep-seated psychological problems and as a result can make a bad situation worse.

Jerry Flynn (*Continued*)

After deciding that he was too valuable to terminate, the head partner assigned Jack Weston to coach Jerry Flynn. Weston, a "retired" college football coach turned executive coach, worked with Flynn weekly for 12 months. Rather than exploring Flynn's mistreatment of his staff, Weston focused on and taught him techniques for "winning friends and influencing people." Gradually, Flynn seemed to become more "congenial" with his staff and morale seemed better.

About 2 months after Flynn and Weston finished working together, Flynn verbally humiliated one of the partners. When confronted about his behavior, Flynn said he just needed a little more coaching and sought to work with Weston again. The head partner suspected that something more was going on, denied Flynn's request, and engaged an outside psychological consultant, a Ph.D. in clinical and organizational psychology, to evaluate the situation.

During their consultation session, the consultant quickly recognized Flynn's exaggerated sense of entitlement and grandiosity, patterns of contemptuous behavior toward others, and other indications of a narcissistic personality disorder. The consultant recommended to the CEO that Flynn could conceivably need therapy rather than coaching and that a psychologically trained coach was worth a try. If that was unsuccessful, it was recommended that Flynn's continued employment be contingent on specific changes that might be achieved with psychotherapy.

It is inconceivable that standard executive coaching provided by someone like Weston could have substantially redirected Flynn's pattern. Executives with the kind of narcissistic personality pattern exhibited by Flynn rarely change their behavior unless they experience extraordinary psychological pain, such as the threat of losing their jobs or prized relationships such as their marriages. However, they may, as a result of coaching, manifest some superficial modifications in the way they relate to others, i.e., act more congenially when it is in their best interests. Treating others more civilly would presumably have netted Flynn the partner status he wanted. The paradox of Flynn's situation was that working with his executive coach had not only shielded him from pain, but apparently also reinforced his sense of entitlement and grandiosity. Unfortunately, such coaching too often engenders a common belief among narcissistic executives: "I'm so important that my superior boss paid for a special coach to assist me." Furthermore, such coaching inadvertently eroded Flynn's job performance, as typically occurs when executives with narcissistic personality disorders are not held accountable. A major objective of psychologically trained executive coaches is to heighten awareness of the difference between a "problem executive" who can be trained to function effectively with coaching and an "executive with a problem" who can best be helped with psychotherapy.

Nonpsychologically Trained Coaches: Some Major Concerns

There are four major concerns involving executive coaches who lack training and experience in psychodynamics and psychotherapy. First, such coaches typically take a limited focus and emphasize quick results. Second, such coaches tend to rely primarily on behavioral interventions and methods. Third, such coaches may misuse or exploit their relational power over clients. Finally, because they lack the training and capacity to effectively assess suitability for coaching, they may inadvertently complicate the situation or create new problems, possibly with significant financial and legal consequences. Furthermore, psychologically naive coaching can unwittingly foster psychological problems that may require psychotherapy to repair (Berglas, 2002). This section discusses each of these four concerns.

Limited Focus and Quick Results

The popularity of executive coaching owes much to the American quest for the "quick fix." Businesses constantly seek new ways to achieve results quickly and painlessly. In such an environment, counseling and psychotherapy, which are perceived as change efforts that take time and may be painful, have become marginalized. Not surprisingly, executive coaching is viewed as an instant alternative to therapy. Furthermore, executive coaching is viewed as safer and more acceptable than psychotherapy. Many executives find it easier and more politically correct to say that they are working with an executive coach than to say they are seeing a psychotherapist.

To achieve quick results, many executive coaches model their interventions after those used by top professional sports coaches. Needless to say, such techniques seldom, if ever, involve the kind of self-analysis and introspection characteristic of therapy. Billing executive coaching as a shortcut to improving executive performance is an irresistible selling point. Yet, approaches that ignore or gloss over unconscious conflicts can have disastrous consequences for corporations in the long term and can exacerbate the psychological damage of the executive being coached (Berglas, 2002).

Reliance on Behavioral Interventions

Nonpsychologically oriented executive coaching characteristically focuses on symptoms rather than causes—on external behaviors such as skill deficits, rather than on underlying psychodynamics such as narcissistic personality style or disorder. Consistent with this focus on external behaviors and skills is a tendency for most executive coaches to rely on behavioral interventions.

A common behavioral strategy is assertiveness training. This strategy can be used to help individuals cope with circumstances that produce intense discomfort, such as helping substance abusers deal with the allure of and craving for drugs. Executive coaching utilizes assertiveness training in various situations. For example, assertiveness training can be used with executives who seem to lack confidence and thus underperform. Not surprisingly, learning effective responses to stressors seldom leads executives to deal effectively with internal conflicts and struggles.

Presumably, psychologically trained coaches have broader training and experience and thus should be able to bring various other intervention strategies to bear in their coaching. This is not to imply that such coaches are or should covertly practice psychotherapy under the guise of executive coaching, but rather that when appropriately modified, certain cognitive, psychodynamic, and systemic intervention methods and techniques can have considerable value in achieving the goals of executive coaching

Misuse of Relational Power

Executive coaches who functioned as executives prior to becoming coaches are likely to connect to the executives they are coaching more readily than most psychotherapists. Thus, executive clients can easily identify with coaches who have executive experience, and unless these coaches understand the dynamics of interpersonal relations, they may unwittingly misuse their relational power. "Indeed, many coaches gain a Svengali-like hold over both the executives they train and the CEOs they report to, sometimes with disastrous consequence" (Berglas, 2002). The nature of this relational process is transference.

Transference is basically an intense feeling—positive or negative—for an individual whose traits mirror those of a significant individual—like a parent—from the past that manifests in relationships in the present, such as with an executive coach or a therapist. While transference is not inevitable in executive coaching, it is nevertheless a common element of influence or power in the relationship of coach and client. Because it is an unconscious process, the coach (the object of such transference) can exert considerable influence in the relationship with the client. The issue becomes how the executive coach handles transference, how he or she handles this relational power. Presumably, psychologically trained coaches should be able to effectively deal with it in an ethical and competent manner. On the other hand, coaches without such training may unwittingly or deliberately exert undue influence over their clients.

Executive clients experience transference toward executive coaches and so do some CEOs who hire executive coaches. Of course, not all CEOs experience transference toward coaches they engage to work with their executives, but transference is not uncommon among CEOs. Thus, coaches can easily expand their influence over CEOs, from focused coaching to general consultation and advisement. Not surprisingly, CEOs do not like to lose face and often feel personally responsible for selecting coaches. Accordingly, they tend to feel more accountable for their coaches' successes or failures than for therapists who might be assigned to particular executives.

Problem Exacerbation

Another drawback of nonpsychologically trained coaches is that their efforts may actually exacerbate or complicate a condition, situation, problem, or concern either because they are unaware of psychological dynamics or are unable to effectively deal with them. In referring to nonpsychologically trained executive coaches, Berglas (2002) notes: "By dint of their backgrounds and biases, they downplay or simply ignore deep-seated psychological problems they don't understand. Even more concerning, when an executive's problems stem from undetected or ignored psychological difficulties, coaching can actually make a bad situation worse" (p. 87).

Value-Added Benefits of Psychologically Trained Coaches

While nonpsychologically trained coaches may possess many of the requisite skills of executive coaching, there are certain coaching situations in which clinical training is invaluable. One such situation is referral for medical or psychiatric evaluation or psychotherapy. Wasylyshyn (2001) contends that: "Coaches who have not had training in psychology or in a related behavior science are less likely to be successful in handling referrals where an executive must change a deeply entrenched and dysfunctional behavior pattern" (p. 17). Another coaching consideration is where the desired coaching outcome involves maintaining or sustaining a hard-won behavior change or preventing relapse, both of which require the specific expertise provided by clinical training.

Corporations may be better served by drawing on the expertise of psychological consultants, psychotherapists, and executive coaches with legitimate skills. There is a growing consensus that every executive slated for coaching should first undergo a psychological evaluation (Berglas, 2002). By screening out executives not psychologically predisposed or ready to benefit from coaching, corporations avoid putting executives in deeply uncomfortable—even damaging—positions. Equally important, corporations would do well to engage external mental health professionals to review coaching outcomes. Such a strategy can ensure that coaches do not overlook underlying problems or create new ones.

Psychological assessment and treatment are not magic bullets and can even be misapplied. For example, an individual does not need to be a psychotherapist to coach executives to enhance their strategic planning skills and should not assume that all executives who have planning problems lack the necessary skills. The reality is that psychological disorders can and do interfere with developing and executing business plans. For instance, clinical depression can block an executive's ability to engage in constructive, goal-oriented behavior. Thus, it is essential to recognize that coaching executives whose problems stem not from a lack of skills but from psychological problems can be hazardous to both the coached executives and their corporations.

In short, mental health professionals with interests in workplace problems and some related experience can offer considerable value to corporations that utilize coaching. By virtue of their clinical expertise, mental health professionals are uniquely qualified to provide corporations with psychological screening and referrals when indicated, in addition to standard executive coaching and consultation.

Requisite Psychological Skills of Effective Executive Coaches

Finally, certain general psychological skills appear essential for effective coaches. These include interpersonal effectiveness, listening, empathy, patience, adaptability, analytical problem solving, humor, and creativity (Wasylyshyn, 2003). Other psychological skills useful in executive coaching are building rapport, encouraging, facilitating change, intuition, strong boundaries, reframing, objectivity, unconditional positive regard, acceptance of emotions, and being nonjudgmental (Auerbach, 2002).

Modoono (2002) developed a self-assessment inventory of the requisite psychological competencies needed by executive coaches. The inventory reflects the competencies demonstrated by effective executive coaches. Table 4.3 lists the competencies.

Concluding Note

In addition to the executive client, the executive's boss, and the executive coach, other professionals such as psychiatric consultants and psychotherapists can be key players in decisions about executive coaching. This chapter emphasizes the importance and value of assessing the suitability of both executive clients and coaches for executive coaching. We have highlighted the value-added benefits that psychologically trained executive coaches bring to corporations: they have the capacity to competently screen and make referrals to appropriate medical, substance abuse, and psychological treatments, as well as provide psychologically informed executive coaching.

We and others (Berglas, 2002) contend that all potential candidates for executive coaching should be screened for their suitability for coaching and those who are better suited for psychotherapy or other psychologically

TABLE 4.3 Psychological Competencies Demonstrated by Effective Executive Coaches

Self-awareness of feelings toward others
Capacity to monitor own feelings when dealing with others
Ability to understand own strengths and weaknesses
Ability to view situations from another's perspective
Ability to read another's underlying emotions
Skill at developing rapport with others
Capacity to assess impact on others in real time
Ability and willingness to adapt approach
Capacity to quickly assess individual and organizational dynamics
Capacity to balance interests of an individual with organization's needs
Capacity to effectively help others solve organizational and management problems
Capacity to aid executives in creating realistic personal development plans that positively impact organizational outcomes
Capacity and willingness to hold individuals accountable for their behavior
Ability to understand how an executive's behavior affects the economic value of the organization
Refusal to be easily intimidated by individuals in positions of power
Ability to be energized by helping others achieve success
Capacity for providing effective feedback in an unambiguous fashion without fear of conflict

Source: Derived from Modoono, S. (2002). *Journal of Consulting Psychology*, 54, 43.

oriented treatments should be referred for such treatment. This is not to suggest that nonpsychologically trained coaches do not or cannot provide effective executive coaching. On the contrary, they can, provided that they work with suitable clients. However, given the propensity for top management to view coaching as a quick and relatively inexpensive form of therapeutic change, many executives who really need professional counseling or psychotherapy are sent to executive coaching instead. As noted earlier, I believe that when the last three markers of nonsuitability (significant psychological immaturity and/or Axis I psychopathology; lack of self-responsibility; and difficulty with cooperativeness—the latter two indicative of Axis II personality disorders) are present, such executives are usually not candidates for executive coaching even if it is provided by experienced psychologically trained coaches. Instead, they should be referred for appropriate psychological treatment and/or management action.

A basic theme of this book is that coaching is not a panacea nor a substitute for professional counseling or psychotherapy. Hopefully, after reading this chapter, executive coaches with and without psychological training will more clearly understand an executive's suitability for coaching and will not attempt to provide psychotherapy under the guise of executive coaching to those poorly suited for coaching.

References

Auerbach, J. (2002). *Personal and executive coaching: The complete guide for mental health professionals.* Ventura, CA: Executive College Press.

Berglas, S. (2002). The very real dangers of executive coaching. *Harvard Business Review, 80,* 86–92.

Bromet, E., Parkinson, D., Curtis C. et al. (1990). Epidemiology of depression and alcohol abuse/dependence in a managerial and professional work force. *Journal of Occupational Medicine, 32,* 989–995.

Cloninger, R., Svrakic, D., & Prybeck, T. (1993). A psychobiological model of temperament and character. *Archives of General Psychiatry, 50,* 975–990.

Kets de Vries, M. (1989). *Prisoners of leadership.* New York: Wiley.

Kiechel, W. (1990). The executive insomniac. *Fortune, 122,* 183–184.

Kiechel, W. (1988). Looking out for the executive alcoholic. In *Office hours: A guide to the managerial life.* Boston, MA: Little, Brown, pp. 216–233.

Modoono, S. (2002). The executive coach self-assessment inventory. *Journal of Consulting Psychology, 54,* 43.

Moss, L. (1981). *Management stress.* Reading, MA: Addison Wesley.

Pasick R. (1990). Raised to work. In R. Meth & R. Pasick (Eds.). *Men in therapy: The challenge of change.* pp. 35–53. New York: Guilford.

Prochaska, J., Norcross, J., & DiClemente, C. (1994). *Changing for good.* New York: Morrow.

Smith, E. & Siwolop, S. (1988). Stress: The test Americans are failing. *Business Week, 30,* 74–78.

Speller, J. (1989). *Executives in crisis: Recognizing and managing the alcoholic, drug addicted or mentally ill executive.* San Francisco: Jossey-Bass.

Sperry, L. (2003). *Becoming an effective health care manager: The essential skills of leadership.* Baltimore: Health Professions Press.

Sperry, L (1993). Working with executives: Consulting, counseling and coaching. *Individual Psychology, 49,* 257–266.

Wasylyshyn, K. (2003). Executive coaching: An outcome study. *Consulting Psychology Journal: Practice and Research, 55,* 94–106.

Wasylyshyn, K. (2001). On the full actualization of psychology in business. *Consulting Psychology Journal: Practice and Research, 53,* 10–21.

5
The Process of Executive Coaching

Executives are referred for executive coaching for a number of reasons ranging from increasing their overall productivity and effectiveness to improving relations with their staffs and even fostering personal and professional well-being. Previous chapters described coaching as a professional service related to but distinct from consultation and psychotherapy and discussed the needs of executives who present themselves for coaching. Because most mental health professionals have limited knowledge of the business sector, we have explored the organizational context in which coaching takes place and various personal and systemic dynamics that impact executives. We have also highlighted the importance of evaluating a client's suitability and readiness for executive coaching. Now we are ready to turn to the actual process of executive coaching.

This chapter begins with a brief discussion of the theoretical models that inform most coaching practice today. It then goes on to describe different modes in which executive coaching tends to be practiced. While the most common mode involves a coach and client in a one-to-one relationship, situations require executive coaches to function in other modes as well. Following this is a discussion of the focus of coaching and three common types of executive coaching. Finally, the phases or stages of the coaching process are described.

Models of Coaching

Generally speaking, coaches are informed by one of three main models of coaching thought and practice: expert, person-centered, and blended (Campbell, 2001). In the section that follows, the basic assumptions and the roles of coaches and clients are briefly discussed for each of these models.

Expert Model

The expert model of coaching is based on an assumption that most individuals desire improvement, recognition, and advancement and that executive coaching can foster these outcomes through teaching specific skills, improving job performance, and fostering career advancement in an organizational context. The role of the executive coach is to guide and assist clients in achieving "a mutually identified set of goals to improve his or her professional performance and personal satisfaction and, consequently, to improve the client's organization within a formally defined coaching agreement." (Kilburg, 1996, p. 142). Not surprisingly, the assumptions of this model are acceptable to most executive clients as well as to many who provide executive coaching, particularly nonpsychologically trained coaches.

Person-Centered Model

The person-centered approach to coaching reflects the work of Carl Rogers (1996) and others in humanistic psychology and in the human potential movement. The basic assumption of this model of coaching is that clients have within themselves the wisdom to solve their problems and concerns; the coach's role is to serve as a partner on the journey. More specifically, a person-centered coach provides a supportive context so that clients can find their own answers and helps clients implement changes in their lives. This model seems to be more compatible with coaches who practice life coaching than those who practice executive coaching.

Blended Model

This model "blends" elements of both the expert and person-centered models. The underlying assumption of this model is that individuals possess inner wisdom but need guidance and challenge in addition to support in order to resolve problems and develop their potential. The coach's role in this model serves as both partner and guide. This model requires that coaches have considerable skill and experience that ranges from asking clients for their own solutions to assisting clients to utilize their strengths and capabilities to overcome obstacles as well as challenging them to make important life changes. Largely, this model informs the work of many executive coaches, particularly those who are psychologically trained.

While all three models hold that the goals of effective coaching are increased competence and personal and professional development, the person-centered and blended models have additional goals: to promote vision and focus energy on personal values, to assist clients in seeking new directions and purposes in their lives, and to inspire clients to be more effective and creative in finding solutions to life's problems (Campbell, 2001).

Modes of Executive Coaching

When most individuals think about the process of coaching, they visualize a one-to-one exchange between an executive coach and an executive client. For the most part, executive coaching typically occurs in such a one-to-one mode. However, effective executive coaching must respond to the reality of corporate situations and circumstances and thus two other modes of executive coaching exist. These as well as the typical one-to-one mode will be described in this section. A somewhat different perspective on modes articulates four "levels" of coaching (O'Neil, 2000). Table 5.1 lists these modes.

TABLE 5.1 Three Modes of Executive Coaching

1. Two-way coaching: includes coach and executive client
2. Three-way coaching: includes coach, executive client, and a third individual
3. Team-based coaching: includes coach, executive client, and executive's team

Two-Way Coaching

In what is the most common coaching mode, the executive meets with the coach to set goals, plan for action, and debrief the executive's efforts to accomplish the action plan. While the coach and client do meet formally on a scheduled basis, it would be erroneous to conclude that the coaching process is conducted only during those encounters. Actually, the coaching process extends beyond those scheduled sessions and includes all instances in which the executive is engaged in implementing the agreed-upon coaching plan, even when the executive is with his team, colleagues, or family and not in the presence of the coach. In a sense, this part of the coaching process takes place "behind the scenes." The other two modes directly involve the executive coach and the executive in executing the agreed-upon course of action.

Three-Way Coaching

This mode of coaching involves three individuals: the executive coach, the executive client, and a third individual, usually a staff member or other employee. The coach is present while the executive is engaged in a one-to-one session with the other person. This type of executive coaching provides live feedback to the executive client in the midst of what could be a highly reactive, difficult, or deadlocked situation. The coach can suggest alternatives or process issues so that the impasse or conflict can be resolved. More than any of the other coaching modes, this one exposes the client's vulnerability and thus requires that the executive has considerable psychological resilience and self-esteem as well as a high level of trust in the coach. Probably for this reason, this may be the least frequent coaching mode (O'Neil, 2000).

Team-Based Coaching

In this mode, the coach works with the executive and his or her staff in the context of a team setting. This mode has two variants: coaching the whole team including the executive, and coaching the executive in a team context.

In the first variant, coaching takes place in a team setting while the executive and team members are engaging in reviewing, strategizing, decision making, or problem solving. The executive coach is also present and selectively intervenes in the process. This coaching mode allows the coach to emphasize team strengths and accelerate the team's performance. It also provides the executive and team with feedback and suggestions to get the team back on track when they have lost focus. Also called *group process consultation*, this form of coaching championed by organizational consultants has long been shown to be a powerful change strategy.

In the second variant, the executive coach works with the executive to effect change in the executive's team leadership behavior in the context of team meetings. The executive's effectiveness in a team setting becomes the focus of coaching. While this may appear similar to the coaching-a-team-including-the-executive-client mode, it is actually quite different. In the first variant, the client is the entire team, whereas in the second, the client is the executive who is coaching in a team context. In the second variant, the executive coach does not directly address or facilitate the team; these functions are handled by the executive client who is the team leader. The focus of this coaching is enhancing the executive's competency in team leadership.

Types of Executive Coaching

As we have pointed out, executive coaching is a strategy or method for improving an executive's personal and professional effectiveness. Depending on the specific goal or focus of coaching, three different types or approaches can be specified (Sperry, 2002). When the focus is on the individual's current task or project, skill-based coaching is the appropriate type. If, however, the focus is on the individual's effectiveness or competence, performance-based coaching is the appropriate type. Finally, when the focus is on the individual's future job responsibilities or career, developmental coaching is appropriate (Witherspoon, 2000). Each type is described and illustrated with case studies in this section. Table 5.2 summarizes these types.

Skill-Focused Coaching

Skill-based coaching is typically what most people associate with the term "coaching." Skill-focused coaching is both a process and method for developing or enhancing technical, operational, analytic, relational, strategic, or self-management skills that occurs within a collaborative relationship with a coach. The goals and outcomes can be short or long term. In the short term, the objective is typically to reverse a skill deficit or enhance a specific leadership skill, whereas in the long term, the goal and outcome are to increase the executive's overall leadership competencies. The primary purpose of skill-focused coaching is to sharpen skills in one or more areas that will facilitate the executive's efforts with a current project or task.

Performance-Focused Coaching

"Performance" refers to an individual's competencies and personal styles as they impact work outcomes positively or negatively. As distinct from skill-focused and developmental coaching, performance-focused coaching is a process and method for increasing performance and job effectiveness. In the short term, its primary objective is to increase leadership performance in a specific area. In the long term, such coaching would endeavor to increase overall leadership performance so that an executive can more consistently function effectively.

TABLE 5.2 Three Types of Executive Coaching

Type	Description	Goals
Skill-focused coaching	Process and method for learning or enhancing technical, operational, analytic, relational, strategic, or self-management skills	*Short term*: reversing a skill deficit or enhancing a specific leadership skill *Long term*: increasing leadership competencies
Performance-focused coaching	Process and method for increasing performance and job effectiveness	*Short term*: increasing leadership performance in a specific area *Long term*: increasing overall leadership performance; functioning consistently as an effective executive
Development-focused coaching	Process and method for fostering professional, career, and personal growth in executives and their employees	*For the executive*: increasing personal and professional transformation *By the executive*: professional and career development of employees *For the organization*: developing leadership potential, skills, and performance in potential or existing executives

Performance-based coaching is a strategy for increasing, correcting or recalibrating an executive's overall performance and job effectiveness as a function of leadership competencies and personal style. Coaching to improve performance typically focuses on either enhancing competencies or removing barriers that interfere with job performance and may even jeopardize an executive's career. In short, this type of coaching focuses both on increasing performance and decreasing or eliminating impediments to higher level executive performance.

Development-Focused Coaching

Developmental coaching is a process and method for fostering professional, career, and personal growth of executives and of the employees they manage. The goals and outcomes of this kind of coaching vary, depending on the target.

Typically, the expected outcome for executives is to increase their personal and professional transformations. Because executives are expected to assume coaching functions, the goal is to foster professional and career development in the employees they lead. For the organization, the expected outcome of developmental coaching is promoting leadership potential by means of developing or enhancing skills and performance of executives

Phases of Coaching Process

Although various descriptions of the executive coaching process exist, most include at least four phases. This section describes the four-phase model of coaching that I use with executives. See Table 5.3.

Phase 1: Engagement and Contract

Phase 1 involves establishment of a viable relationship and some agreement about the nature of the coaching. Establishing a collaborative relationship is considered by many as a necessary condition of success of the undertaking. A collaborative relationship presumes that both coach and client are ready and motivated to participate in the coaching process. The coach cannot blindly assume readiness and motivation, because if it is lacking, the coaching effort will surely fail. The agreement or contract for coaching usually specifies the goal, method, frequency and duration of meetings, and remuneration.

Phase 2: Initial Assessment

Phase 2 includes assessment of the executive. This may be quite broad or narrow. It might include an evaluation of job description, functions, and performance standards, skills, talents and competencies, reporting relationships, etc. An increasing number of executive coaches incorporate some form of 360-degree evaluation that serves as a baseline to monitor and evaluate progress. Sophisticated coaches also assess the executive's motivation and level of readiness for coaching.

This initial or preintervention assessment is only part of the process which, in my view, must be an ongoing process providing continuous feedback on all phases of the coaching process. Just as in strategic planning and implementation processes wherein ongoing evaluation and monitoring provide feedback for making necessary course corrections in the direction and focus of the organization's strategy, ongoing assessment provides essential feedback to modify the direction and focus of coaching.

TABLE 5.3 Four Phases of Coaching Process

1. Engagement and contract
2. Initial assessment
3. Coaching plan and implementation
4. Evaluation of progress and outcomes

Phase 3: Coaching Plan and Implementation

Phase 3 includes some action planning that specifies the goal to be achieved and articulates the methods and techniques for achieving it. The goal usually is learning a new skill, improving performance, developmental or career planning, etc. Establishing specific coaching targets is a way to operationalize the goals in behavioral, measurable terms.

Goal setting is the key to successful executive coaching. Goal setting provides a structure for the coaching session and provides a clear focus for resulting actions and outcomes. Many coaches use the mnemonic SMART to focus on achievable results. The S stands for *specific*: one must precisely define the aim. The M stands for *measurement*; there is an identifiable standard with which to assess achievement. The A means *achievable*; it ensures the employee or team has the resources needed to accomplish the goal. The R is for *relevant*; the goal must be worthwhile for the employee or team. T means *time-bound*; it specifies the targeted completion date.

Implementing the coaching plan is the heart of the executive coaching process and usually the longest phase during which various coaching interventions are initiated. These typically include skills training, modeling, role playing, writing a personal mission statement, journaling, and the use of executive resources. They may also include interventions from counseling and psychotherapy, such as the miracle question from solution-focused therapy and circular and strategic questioning from systemic therapy.

Phase 4: Evaluation of Progress and Outcomes

Assessment continues throughout the coaching process. Monitoring and evaluation of outcomes against the agreed-upon goals and targets are essential components of the coaching process. In this phase, two kinds of assessment are important. The first is monitoring incremental progress in terms of achieving coaching targets on a session-to-session basis, and the second is evaluation of the achievement of overall coaching outcomes that are usually specified as the coaching goals.

Scaling is an easy and accurate way to monitor an individual's progress with regard to the coaching targets. The executive is asked to rate his or her current level of performance on a scale of 1 to 10 where 10 is the highest and 1 is the lowest. If the executive's rating is 4, pose the question: What has to happen for you to get to 5 on this scale? Spend some time discussing and providing feedback on the answer to this question. Is the answer realistic? What support or resources might be needed for this to be accomplished? Record this self-rating and explanation for comparison when you monitor performance changes.

Momentum for existing changes will slow down as the executive becomes more experienced. Coaching requires that the employee is continually stretched or challenged in order to improve on past levels of performance. For example, when an executive reaches 6 on the performance scale, challenge him or her to rescale performance efforts by asking what it will take to progress to 7.

Illustration of Phases of Coaching

An executive who consistently met his productivity quotas had problems with employee morale and turnover, and because of his hard driving, overbearing and somewhat arrogant style, took excessive sick and personal days. Because he was being groomed for a promotion, his superior wanted him to work with an executive coach. The executive agreed.

Phase 1

The executive's superior introduced him to the coach in a short meeting. After that, the executive and coach met about 30 minutes to discuss the process. The executive said he was glad he was being considered for the promotion, knew he needed to work on his "issues," and thought coaching could help. He said he was willing to commit to the process. During that time the coach gave the executive a 12-page questionnaire to complete and deliver the day before their first scheduled session. Before their meeting, the coach reviewed the questionnaire to determine focused work issues, indicators of readiness, and success in other planned change efforts. When they met next day, the coach endeavored to further engage the client.

Phase 2

In addition to the questionnaire data, additional assessments were undertaken. These included the Myers–Briggs Type Indicator (MBTI), the Emotional Competency Inventory (ECI), and two different 360-degree feedback instruments containing data collected from the executive, his superior, his employees, and his executive peers. This information was analyzed and integrated into a case conceptualization.

Phase 3

The coach and executive met a third time and collaborated on establishing goals, targets, and a counseling plan to achieve the goals. Three *coaching goals* were set: (1) reducing unit turnover and improving morale; (2) improving health and reducing the number of sick days taken; and (3) assessing and fostering the executive's promotability to COO. The following *coaching targets* that operationalized the coaching goals were specified: (1) improving listening and communication skills; (2) increasing health status and stamina; (3) increasing awareness of insensitivity and arrogance; (4) improving relational sensitivity, particularly with an engineer in his unit; and (5) enrolling in a corporate leadership development program. The specifics of the *coaching plan* involved three elements: (1) face-to-face (two-way) coaching meetings of 90 minutes every week; (2) team-based coaching to foster improved unit functioning; and (3) referral for an executive health evaluation and recommendations; regular between-meeting assignments (homework).

Over the next 3 months, the focus of coaching was directed to the first two coaching goals and the first four coaching targets. Coaching began with two-way sessions. After 4 weeks, the coaching also included four separate sessions of team-based coaching. The third goal and the fourth coaching target were longer term goals that started in the second month of coaching. Weekly progress was monitored for each coaching target on a rating scale of 1 to 10.

Phase 4

As planned, at the end of the third month, the coach and executive reviewed the weekly progress ratings in addition to a second set of 360-degree evaluations. Significant progress was noted on all four coaching targets, with the most progress noted in the areas of health and stamina and interpersonal relations with the executive's engineer. As anticipated, the executive made less (but sufficient) progress on the increased sensitivity target. Although they were longer term goals, some progress was also noted on the third goal and the fourth coaching target. It was decided to continue coaching for 3 months, but on a biweekly basis, to both increase gains and sustain progress, particularly with regard to goal 3.

Phases of Psychotherapy Process

Executive coaching and psychotherapy share several commonalities as well as differences. The commonalities and differences were noted in chapters 1 and 4. The comparisons in those chapters primarily described the structures of psychotherapy and executive coaching. For executive coaches without psychological training and psychotherapy experience, a structural comparison may have been sufficient. However, mental health professionals in my seminars and workshops on executive coaching find this type of comparison superficial because it does not compare or reflect the actual processes of psychotherapy and coaching. For that reason, this section offers a side-by-side comparison of the processes of psychotherapy and executive coaching.

Basically, the course of psychotherapy can be understood as having a beginning point, a middle, and an end point. Various efforts to describe the course and process of psychotherapy have yielded various formats, but the phase model described here reflects commonalities among both eastern and western therapy systems and approaches (Beitman,1993). Four essential phases based on Beitman's research and articulated by Sperry (1999) are as follows:

Phase 1: Engagement

Engagement is the first and most important stage of treatment. Effective treatment outcomes require that clients be sufficiently engaged—committed to and actively involved—in the treatment process. In other words, engagement is required for any therapeutic change to occur. Typically, therapists assume that a client who appears for sessions and talks about his concerns is engaged in treatment. However, it only takes an instance or two of nonadherence to treatment activities—such as failing to do homework—for the therapist to begin to question the client's degree of engagement. A general rule is that until an optimal degree of engagement is achieved, formal treatment should not proceed. What is the optimal degree of engagement? Optimal engagement is indicated by a client's active involvement in negotiating treatment goals, and realistic expectations for his role—and the therapist's role—in the change process; by the client's willingness to follow the ground rules of therapy when a formal or informal treatment contract is negotiated; and by a high level of client motivation or readiness for change. A high degree of readiness for change predicts collaboration, compliance, and positive change; a low level predicts resistance, noncompliance, and no change.

The goal of the engagement phase is to develop a working therapeutic relationship and maximize the client's readiness for change. Therapeutic strategies to facilitate optimal engagement are many. They include manifest empathic listening; triggering the placebo effect; reversing the client's demoralization; and providing effective suggestions and socialization to therapy.

Phase 2: Pattern Identification

Identification means a focused assessment of a client's maladaptive patterns. A *pattern* is a predictable and consistent style or manner in which a person thinks, feels, acts, copes, and defends himself or herself in stressful and non-stressful circumstances. It reflects an individual's baseline functioning. A pattern has physical, psychological, and social features, such as a hard driving, Type A lifestyle, narcissistic personality style or disorder, or domineering manner among workplace peers. *Maladaptive* actions are detrimental or harmful to self or others. Maladaptive actions are predictable patterns of detrimental behavior and thinking. One way of specifying a behavioral component of a pattern is with DSM-IV Axis II personality traits or disorder terms. *Schema* is a specific way of describing the content and style of the thinking component.

The goal of the identification phase of treatment is to specify a client's maladaptive pattern including behavioral, effective and cognitive (schema) components, which, if changed, will lead to more adaptive functioning. Common therapeutic methods useful in pattern assessment are diagnostic questioning protocols or strategies, interventive questioning strategies, and assessment by means of psychological inventories or other questionnaires. In addition, the therapist may also utilize role playing or other forms of in-session enactment to elicit and/or clarify client patterns.

Phase 3: Pattern Change Interventions

The goal of the intervention phase is straightforward: to modify or transform a client's maladaptive pattern into a more adaptive pattern. Intervention methods potentially include all therapeutic intervention strategies and tactics, for example, focused pattern interruption strategies, cognitive restructuring, interpretation, and/or reframing methods. One significant intervention method is so obvious that it is often overlooked in discussion—eliciting and supporting internal and external client resources.

Maladaptive patterns often manifest themselves with symptomatic distress and functional impairment. Thus, decreasing symptomatology and/or increasing life functioning are usually treatment goals related to intervention. Individuals and couples who present for psychological treatment in symptomatic distress are seeking relief from symptoms they have not be able to reduce by their own efforts. Thus, symptom reduction or removal is one of the first goals of treatment. Usually, this goal is achieved with medication and/or behavioral intervention. Research indicates that as symptoms increase, one or more areas of life functioning decrease; and therapeutic efforts to increase functional capacity tend to be thwarted until symptomatology is decreased (Sperry, Brill, Howard, & Grissom, 1996).

Phase 4: Pattern Maintenance and Termination

The goals of this phase of treatment are to maintain the newly acquired adaptive pattern, to prevent relapse, and to reduce or eliminate the client's reliance on the treatment relationship. Technically, a *relapse* is a continuation of an original episode, while recurrence is the instigation of a new episode. In order to prevent relapse, a therapist must assess a client's risk factors and potential for relapse and incorporate relapse prevention strategies into the treatment process. Therapeutic methods to accomplish these goals are employing relapse prevention strategies; setting or negotiating a termination date; scheduling weaning sessions; and, when indicated, to increasingly spacing medication maintenance sessions when continued use is warranted.

Comparison of Phases of Psychotherapy and Executive Coaching

For all practical purposes, executive coaching can be described in terms of the four phases of psychotherapy with some modification. Certainly, the engagement phase is central to both effective psychotherapy and effective executive coaching. As noted earlier, engagement is not as critical in teaching or training and development as it is in coaching or psychotherapy.

While pattern recognition is also common to both therapy and coaching, coaching focuses more on limiting patterns instead of the maladaptive patterns associated with psychotherapy. A limiting pattern is a predictable and consistent style or manner in which an executive thinks, feels, acts, and copes that may or may not be particularly effective. A limiting pattern is not harmful or detrimental to self or others. Because limiting patterns tend to be "rate limiters" of an individual's functional strengths and talents, executive coaching focuses on reducing and eliminating limiting functions.

While pattern change can also be a focus of executive coaching, it is not the only intervention strategy as tends to be the case in psychotherapy. Certainly,

TABLE 5.4 Comparison of Four Phases of Psychotherapy and Coaching

Phase	Psychotherapy	Executive Coaching
Engagement; *engagement and contract*	Critical to successful therapy process and outcomes	*Critical to successful coaching process and outcomes*
Pattern identification; *initial assessment*	Maladaptive pattern focus	*Limiting pattern focus*
Pattern change; *coaching plan and implementation*	Main psychotherapy strategy; emphasis on past, symptoms, and return to baseline functioning	*One of many coaching strategies; emphasis on present and future, strengths and development*
Pattern maintenance and termination; *evaluation of progress and outcomes*	Formal evaluation tends to be less common, relapse is a major concern; termination tends to be difficult because of client dependency on therapist	*Ongoing evaluation of process and outcome of change is common; relapse is major concern; termination is relatively straightforward and easy*

skill building is another key focus or strategy of intervention in executive coaching. As noted previously, a focus on building on strengths and emphasizing positive learning and experience in the present characterizes change in coaching. A focus on the past, on reducing symptoms and returning to baseline functioning, is more likely to be emphasized in psychotherapy

In terms of the fourth phase, both executive coaching and psychotherapy are concerned with maintaining the new, often hard-won changes and incorporating them within the client's behavioral repertoire. Reducing backsliding or relapse is a concern for both coaching and psychotherapy. A formal, ongoing evaluation of the process and outcome of change is more likely to occur in executive coaching than in psychotherapy. Finally, termination from coaching is less likely to be as problematic and challenging as it is in psychotherapy, since client dependency on a coach tends to be less of an issue than client dependency on a therapist. Table 5.4 summarizes these commonalities and differences. The phases of coaching are shown in italics.

Differential Impacts of Psychotherapy and Executive Coaching

In relatively uncomplicated situations, the natural course of a psychological disorder follows a predictable trajectory (Frank & Frank, 1993). First, life *functioning* in one or more areas begins to decline. As this occurs, mild *symptoms* and distress are noted. The affected individual attempts to cope as best he or she can. Demoralization and a decreased sense of *well-being* begin to set in, but the individual keeps trying. However, as coping resources become strained, further declines in functioning occur while acute symptoms become more distressing. Eventually, as the individual continually experiences the failure to cope, he or she moves into the "sick role" that usually follows a call for help. By seeking professional help, the sick role status is confirmed and legitimized.

During this time, individuals are relieved of personal responsibilities to varying degrees. In western culture, social convention allows individuals to remain in their sick roles for a limited time after which they are expected to recover and increasingly return to their previous responsibilities. Situation 1 in Figure 5.1 illustrates the usual course of a psychological disorder and its natural recovery process without psychotherapy or other treatment. Executive B formerly had a relatively high level of psychological functioning as indicated by a Global Assessment of Functioning (GAF) score of 75. This changed abruptly following the death of her mother after which Executive B experienced an acute, reactive depression reflected in a GAF of 50.

The rate of recovery following the application of psychotherapy or other clinical intervention tends to be faster and shorter than the rate when a condition is left untreated. Recall that the sick role is legitimized when professional treatment is sought. Recovery typically follows the pattern of increased hopefulness, followed by decreased symptomatology, followed by return of functional capacity. Kenneth Howard, Ph.D. has operationalized this healing sequence as *remoralization, remediation, and rehabilitation* and designated this predictable sequential process of treatment recovery the *Phase Theory model* (Howard et al., 1993).

For some acute Axis I diagnoses, such as depressive and anxiety disorders, this recovery process is approximately 4 to 9 or even 12 months. Remaining in the *sick role* for longer periods of time usually suggests a complicated case that may be interpreted by caretakers and health care providers as representing disability proneness. Not surprisingly, indices of well-being or remoralization tend to not rise much, if at all, even when treatment is provided. Similarly, life functioning remains low while symptoms may or may not remain at high levels. Situation 2 in Figure 5.1 illustrates the usual course of successful psychotherapy. Executive B was able to be treated with brief psychotherapy without hospitalization or medication. Her prognosis was good, given her high level of premorbid functioning and no apparent genetic loading or family history of psychiatric or substance disorders. She responded quickly to treatment and returned to her prior baseline functioning within 8 weeks.

What about Axis II diagnoses? Executives who meet criteria for personality disorders typically have difficulties with responsibility, collaboration, and cooperation. Rather than taking responsibility for their behaviors, they are likely to use avoidance, refusal, manipulation, procrastination, and/or blame. Instead of a cooperative attitude and the types of collaborative behaviors expected of effective team members, an executive's noncooperativeness may cause others to feel dissension and lowered morale. As illustrated in Situation 3 of Figure 5.1, Executive C has a lower GAF score than Executive A and probably most others in the team or unit.

After a point, an executive's superior may consider actions such as referral to executive coaching or psychotherapy. We previously indicated that psychotherapy or administrative action is appropriate in such situations, while executive coaching is not. Situation 4 represents the impact of successful psychotherapy with a personality-disordered executive. Note that the positive impact of the treatment increased Executive C's baseline functioning, i.e., it is higher than his prepsychotherapy GAF level and in the normal range of functioning, consistent with that of Executive A and others.

What about those executives who are good candidates for executive coaching? For example, in Situation 5 of Figure 5.1, Executive D is a relatively effective executive and would be characterized by Level 3 Leadership functioning (Collins, 2001). Skill-focused and performance-focused executive coaching is arranged for this executive whose GAF is 75. Like other executives who function in the adequate to high range of psychological well-being (GAFs over 70), their GAFs tend to remain the same. In circumstances where an executive's baseline of psychological well-being is in the adequate range and he or she experiences a time-limited but significant stressor or minor crisis reflected in a slightly lowered GAF, the GAF is likely to return to the previous baseline as a result of coaching and the passage of time.

Situation 6 in Figure 5.1 illustrates the impact of developmentally focused executive coaching arranged for an executive who is being groomed for promotion to a senior leadership position. More specifically, the coaching is targeted at increasing his self-awareness and psychological hardiness as well as "smoothing some of his rough edges." As a result of such developmental coaching, Executive E increases his functioning beyond his prior baseline. This is not an uncommon outcome of developmentally focused executive coaching.

Concluding Note

This chapter has introduced the process of executive coaching. It provides an overview of some of the basic conceptual models that inform the practice of executive coaching as well as the common modes in which executive coaching is practiced. We also described the three basic types or functions of coaching executives: skill focus, performance focus, and developmental focus. Five phases of the coaching process were then noted. In a sense, this chapter completes our discussion of the background and context of

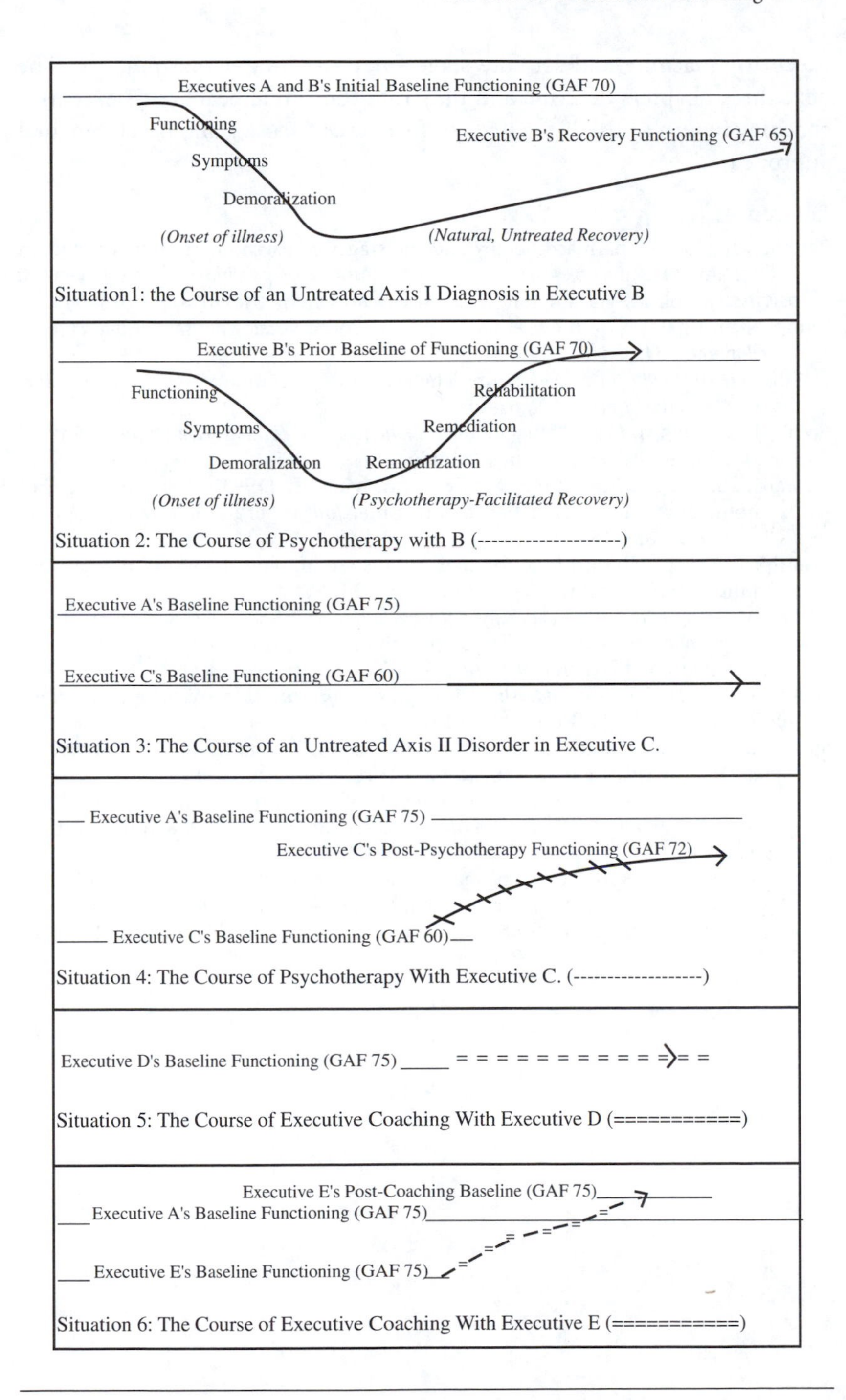

Fig. 5.1 Impacts of psychotherapy and executive coaching on executives.

executive coaching and sets the stage for describing actual practice. The next three chapters describe and illustrate the actual practice of executive coaching in terms of skill-focused, performance-focused, and developmental approaches.

References

Beitman, B. (1993). Pharmacotherapy and the stages of psychotherapeutic change. In J. Oldham, M. Riba, & A. Tasman (Eds), *American psychiatric press peview of psychiatry*, Vol. 12. Washington, D.C.: American Psychiatric Press, pp. 521–540.

Campbell, J. (2001). Coaching: A new field for counselors? *Counseling and Human Development, 34*, 1–14.

Collins, J. (2001). Level 5 leadership: The triumph of humility and fierce resolve. *Harvard Business Review. 79*, 67–75.

Frank, J. & Frank, J. (1993). *Persuasion and healing: A comparative study of psychotherapy*, 3rd ed. Baltimore: Johns Hopkins Press.

Howard, K., Lueger, R., Maling, M., & Matinovich, Z. (1993). A phase model of psychotherapy: Causal mediation of outcome. *Journal of Consulting and Clinical Psychology, 61*, 678–685.

Kilburg, R. (1996). Toward a conceptual understanding and definition of executive coaching. *Counseling Psychology Journal, 48*, 134–144.

O'Neil, M. (2000). *Executive coaching with backbone and heart: A systems approach to engaging leaders with their challenges.* San Francisco: Jossey-Bass.

Rogers, C. (1996). *On becoming a person.* New York: Mariner Press.

Sperry, L. (2002). *Effective leadership: Strategies for maximizing executive productivity and health.* New York: Brunner-Routledge.

Sperry, L., Brill, P., Howard, K., & Grissom, G. (1996). *Treatment outcomes in psychotherapy and psychiatric interventions.* New York: Brunner-Mazel.

Sperry, L. (1999). *Cognitive behavior therapy of DSM-IV personality disorders: Highly effective interventions for the most common personality disorders.* New York: Brunner-Mazel.

Witherspoon, R. (2000). Starting smart: Clarifying coaching goals and roles. In M. Goldsmith, L. Lyons & A. Freas (Eds.), *Coaching for leadership: How the world's greatest coaches help leaders learn.* San Francisco: Jossey-Bass/Pfeiffer, pp. 165–185.

6
Skill-Focused Coaching with Executives

Skill coaching, also referred to as skill-focused coaching, is typically what most individuals associate with the term *coaching*. Actually, executive coaching has three different varieties or types: Skill-focused, performance-focused, and development-focused. Because *types* suggests specialized areas of coaching, it may be more accurate to think of each form of coaching as a function rather than as a type or area of specialization. The reality is that in most executive coaching situations, two or all three of these coaching functions are likely to be involved.

Nevertheless, for didactic purposes, we describe the three functions in separate chapters. Chapter 7 describes and illustrates performance-focused executive coaching, and chapter 8 describes and illustrates development-focused executive coaching. This chapter describes and illustrates skill-focused executive coaching. It briefly distinguishes coaching from teaching and training and development, identifies some 50 possible coaching targets, and then proceeds to discuss some of the more common targets for skill-focused coaching. These include team development, strategic thinking, delegation, commitment building, communication, conflict management, and stress management.

Skill-Focused Coaching: Distinct from Teaching and Training and Development

Skill-focused coaching is distinct from both teaching which largely relies on one-way instruction, and training and development which is a more sophisticated form of instruction that is typically two-way or interactive. Skill-focused coaching emphasizes learning in the context of a professional relationship with a coach who is both process- and content-oriented.

With executive coaching, the nature of the relationship between coach and client is qualitatively different from a relationship in teaching or training and development. In some ways similar to the relationship of a client and therapist, the relationship in executive coaching involves respect, trust, concern, caring, and confidentiality. Unlike teaching or training wherein the teacher or trainee assumes the role of expert, the relationship in coaching is typically collaborative. Such a collaborative relationship can effectively facilitate the processes of learning or enhancing new skills, improving performance, and fostering personal, professional, and career development and well-being.

With regard to the focus on both process and content in executive coaching, it has been noted that executive coaching that relies on "observation, inquiry, dialogue and discovery. The essence of coaching executives is helping them learn, rather than training or tutoring them. To coach in this sense is less to instruct than to facilitate" (Witherspoon, 2000, p. 168). Skill-focused coaching addresses deficits in the core leadership skill sets: technical-analytic, relational, strategic, financial informational, and self-management skills. It is interesting to note that some executive coaches specialize in certain skill sets. Coaching executives to develop relational skills is an area of focus for many coaches. Many coaches share Harry Levinson's view that of all the strategies for enhancing executive performance, executive coaching is the most useful means of teaching human relations skills to senior managers (Levinson, 1981). Similarly, D.A. Benton (1999), in *Secrets of a CEO Coach*, describes eight cases in which she coached senior executives to increase their capacities for relating to subordinates, peers, and customers more effectively.

Skill-Focused, Performance-Focused, and Development-Focused Coaching

For purposes of discussion, three different types of executive coaching can be described. Table 6.1 lists and briefly distinguishes the three types. Skill-focused coaching is both a process and a method for developing or enhancing technical, operational, analytic, relational, strategic, or self-management skills that occurs within a collaborative relationship with a coach. The goals and outcomes can be short term or long term. In the short term, the objective is typically to reverse a skill deficit or enhance a specific leadership skill, whereas in the long term, the goal and outcome is to increase overall leadership competencies.

The primary purpose of skill-focused coaching is to sharpen skills in one or more areas that will facilitate efforts with a current project or task. Typically, an executive will work collaboratively with a coach to achieve the following objectives: First, the coach assesses the executive's current levels of skills. The second step is clarifying expectations, stated performance standards, and priorities for current projects or tasks on the part of the coach and executive. Third, they develop plans for skill building. Fourth, through the use of modeling and other methods, the executive learns and practices the new skill or skills. The fifty step is evaluating the results of skill building. Coaching for skill acquisition typically occurs in a relatively short period, usually over a matter of weeks and sometimes longer. Only a session or two may be required.

Executive Coaching Targets

As noted earlier, the skill-focused coaching function is commonly involved in the course of providing executive coaching to executive clients. Sometimes skill-focused coaching is the main reason for seeking coaching and serves as the primary or only agenda and goal for coaching. For example, executives who need to improve their performance in the area of giving media interviews

TABLE 6.1 Three Types or Functions of Executive Coaching

Type or Function	Description	Goals
Skill-focused coaching	Process and method for learning or enhancing technical, operational, analytic, relational, strategic, or self-management skills	*Short term*: reversing skill deficits or enhancing specific leadership skills *Long term*: increasing leadership competencies
Performance-focused coaching	Process and method for increasing performance and job effectiveness	*Short term*: increasing leadership performance in a specific area *Long term*: increasing overall leadership performance; functioning consistently as an effective executive
Development-focused coaching	Process and method for fostering professional, career, and personal growth of executives and their employees	*For executive*: increasing personal and professional transformation *By executive*: professional and career development of employees *For organization*: developing leadership potential, skills, and performance in potential or existing executives

or delivering more compelling speeches might seek coaches with special expertise in these areas. In other situations, a skill deficit may be noted in the course of assessing overall competencies and subsequently skill-focused coaching becomes part of the coaching agenda (Sperry, 2002). Table 6.2 lists some 50 targets in which skill-focused coaching might be involved.

TABLE 6.2 Fifty Executive Coaching Targets

Personal
Self-awareness
Active listening; empathy
Assertive communication
Two-way communication
Increased decisiveness
Becoming less dominating
Relaxation

TABLE 6.2 (*Continued*)

Becoming more spiritually centered
Smoothing "rough edges"
Generosity
Broadening perspective
Relational responsiveness and intimacy
Psychological and physical hardiness
Strength and endurance training
Weight management
Nutrition
Enhance people reading skills
Improve stress management
Professional (Directly Job Related)
Strategic thinking
Strategic implementation
Conflict management and resolution
Delegation
Strategic interviewing
Employee coaching
Employee counseling
Team development
Effective meeting facilitation
Enhancing employee commitment
Writing effective memos and reports
Preparing budgets
Reading financial reports
Effective performance appraisal interviewing
Increasing computer and technological savvy
Professional (Indirectly Job Related)
Board of directors training
Leading professional organizations
Writing for business publications
Delivering more compelling speeches
Oral presentations
Increasing political savvy
Giving media interviews
Terminating employees
Career
Enhancing job interview skills
Strategic career planning
Requisite job skills
Time and priority management
Life–work balance
Life stage–dual career synchrony

TABLE 6.2 (*Continued*)

Work stress management
Organizational assessment
Optimizing job–team–organization–family fit

Skill-Focused Coaching: Team Development

Effective team leadership is another essential skill of effective executives. Teams are small groups of individuals who have complementary skills, are committed to common performance goals, and hold themselves accountable for achieving those goals. For the past two decades, teams have become dominant forces in increasing productivity and commitment in the corporate world. This section describes the stages of team development. It then describes the importance of team building, characteristics of highly productive teams, and some strategies for building teams. Finally, it provides a case example.

Stages of Team Development

Team performance is anything but constant, yet the observant manager can note predictable or patterns or stages through which a team evolves. Various markers in team behaviors, relationships, and leadership demands are associated with four evolving stages: forming, storming, norming, and performing (Tuckman, 1965).

Forming This is the beginning stage of development in which team members start becoming acquainted with each other, with the team's purpose, and with its boundaries. At this stage, members tend to experience a sense of anticipation along with uncertainty because they lack boundaries and rules. Accordingly, they may focus attention on leaders and demonstrate some degree of dependency on such leaders. The goal is not so much to be productive as it is to establish a sense of purpose. The main task of this stage is to orient members, establish relationships, and develop a sense of trust. The basic task of the team leader is to provide clarity of direction.

Storming At this stage, members start feeling more independence and a sense of individuality. In the process, they begin reacting against their dependency on the team leaders and each other. Accordingly, teams must contend with competition among members, dissension, testing of rules and boundaries, negative dependence, and violations of team expectations. The main tasks of this stage are effectively managing conflicts and turning negative dependence into interdependence. This stage truly tests the mettle of team leaders because the very viability of the team is at stake. In order to emerge from this very trying but necessary stage, effective leadership is essential. Accordingly, team leaders must strive to foster consensus building, recognize team achievement while legitimizing productive expressions of individuality, and at the same time encourage win-win relationships.

Norming The team is faced with reestablishing the sense of stability, loyalty, and focus that was challenged in the storming stage. To become highly effective, a team must share a common vision and develop a cohesive team culture. As a team increases its commitment and clarifies norms and expectations, members experience increasing peer pressure to those norms and expectations. Not surprisingly, dealing with the tendency toward "groupthink" (the agreement by the team not to disagree) and exclusivity (decreasing receptivity to diversity and "outsiders") are major challenges for the group at this stage. The main tasks are to foster empowerment and participation, increase and maintain a sense of cohesion, and provide feedback to members on their performance. The leader's tasks are fostering cooperation and commitment to a common vision, providing supportive feedback, and managing tendencies toward groupthink.

Performing At this stage, the team is able to experience high levels of efficiency and effectiveness because it worked through the challenges of the previous stages of development. It has developed high levels of trust, loyalty and morale, as well as strong personal commitments to the team. Because it has overcome the tendencies of groupthink and exclusivity and can function interdependently, it is on its way to become a high performing team. The main tasks at this stage are to foster a culture of innovation and continuous improvement, encourage creative problem solving, and capitalize on core competencies. The leader's basic task is to upgrade and elevate team performance to the level of a high performing team.

Process of Team Building

Team building is a systematic process for unifying the efforts and galvanizing the commitment of a group of employees with common objectives into an effective and efficient functioning work team. The goals of team building are quite lofty in that team building attempts to foster increased productivity while maintaining high levels of quality as well as to improving work relationships, commitment, and job satisfaction.

Team building is a continuous process that requires a number of basic changes in manager attitudes and behavior, employee attitudes and behavior, reward systems, and corporate culture. Successful team building requires both shared power and authority and increased employee participation.

The basic premises of team building challenge traditional managerial attitudes regarding control and command. Not surprisingly, team building is bound to fail if managers insist on exerting control over a team and its members. Similarly, team building requires a high degree of cooperation and collaboration among team members. Employees who prefer to work alone and compete with coworkers for rewards and recognition may find team building efforts exasperating and threatening. An inability or unwillingness to cooperate is a prelude to failure. Additionally, organizational culture can either foster or inhibit team building efforts. A culture that fosters competition and individual accomplishment and downplays the value of information sharing among individuals and units cannot support team building efforts.

Implementing team building in a medical practice group organization begins at the top. First of all, top management must visibly demonstrate its commitment to and support for a team approach. At a minimum, team building requires a concerted effort to educate managers and employees about teams and modify management attitudes, reward systems, and culture so that management facilitates rather than impedes the team building process. In addition, staff must be expected to take responsibility for the success of team building. They must be willing and able to cooperate and collaborate with other team members.

How is the team building process actually initiated? Ideally, a manager with previous successful experience in team building initiates the process on-site by selecting appropriate team members and coaching them about what it means to function as a team, or an internal or external consultant may be asked to initiate this process in conjunction with the manager.

As a team continues to develop it is essential to meet periodically, usually quarterly for a day or so, to formally address the team building process and issues involving goals and performance. The more team building becomes an integral part of a team's operations, the more likely the team will increase its effectiveness and productivity.

Characteristics of High Performing Teams

It has been estimated that more than 80% of employees are involved in some form of teamwork. Although teams are used extensively today, not all these teams are particularly effective. Team effectiveness spans the continuum from very low to very high. High performance is the designation for teams with very high levels of effectiveness. High performance teams share a number of common characteristics. The reader will note that these characteristics are integrally related (Katzenbach & Smith, 1993; Sperry, 2003).

Shared Vision

High performance teams share a specific purpose and vision. The specificity of this vision and short-term goals serve as sources of both motivation and commitment to their mutually coordinated efforts.

Outcomes Orientation

The primary focus is on achieving results or outcomes. The expected outcome is the team's central preoccupation from initial planning through implementation and on to monitoring performance. To achieve this result requires a high degree of single mindedness and closely coordinated team effort.

Coordination

Work roles are shared and coordinated in such a manner that the outcome is a team accomplishment rather than a set of individual accomplishments. Such a level of coordination requires a high degree of mutual trust and commitment. It also requires that team members possess high levels of technical, conceptual, and interpersonal skills.

Quality

Team members seek to achieve the highest levels of quality and ongoing or continuous quality improvement. Their goal is achieve a level of quality above the expected standard of performance and then supersede that level in subsequent efforts. This requires very high levels of commitment, coordination, and competency.

Competency

Team members exhibit very high levels of skills and competencies including interpersonal skills such as empathy, two-way communication, and conflict resolution in addition to proficiency in conceptual or analytic skills such as strategic thinking, problem solving, decision making, and finely honed technical skills.

Strategies for Building High Performing Teams

Although many methods for improving team performance have been suggested, here are eight strategies that I have found useful in helping coaches work with executive clients to increase team performance (Sperry, 2003).

1. Foster an organizational culture that values teams

One aspect of creating such a team-friendly culture is to review and reconsider reward structures as well as policies and procedures that may foster individual achievement and competition.

2. Foster team decision making

A manager who is successful with team building recognizes that giving team members voices in decision making is not a sign of weakness or abrogation of the manager's responsibility, but rather demonstrates the manager's confidence in his employees. Team decision making increases the team's ownership of those decisions and improves their commitment to productivity as well as to the organization.

3. Select job candidates who have proven team skills

Not all job candidates have the desire or capability of serving as effective team members. Some individuals prefer to work alone. It cannot be assumed that a candidate who has the requisite technical skills can learn to work collaboratively on a team. Instead, in addition to technical skills and experience, look for candidates who have the requisite interpersonal and decision-making skills to function as team members.

4. Clarify the mission and articulate a vision and goals for the team

Articulating a motivating vision for a team is a manager's main task. That is because a vision gives a sense of direction, evokes commitment, and serves to bind a team together. Flowing from this vision is a particular mission and set of goals that the manager must clarify and routinely reassert. It can be useful to draft a team mission statement, for example, "Our team is committed to providing quality care at low costs to cardiac bypass patients. Staff maintains their expertise and commitment through continuing education and team building retreats."

5. Provide training to develop or enhance team skills

Training that increases requisite team skills such as supportive communication, empowerment, active listening, and decision making increases the likelihood that a team will be committed, efficient, and productive.

6. Provide opportunities for autonomy

Managers who need to exert command and control over a team cannot fathom a team that functions with autonomy. Autonomy is essential for a team to become highly effective and efficient. Thus, managers need to provide teams with opportunities to function independently as well as interdependently. Delegation of given tasks and specific decisions, such as letting team members select new members, fosters autonomy.

7. Demonstrate integrity and credibility

Being believable, honest, trustworthy and fair are characteristics of an individual with a high degree of credibility. Credibility is considered the essential requirement for leadership effectiveness. Credibility increases not only an employee's confidence in a leader but also the leader's influence over the employee. Integrity, a prerequisite of credibility, refers to the soundness of one's moral character. A manager who is not viewed as credible is unlikely to develop a high performance team.

8. Be readily available to team members

Availability and visibility reinforce a manager's commitment to the team and provide assurance of assistance and support. Managers who are perpetually tied up with meetings and special projects or are frequently out of town are not viewed as true team members by employees. A manager who is not available is not likely to succeed at building an effective team.

Case Study: Team Building

Like many of its competitors, a national corporation processes several thousand customer payment checks each week. With that volume, operators posting the checks were frequently so overwhelmed that several hundred checks a day were often not posted and deposited for a day or more which resulted in lower corporate return on assets. While the operators were assigned in teams, for the most part they acted more as individuals than as team members.

The director of operations thought team building could have a place in improving the operation. He provided a consultant to coach the operators. After an assessment of the work flow and team functioning, the coach proposed a plan that would reward teams that found ways to cut costs or improve quality. The coach offered herself as a resource to the teams on each shift during the week and on weekends.

The Saturday day shift team was relatively cohesive and it was no surprise to the coach that they took up the challenge and set out to find a solution to the delayed posting–depositing problem. The team developed a survey and did a productivity audit. They found that productivity, communications, and morale were better on Saturdays than they were on Mondays through Fridays. Interestingly, they found that total postings were actually lower during the week. While work flow was managed through a coordinator during the week, the operators managed flow on Saturdays. They "huddled" together as a team at the start of the shift, distributed work, and juggled lunch breaks. They felt more in control of their work when they had responsibility over assignments than when the coordinator distributed the work. They made a proposal to the director of operations to eliminate the coordinator position and coach other operator teams on devising team strategies for dividing up their work.

The director of operations approved the plan and redeployed the coordinator. He also provided coaching on team building to the other operator groups. The coaching was informed by the eight strategies for building high performing teams cited above. The end result was a 21% reduction in the number of delayed check postings, a 60% decrease in overtime, greatly improved employee job commitment, and better communication.

Skill-Focused Coaching: Strategic Thinking, Planning, Communication, and Action

While many executives have become quite proficient and even brilliant in their strategic planning, a much smaller number have become proficient in strategic implementation. The reality is that a brilliant strategy is worthless without brilliant execution. Strategy implementation requires a number of skills related to strategic planning such as strategic thinking, strategic communication, and strategic action. This section describes and illustrates these skills.

Strategic Thinking

Strategic thinking is similar but differs from strategic planning. While strategic thinking is inevitably a skill in effective strategic planning, some of what passes for strategic planning is really long term planning with little or no recourse to strategic thinking. So what is strategic thinking? It is a mental discipline consisting of broad ranging, flexible, and creative thinking that involves finding connections in apparently unrelated events or circumstances and understanding how various trends and occurrences interrelate to affect a specific organization. In short, strategic thinking is thinking "outside the box" and about the future while being mindful of the limitations of the here and now.

Strategic Thinking Cycle

Strategic thinking can be summed up by three simple questions: What seems to be happening? What possibilities do we face? What are we going to do about them? These three questions reflect the natural flow or cycle of strategic thinking (Wells, 1998). This cycle of strategic thinking lays the groundwork for taking action, although the processes of data gathering, i.e., situational or SWOT analysis, and implementing the strategy is outside the cycle. SWOT is an acronym for strengths, weaknesses, opportunities, and threats.

The "What seems to be happening?" question characterizes the first phase of the cycle of the strategic thinking process. This phase facilitates visualizing the medical practice within its larger context. The manager distinguishes the details of what has happened and what is currently happening and looks in depth at the various forces, circumstances, and individuals and casts them together into a focused picture that provides alternative views of the future. The purpose of this phase is not to collect data, as so often happens in traditional strategic planning, but rather to build the necessary knowledge base for the other phases of this process of thinking strategically.

The "What possibilities do we face?" question characterizes the second phase of the cycle. This phase identifies strategic possibilities, i.e., the most advantageous possibilities and opportunities for both taking in and influencing the practice's external environment, and matches these opportunities with existing and potential strengths. This step involves looking at the interplay of the weaknesses of the practice against the threats posed by the environment. It also articulates how the practice can focus on a limited number of its strengths in order to form the base of a strategy.

The "What are we going to do about them?" question characterizes the third phase of the strategic thinking cycle. This phase narrows and refines the strategy and begins the process of enacting it. It involves making a decision about the best fit strategy from among all the generated strategic possibilities and focuses on thinking about various ways and means of implementing the strategy.

Strategic Communication

Strategic communication is a way of thinking about how to communicate your message to those you wish to inform or influence (Parsons, 2001). It is an intentional process of presenting ideas in a clear, concise, and persuasive way that contrasts with the off-the-cuff oral and written communications that characterize the communication efforts of too many managers. It requires some forethought about the purpose and outcome of the message: how it relates to the needs of staff and the mission, budget, and deadlines of the practice. It should not be surprising that among highly effective group practice managers, strategic communication is probably the most common outward manifestation of strategic thinking.

How does one learn to communicate strategically? First, by mastering the requisite communication skills. Second, by making an intentional effort to use these communication skills in a strategic manner, i.e., in ways that are consistent with the practice's values, mission, and strategy.

Strategic Action

Strategic action differs from strategic thinking and strategic planning in that it emphasizes action or implementation over thinking or planning. Strategic action is a term we coined to designate a method by which managers can implement a segment of an organization's strategy. While strategic action seems as if it should be a reasonable and inevitable outcome of strategic thinking and planning, the reality is that too often excellent strategies are not implemented or implemented fully. Thus, strategic action is proposed as an intentional and systematic method for implementing a particular aspect of the group practice's mission or strategy. It should not be surprising that highly effective group practice managers utilize strategic action although they might not use the term. Strategic action is a manifestation of strategic thinking.

How does one learn to act strategically? First, by mastering the requisite skills of strategic thinking, strategic planning, collaboration, and effective listening and communication. Second, by making an intentional effort to use these activities in a strategic manner, i.e., in ways that are consistent with the practice's values, mission, and strategy.

Executives find that a straightforward, five-point, strategic acting map (SAM) can be invaluable in their efforts to act strategically. The map is a method for mentally preparing and implementing an effective course of action for many everyday responsibilities that executives do not usually consider important from a strategic perspective, but in reality are important (Sperry, 2003). These include memos, meeting agendas, meetings, and other activities. The five points of SAM are:

Outcome: the specific result to be achieved
Context: the organizational importance of the action
Message: the key information to be understood and shared
Tactical reinforcement: tactics and methods to reinforce the message and outcome
Feedback: the way the effort or message was received and its impact on the individual, team, unit or organization

In short, SAM helps executives exercise their capacities to strategically think, plan, communicate, and act in their everyday work lives.

Case Study: Strategic Thinking and Acting

Nathan Stroberg has been the vice president of administration at a regional medical center for the past year. He has been working with an executive coach for the past 9 months to enhance his leadership skills and competencies. Prior to his promotion, Stroberg had been the director of a very successful surgical center. Recently he had been appointed the chief compliance officer for the entire medical center. This new responsibility was added just after the center's board of directors had voted to adopt a Code of Professional Conduct in an effort to increase the center's compliance with state and federal laws and regulations and reduce spiraling liability costs. Stroberg's responsibility is to see that the code is implemented. In discussing the challenge of this new responsibility with his coach, it became clear that Stroberg had to be more strategically focused in his job more than ever.

The coach worked with Stroberg on utilizing SAM to think, communicate, and act more strategically. Before learning about SAM, Stroberg would typically "shoot from the hip" although he considered himself a key player on the center's strategic planning committee. When drafting memos or staff meeting agendas, he made no connections between the correspondence and agendas and the group practice's overall strategy or the impact of these communications on the practice. Now he spends a few extra minutes thinking strategically

TABLE 6.3 Nathan Stroberg's SAM for Adoption of Professional Code

Outcome	My staff will 1. understand and accept, and most importantly 2. implement the new code of ethics, particularly the section on billing irregularities (as per HIPPA regulations) and 3. achieve a 90% compliance rate over the next three quarters.
Context	1. The previous compliance rate was 71% (last year the center was fined $12.8 million for being out of compliance with Medicare regulations alone). 2. The code is so important that the management team has set an incentive: 2 extra personal days for all staff in clinical units if compliance reaches 90%.
Messages	Since staff is likely to balk at another set of regulations, I need to draft a memo and bullet points for discussion that: 1. Emphasize the impact of poor compliance in the past 2. Explain that we are most vulnerable to noncompliance with billing problems 3. Focus on billing issues and everyone's role in compliance in all clinical units from physicians to billing clerks. 4. Emphasize the incentive and have them start dreaming about what they'll do with the extra personal days off.

TABLE 6.3 (*Continued*)

Tactical Reinforcement	1. Post a copy of the code and this memo on all bulletin boards. 2. Plan to begin meetings with each unit in 2 days for open discussion with all staff. 3. Include code adherence as a written performance standard for managers in every clinical unit.
Feedback	1. Ask Jack W. to review the memo for clarity and tone before it is finalized and distributed. 2. Encourage staff to e-mail me with their ideas for implementing the code—ideas that will discussed at our next staff meeting. 3. Listen to staff discussion of the code, gauge their reactions, and incorporate their ideas in further implementation planning.

as he plans his written communications and his oral presentations as well. Based on SAM, Stroberg will draft a memo that will be attached to the code that will be delivered to all staff in clinical units and will also put into motion the first of several initiatives to successfully implement the code.

Skill-Focused Coaching: Delegation

Traditionally, delegation is understood as entrusting an employee with a task for which the manager remains ultimately responsible. Delegation can range from a major appointment, such as the leadership of a project review team, to smaller tasks in the everyday life of an organization such as interviewing a job candidate.

Two basic issues involved in the process of delegation are control and autonomy. The first issue is the matter of authority and control for manager and employee. How much authority will the delegated employee be able to exercise without referring back to the manager; and how far should the manager exercise direct influence over the work of the employee? When choosing a delegate, a manager assesses whether a given employee is capable of performing the task with available resources and can, in fact, perform the task. The second issue is autonomy. Will the employee be given sufficient autonomy to undertake the task in his or her own way?

Delegation has a number of benefits. First and foremost, delegation allows managers to unburden themselves of less essential tasks and free up time for more essential functions (Roebuck, 1999). More streamlined workloads will allow managers to engage in essential managerial tasks such as coaching, encouragement, and monitoring performance. In other words, delegation increases a manager's efficiency, but not necessarily his or her effectiveness.

Empowerment is a strategy for helping others to act and feel more competent and confident. An executive cannot empower employees, but rather create situations in which employees can empower themselves. Empowerment results when managers are successful in fostering five attributes: self-efficacy, self-determination, personal control, trust, and a sense of meaning (Whetten & Cameron, 2002). Self-efficacy is the sense of possessing the capacity and competence to perform a task successfully. Self-determination is the sense of having a choice and the freedom to initiate and be involved in tasks of one's own choosing. Personal control refers to the capability to effect change and exert a measure of control over the external environment. Trust is a sense of security and the assurance of being treated fairly. A sense of meaning refers to the sense of purpose, involvement, and caring about the activities in which one engages.

How can coaches actively foster empowerment? Several strategies are suggested: (1) articulate a vision and goals that specify desired outcomes; (2) assist employees to master challenges or problems; (3) model the correct behavior; (4) provide social and emotional support; (5) replace negative emotions with positive emotions; (6) provide resources needed to accomplish the task; (7) connect efforts to outcomes; (8) create a sense of confidence in the trustworthiness of the manager (Sperry, 2003).

Empowered Delegation

Empowered delegation stands in contrast to the traditional view wherein burdensome tasks are basically shifted from managers to employees which may result in resentful feelings and a sense of disempowerment. As noted above, empowered delegation is a strategy by which managers assign a task while simultaneously empowering employees. Whetten and Cameron (2002) indicate that empowered delegation typically develops employees' knowledge bases, capabilities, and senses of personal mastery. They point to research that indicates that empowered delegation also increases employee involvement, commitment, and job satisfaction. Unlike the traditional view of delegation wherein the manager's efficiency is increased, empowered delegation increases productivity and effectiveness as well as efficiency.

Here are some guidelines to empower employees: begin with the end in mind; allow employee participation in the assignment of tasks; establish parity between authority and responsibility; focus accountability on results; delegate consistently; and clarify consequences (Whetten & Cameron, 2002).

Barriers to Delegation

While some managers are in favor or delegation others are not. Barriers preventing delegation are often based on negative feelings of insecurity and mistrust. Lack of confidence in employees is a common barrier to delegation. Managers who subscribe to the philosophy that "if you want it done right, do it yourself" are basically asserting their lack of trust that employees are sufficiently resourceful and responsible to handle delegated tasks. Even though a manager may be more proficient and efficient at many tasks than his or her staff, efforts to do many of those tasks inevitably causes the manager to be overburdened. As a result the manager will have less time to spend on higher level tasks that cannot be delegated. Furthermore, employees cannot increase their proficiency and efficiency unless they are given the opportunities to learn and perform a broader range of tasks.

Besides personal barriers, there are also organizational barriers to delegation. Such barriers usually reflect the organization's systems of incentives, delegation practices of senior management, and the culture of the organization. When incentives are based solely on measures such as quarterly productivity targets and do not recognize the value of developing employee competence and commitment, managers may be less inclined to delegate, particularly if senior management does not model empowered delegation. Furthermore, organizations that have adopted a "crisis management" culture tend to downplay delegation, regarding it as time consuming and diverting managers' attention away from "more important matters." Similarly, organizational cultures that are highly competitive or individualistic may reinforce managers' beliefs in doing things themselves so they are done correctly. On the other hand, organizations that are receptive to empowerment are most likely to favor and support delegation.

Decisions to Delegate: What and to Whom

The decision to delegate begins with a determination of what task and responsibilities you as a manager can and probably should delegate and those responsibilities which you cannot delegate. This decision process involves assessing your time and the time of your employees and grouping and prioritizing your current responsibilities. The list below contains examples of tasks that executives usually can delegate (D) and those that cannot or should not be delegated (ND).

Strategic/Tactical Tasks

Clarifying the unit's vision; establishing key goals, targets, and implementation plan (ND)

Planning operational initiatives; implementing strategic initiatives (D)

Leadership/Staff Functions

Overall responsibility for providing direction and stewardship to a project or work unit; negotiating the annual budget; representing the unit's needs with management; developing and challenging staff to maximize their performance (ND)

Drafting routine administrative reports; compiling and analyzing data; program development; selected project management tasks; writing proposals; preparing computer-assisted instruction and other training programs (D)

Personnel

Hiring decisions; performing annual performance reviews; coaching employees; disciplinary actions; setting parameters for salaries, bonuses, and significant nonfinancial rewards (ND)

Serving on search committees; proposing salary, bonus, benefit, and nonfinancial reward criteria; performing feasibility studies (D)

Outcomes and Quality

Setting goals; monitoring progress toward goals; setting quality standards; ensuring standards are met (ND)

Collecting and analyzing productivity, performance outcome, and quality data (D)

Highly Sensitive and Less Sensitive Tasks

Confidential personnel and operational matters, often involving contract negotiations, legal or compliance issues (ND)

Other routine tasks (D)

Strategies for Effective Delegation

The process of delegation begins with a manager's decision to delegate a given task and deciding to whom the responsibility will be delegated. Assuming the employee agrees to handle the delegated responsibility, the process of delegation moves into high gear. An initial meeting is held to formalize the delegation and followed up with ongoing meetings to review progress. Six strategies are involved in effective delegation, the first five of which should be accomplished in the initial meeting (Sperry, 2003).

1. **Specify the task and expectations for performance**—Describe the task and its purpose, importance, and your expectations for (a) work product or deliverables and (b) performance standards.
2. **Define the parameters and boundaries**—Indicate the specific direction and limits you want heeded in terms of (a) time line, i.e., deadlines; (b) budget; and (c) decisional authority.
3. **Provide the necessary resource allocation**—Discuss with the employee the resources needs, and allocations, i.e., personnel, adjustments in priorities and duties, training or coaching, expenses, materials, etc.
4. **Recap the employee's understanding of the task**—Verify the employee's understanding of the task and expectations by asking: "Please recap for me what you're being asked to do and the expectations for it." Asking "Did you understand what I want you to do?" will not elicit the required understanding.
5. **Schedule progress reviews**—Set up a schedule of checkpoint meetings to regularly monitor progress. When you first delegate assignments to an employee, more frequent meetings should be scheduled.
6. **Evaluate and provide feedback**—Each checkpoint meeting should recognize the progress made. Provide both positive and negative feedback, as indicated, to keep the task on course.

An initial delegation meeting usually takes 10 to 30 minutes. In preparation, the manager could use the six-step protocol to think about expectations, consider parameters, and project anticipated resource allocation and reallocation. The following case example provides a detailed account of how such a meeting would proceed.

Case Study: Delegation

Jeff Gerlach is the executive director of a large professional engineering organization with a membership of nearly 20,000 and a staff of 130. For the past few years, the organization's executive committee has wanted to establish an on-line capacity to extend its continuing education (CE) programs to engineering personnel throughout the U.S. While the organization offers CE programs at its annual conferences and nearly every university has continuing education programs with offerings to engineers, a needs assessment among the membership noted a desire for such training programs among engineers who were unable to take time off and travel to the university medical center. Gerlach's CE department has three program specialists and an administrative assistant who present nearly 40 on-site programs annually. The board has asked Gerlach to submit a proposal for a full scale on-line CE program to be reviewed at its next quarterly meeting.

Gerlach anticipated that the project had potential, but represented a number of risks such as competition from other on-line vendors, start-up costs, increasing staff, etc. He was already swamped with several other new challenges in addition to his stated responsibilities. In discussing the matter with his executive coach, Gerlach admitted that delegation was not one of his strong suits. They decided that this was as good a time as any to work on enhancing his delegation skill. The plan was for the coach to work with Gerlach on both delegation and coaching skills. They agreed that this could serve as an experiment in delegation that presumably could extend to other projects and staff members.

Gerlach had already considered Stinley, manager of the CE division, for help in preparing the proposal. At their last performance appraisal review, Stinley expressed interest in "stretching" beyond his current job responsibilities. Unfortunately, while Stinley had some experience with CE program planning, implementation, and evaluation he had little if any experience with on-line technology, performing feasibility studies, and writing proposals. Gerlach arranged to meet with Stinley to discuss the delegated task. The coach introduced Gerlach to the six-step delegation protocol. The coach walked through the steps and role played parts that Gerlach thought would be tough for him. When he felt sufficiently confident, Gerlach agreed to utilize the protocol to structure the meeting. Here is how that meeting proceeded.

Step 1—Gerlach described the proposed on-line project in general terms: it was to target engineers who had limited access to on-site CE training or preferred on-line CE training; it would include a feasibility study and marketing plan, and would initially involve reconfiguring three of their most popular courses in an on-line format. The purpose of the delegation was to develop a cost-effective program proposal. Gerlach then outlined the results he expected:

Work products: a detailed proposal containing the results of a feasibility study, program outlines, implementation plan, and budget projections for translating three existing on-site CE courses; the final draft proposal would be presented by Gerlach and Stinley to the executive committee at its next quarterly meeting.

Performance standards: a clear and precise proposal with executive summary, rationale, results of the feasibility and marketing study, sample versions of two units of one of the proposed on-line courses, implementation time lines and detailed staff, and on-line technology, equipment, and budget projections.

Step 2—Gerlach specified the following parameters:

Time line: the first draft of the proposal was due in 60 days. It would be jointly reviewed and a final proposal would be due one week later.

Budget: the cost of preparing a mailed survey and other efforts to establish the feasibility of the project, the ins and outs of licensing on-line technology, a data analysis budget.

Decisional authority: For at least 90 days, a full time staffer would be shifted from another department to serve as Stinley's administrative assistant. She had considerable experience in writing program and grant proposals and would assist Stinley as he saw fit in preparing the CE proposal. In his fact finding meetings and discussions, Stinley was to talk only of the possibility—not the inevitability—of an on-line learning format.

Step 3—Gerlach would send a memo to other department staff briefing them on Stinley's new responsibility. He would also meet with the other program specialists to redeploy some of Stinley's other responsibilities. Gerlach agreed to coach Stinley in preparing the budget portion of the proposal. It was agreed that at least .5 FTE release time was needed for Stinley for 3 months. The reassigned administrative assistant would be available full time to assist Stinley.

Step 4—Stinley was able to summarize the project goals and expectations. He was pleased to be asked to head up the project and expressed his eagerness to get started.

Steps 5 and 6—Gerlach suggested they meet weekly for the duration of the project to review progress. Stinley agreed to develop a list of check points for the project with a timeline and Gantt chart for the next 4 months. They both agreed that the feasibility survey was the first priority and needed to be designed, printed, and mailed within 3 weeks. The review meetings would focus on progress toward meeting the check points. Coaching on budgeting would begin as soon as the survey was mailed.

The meeting went well. Gerlach reported to his coach some sense of trepidation during the first 3 weeks, but with each passing meeting in which Stinley updated progress on the project, Gerlach's confidence in delegation increased.

Skill-Focused Coaching: Commitment Building

Webster's Dictionary defines commitment as "the state or an instance of being obligated or emotionally impelled." In other words, individuals who are committed feel connected and are motivated to maintain that connection. Committed employees are pleasant, hard working individuals who look forward to going to work, put in a full day's effort, are productive, act in the organization's best interest, and stay with the organization. Conversely, uncommitted employees tend to be remote and aloof, may pursue their own interests irrespective of the organization's mission, take full advantage of time off, and never seem to be around when they are needed. Their work output barely meets minimum standards; they may be confrontational, defensive, and oppositional and if a better opportunity arises will move to another organization (Kinlaw, 1999).

Commitment has become a critical problem for corporations today. Surveys report that among first year employees, some 43% indicate that they are highly committed to their jobs (Kinlaw,1999). However, during the second and third years of employment, this percentage begins to drop. By the fourth year, the expressed level of commitment falls to 34% and remains for the same for employees who spend at least 20 years with the same employer. Job commitment appears to be decreasing in every sector of the workplace. A survey conducted by the Hudson Institute and published in 2000 found that only 42% of employees believe that their employers deserved their allegiance (O'Malley, 2000). This decline in commitment comes at a time when major shortages of skilled workers are predicted. Some corporations expect to lose more than half of their workforces to retirement by 2005 and a 1998 Harris poll revealed that over 50% of workers will leave their jobs within 5 years for various reasons (O'Malley, 2000).

Employee turnover rates are telling markers of commitment levels. Turnover rates in the corporate sector are often in the 25 to 40% range. This means that 2 to 4 employees out of 10 must be replaced each year. While turnover is higher in some others sectors, i.e., 75% for fast food restaurants, replacement in those sectors is less problematic. On the other hand, replacing nursing and other professional personnel in corporate settings is a major concern. Why do employees leave or stay in their jobs? Several employee turnover studies offer a possible answer: the major factor accounting for employee retention is the quality of the employee–manager relationship (Sperry, 2003). Essentially, employees working for managers who are caring and concerned about their careers and provide them with challenging work are more likely to remain than leave. Relationships appear to be the keys to employee commitment, productivity, and performance.

Levels of Commitment

Commitment is not a binary phenomenon. One is committed or not committed and commitment has varying degrees or levels. Macher (1988) describes a continuum of seven levels of commitment ranging from extremely low to extremely high levels.

Deep commitment—Employees who possess this highest level of commitment find a deep sense of purpose and meaning in their work and exert themselves in ways that really make a difference.

Divided commitment—These employees work hard and know how to "work the system" to achieve their own personal goals and ambitions. Achieving the corporation's mission is a secondary consideration.

Concerned but with limited sense of power—These employees are technically competent and care about quality but feel victimized by the system. As a result, they limit their efforts and commitments to their jobs and organizations.

Minimal level commitment—These employees do only what is required and will not extend themselves beyond the minimum.

Disengaged—These employees actively dodge work and responsibility and regularly make excuses for low performance or nonperformance. They may appear to be involved and may even volunteer if pushed to do so, but are unlikely to follow through. Macher (1988) refers to this group as ROJ (retired on the job).

Alienated—These employees exhibit considerable mistrust of the organization, coworkers, and customers or patients. While they may not take overt actions to sabotage the organization's mission, they tend to complain, feel resigned, minimally meet performance standards, and are seen as unmotivated.

Actively hostile—These employees possess the lowest level of commitment. They vigorously—although subtly, to avoid firing—work against the organization's basic mission. They tend to be antimanagement, and their only commitments are to receiving salaries and benefits.

Conditions That Foster Commitment

Research on the dynamics of commitment suggests five basic conditions that facilitate the development of commitment and fulfill the five most basic needs of employees (O'Malley, 2000). The five basic conditions are:

Fit and belonging—The extent to which employee and organizational values and interests are compatible, and the degree to which employees feel they belong and develop friendships. This fulfills the need for *acceptance.*

Status and identity—The extent to which employees' self concepts are influenced by their organizational affiliations. This fulfills the employee's need for *esteem.*

Trust and reciprocity—The extent to which the organization acts in such a way that employees and organization become indebted to each other. This fulfills the employee's need for *security.*

Emotional reward—The extent to which employees experience their jobs and work environments as satisfying and supportive. This fulfills the employee's need for *growth.*

Economic interdependence—The extent to which employees believe they are fairly compensated and benefit in such a way that they remain in the organization. This fulfills the employee's need for *sustenance.*

Strategies That Foster and Enhance Commitment

An effective way of establishing and maintaining high levels of employee commitment is to foster what we call a "culture of commitment"—an organizational culture that places a high priority on employee–manager relationships based on trust, belonging, esteem, growth, economic interdependence, productivity, and performance. In short, the qualities of relationships employees have with their managers keep employees committed to their organizations. Here are four strategies for fostering and enhancing commitment (Sperry, 2003).

1. Foster a Leadership Style and Culture Focused on Employee Need Unfortunately, commitment is not something that can be instilled in employees. Rather, commitment must be evoked. Instead of being commanded of employees, it emerges from a leadership style and culture that meet employees' needs for trust, acceptance, esteem, security, growth, and sustenance.

2. Recruit and Hire Employees Compatible with a Culture of Commitment Establishing and maintaining a culture of commitment requires that prospective employees have not only the capacity to meet performance expectations, but share the organization's basic values and mission. If candidates do not have both attributes, they may not be compatible with a culture of commitment and probably should not be hired.

3. Socialize Employees to the Culture of Commitment Efforts to foster commitment do not cease after employees compatible with the culture of commitment are hired. Formal orientation programs must emphasize the importance the organization's basic values and mission in the daily life of employees and work teams, in addition to standard human resources policies and paperwork. Organizations that excel in fostering commitment utilize various means of socializing new employees, for example, some pair new employees with coworkers or mentors to instill the culture over the first 6 months or so of employment.

4. Foster Relationship Management Organizations must endeavor to maintain healthy relationships with employees over time. O'Malley (2000) describes the need for "preventive maintenance to keep relationships moving in a mutually desirable direction as well as corrective maintenance to resurrect relationships that are faltering" (p. 221).

Commitment and Motivation

What is the relationship of commitment to motivation? Commitment and motivation are intimately related in that commitment is a component or dimension of motivation. Motivation can be defined as behavior that is energetic and goal directed. While little agreement exists among motivational researchers about where the energy comes from, there is a growing consensus that motivation involves three factors: ability, commitment, and a goal (O'Malley, 2000).

Case Example: Increasing Commitment

Julian Krathwohl is a 48-year old associate vice president of customer service at a medium-size national insurance company. The organization is attempting to implement a major change initiative intended to increase profitability and meet customers' increasing expectations for quality and service delivery needs. The company knows that to achieve both goals it must reduce high turnover rates (approximately 18% of professional staff and 14% of hourly employees for each of the past 3 years), and must focus on increasing employee commitment to the organization.

The culture of this century old insurance company is proud and staid. Tradition and consistency are valued over creativity and change. Many executives including Krathwohl have been with this company for 15 or more years and have gone through previous change efforts, all of which were championed by the CEO and began with high expectations. Interestingly, grass roots support was never really achieved, and not surprisingly, none of these change efforts succeeded. As a result, employees throughout the organization learned to "play along" with the programs as they played out, knowing that conditions would return to the way they were in time.

The current situation is far different. Many of the previous change efforts were essentially elective—they were not vitally important to the company's existence. This time, the very future of this 100-plus year old corporation was at stake. The board, CEO, and the rest of the top management knew things had to be different. After considerable consultation, individual performance-focused coaching with executives was the key strategy chosen to achieve this overall initiative. The plan was for each executive to meet with an executive coach biweekly for a year (at least 20 sessions lasting 1 to 3 hours). The coaching was to focus primarily on increasing commitment following the four strategies for fostering and enhancing commitment outlined above.

This case is continued in chapter 7 and includes a transcription of a key session in which the executive coach worked with Krathwohl to increase his commitment to the company's initiative. During the year of performance-focused coaching, Krathwohl was successful in implementing the initiative in his unit, i.e., customer satisfaction, a marker of quality, was at 94%, and turnover was reduced to 8%. Among those who left were a number of employees who could have been characterized as ROJ.

Executive Skill Coaching: Stress and Time Management Skills

Stress seems to be increasing in today's fast-paced corporate environment. It tends to affect individuals more than they realize. This is largely due to the increasing influence work exerts on life today. In mainline American culture, individuals typically identify themselves with what they do, e.g., "I'm a senior VP." Individuals in corporate settings spend more hours involved in their work than in any other activity, including sleep. Furthermore, many friendships develop at work. Nearly 80% of all couples are dual-earner or dual-career families. Stress arises in organizations from a variety of causes including work backlogs that continually increase, demanding superiors who exert pressure by adding assignments, changing priorities, and tightening deadlines. Troubling, troubled, and difficult employees who must be dealt with can be particularly stressful for managers. Another type of stress is unique to certain corporate settings, that is, working in an environment of illness, emergencies, trauma, and death.

Stressors

A stressor may be almost anything that adversely affects us (Giordano, Everly, & Dusek, 2001), for example, exposure to high or low temperature, environmental toxins, caffeine, alcohol and drug use, certain foods, lack of exercise, conflicted relationships, and strong emotional reactions. Stressors can compel individuals to smoke, drink, take drugs, and overeat. They can induce back problems, skin disorders, respiratory infections, and circulation problems. Research increasingly demonstrates that stress lowers resistance to illness and weakens the immune system. Three types of stressors are common in corporate settings.

Environmental Stressors Environmental stressors arise from the organizational environment. A situation in which an individual works is referred to as an environmental stressor, e.g., an unfavorable working condition such as a job design that leaves an individual with a perceived loss of control over his or her job and leads to predictable health consequences.

Time Stressors Time stressors result from work overload, i.e., having too much to do in too short a time. Time stressors may be the most common and pervasive sources of stress. While an occasional time stressor may actually energize some individuals to complete a task, a constant state of time pressure is nearly always harmful for all individuals.

Relational Stressors Relational stressor results arise from interpersonal conflicts involving roles, issues, and interactions. Role conflict results from role expectations that are incompatible. Issue conflicts involve disagreement over defining or solving a problem. Interaction conflicts involve mutual antagonism among employees in a work team or unit. This section focuses on environmental and time stressors.

Stress Perspectives Stress can be viewed from two perspectives. The first view is that stress is primarily a function of an executive's perceptions and coping strategies. Accordingly, those who realistically appraise situations and have effective coping strategies will have fewer untoward responses to stressors than others. This "personal view" of stress is ascribed to by many executives and corporate personnel.

One perspective that is gaining support from researchers is that stress is primarily a function of organizational influences, and secondarily a function of personal perceptions and attitudes. This broader view focuses on stressors such as time demands and job control and notes that stress management strategies must target these organizational influences as well as the worker's personal perceptions and attitudes. This section will focus primarily on organizational stressors.

Organizational Stressors Certain work environment factors have been shown to cause feelings of loss of control and powerlessness among workers in certain jobs. Highly stressful environmental conditions that foster feelings of loss of control, helplessness, and hopelessness are associated with high levels of cortisol—the so-called stress hormone—and catecholamines that contribute to heart disease, clinical depression, and neoplastic formations (tumors and cancers).

Karasek and Theorell (1990) reviewed the health effects of job control and note that the risk arising from low job control is about the same as the risks of heart disease presented by smoking and elevated cholesterol levels. Workers with low job control were five times more likely to develop heart disease and three times more likely to develop hypertension than those with high job control. These authors also described other stress-related effects of low job control. Table 6.4 summarizes their findings.

Enhancing Job Control

Consider your current job in terms of its psychological demands and level of control or autonomy. An executive who is overstressed and perceives that his or his employees' decisional control is low can be helped by coaching. The executive can be coached to find ways of increasing decision making related to deadlines, performance standards, flexibility in work hours, etc. In circumstances where increasing decision latitude is not possible or is insufficient, job redesign may be needed (Karasek & Theorell, 1990).

Time Stressors

Effective time management is an essential skill and strategy for stress management because it represents a powerful strategy for gaining control over a job. While it is not the only solution to the workplace stress experienced by managers, it can go a long way toward considerably reducing stress. It is a truism that managers who effectively manage time experience less stress and are more productive than managers who do not.

TABLE 6.4 Health Effects of Job Control Levels

Category	Variables	Description and Representative Job
I	High control–high demand	High level of job commitment and job satisfaction; immune system remains intact, i.e., low cortisol levels; low rates of physical and psychological illness; senior executive
II	High control–low demand	Least pathogenic job category; jobs tend to be stable and satisfying and present few challenges; librarian
III	Low control–high demand	Most pathogenic job category; very high risk jobs; high catecholamine and cortisol levels present; highest rates of physical and psychological illness; security guard, switchboard operator
IV	Low control–low demand	Second most pathogenic job category; boring and repetitive work; janitor, night watchman

Source: Derived from Karasek, R. & Theorell, T. (1990). *Healthy Work: Stress, Productivity and the Reconstruction of Work Life.* New York: Basic Books.

Executives are increasingly aware of the cost of time. They and their units are held accountable for their use of time. Goals are clearly defined and penalties are incurred for missed deadlines. Corporate culture can have an important influence on how employees use their time. In too many organizations, working long hours is equated with working hard. Leaving on time may be interpreted as lack of responsibility and commitment. Interestingly, working longer hours may actually decrease efficiency and productivity.

Few executives readily admit that large parts of their working day are wasted. The only way to make better use of time is to analyze how it is used and consider ways to reallocate it in a more effective way. Every executive faces competing demands on his or her time. It is very easy to spend too much time on routine tasks such as reading mail at the expense of high priority, productive tasks.

A useful strategy for managing such stress is profiling task priorities based on the results of a time log (Sperry, 2003)—a daily log detailing how much time was spent on particular activities. Such a log provides a starting point for determining areas to improve. The length of time for keeping a log is dependent on the nature of the work. For work on a monthly cycle, the log should be maintained for 2 or 3 months. A 2- or 3-week log is reasonable for a weekly work cycle.

List each activity performed from the beginning to end of each work day, then analyze the log. Begin by allocating all 30-minute time chunks into categories according to the nature of each task, then calculate the amount of time spent on each type of task, such as attending meetings, reading and replying to mail, helping colleagues, or making phone calls. Next, calculate the percentage of time spent on each task to determine a baseline of the working day and serve as a rational basis for analyzing time allocations. Categorize the various tasks into three groups: R for routine tasks (e.g. quarterly administrative reports), O for ongoing tasks (e.g. organizing meetings), and D for tasks that would further develop your job and career (e.g. networking and making new contacts). Next, calculate the percentage of time spent on each of the three types of tasks. Effective executives approximate the following profile percentages: 60% on O tasks, 25% on D tasks, and 15% on R tasks. The profiles of less effective executives are likely to have the following profile: 25% on O tasks, 15% on D tasks, and 60% on R tasks

Executives should be coached to strive for 60:25:15 task profiles. If they spend too much time on one group of tasks to the detriment of others, they should be helped to reorganize their daily schedules so that time is distributed more efficiently. For example, if an executive spends time on tasks that could easily be delegated to a staff member, the task should be delegated. Such delegation allows the executive to concentrate energies on the areas where not enough time is spent.

Energy Management

A normal part of the human 24 hour sleep–wake cycle is a series of rest–activity cycles of approximately 90 to 120 minutes. During the first hour or so of each cycle, we experience heightened physical and mental alertness and energy; our skills, memory, and learning abilities are heightened (peaks). For the next 15 or 20 minutes, performance drops to low levels (troughs) during which we may yawn, become easily distracted, and feel like napping.

Body–mind revitalization can occur during such down periods if we allow it. Unfortunately, most of us override the signals for rejuvenation, setting the stage for stress ranging from fatigue to psychosomatic problems. Research indicates that heeding the signals for a few minutes during the down phase of our ten or more daily rest–activity cycles greatly enhances physical and mental well-being and will increase resistance to stress (Rossi, 1991; Loehr & Schwartz, 2003).

Case Example: Stress Management

Sidney Welkert is a senior vice president of engineering. He is 51, has been married for 24 years, and has one married daughter. For the past 3 years, he has worked with an executive coach. They meet for a half day each month to deal with personnel and personal issues. In the previous 2 years, Welkert's division met or exceeded its productivity and profit projections, turnover was less than 3%, and his employees rated him highly as an effective and trustworthy manager. In terms of overall leadership effectiveness, his functioning would be rated in the highly effective range. Were it not for some health concerns, particularly feeling overstressed, having low energy levels, and occasional periods of moodiness and irritability, he might easily be considered a peak performer. He admitted that his energy level was inconsistent throughout the day, that he craved sweet and starchy foods, and that he had been more irritable and impatient for the past year or so and wondered whether that was diet-related. Lately, the only time he seemed energized and exhilarated was when initiating new projects. He was usually overstressed and moody when finishing projects or when engaging in work that was repetitive, detailed, and tedious.

The executive coach suggested a stress and energy management plan that involved a number of health behavior skills. It was noted that Welkert was overly stressed by job functions that required extensive involvement in detail-oriented oversight of ongoing construction sites. The coach asked whether it was possible to shift much of this activity to one of his employees. Welkert indicated that this oversight was actually one of his foreman's duties. While it was not one of his stated job functions, Welkert believed he had to roll up his sleeves and show his employees his personal commitment to projects. When it became clear that Welkert was a "big picture" person rather than a detail person, the task was delegated and that improved Welkert's job fit considerably. It was mutually agreed to try these recommendations for 4 months and evaluate the outcomes.

Welkert also agreed to take 10- to 20-minute stress rejuvenation breaks twice a day just before his energy and mood approached low points, at 10:30 A.M. and 3:00 P.M. Instead of reaching for caffeine and sugary snacks, he mentally disconnected from the task at hand, took a walk, and did some deep breathing or centering exercises to revitalize his energy reserves.

After 4 months, Welkert indicated he was feeling considerably better. The stress rejuvenation breaks resulted in overall higher and constant energy patterns throughout the day. Welkert could not remember when last he felt so energetic and productive. He felt less pressured and irritable since he delegated daily oversight of his project management responsibilities. Now he simply monitored progress weekly. While oversight was not one of his stated job functions, Welkert believed he needed to exhibit his personal commitment to assigned projects. Using his creativity to conceptualize and plan new projects rather than perform routine oversight was not only immensely gratifying for him, but also proved more energizing and less stressful.

This chapter focused on aspects of stress management over a period of 4 months. The full case study is discussed in chapter 8 in the context of development-focused executive coaching conducted over a 3½-year time frame.

Concluding Note

At this point, readers should be able to distinguish skill-focused coaching from teaching and training and development, and differentiate skill-focused executive coaching from performance-focused and developmental executive coaching.

Mental health professionals whose therapeutic training and experience involved problem-solving approaches and interventions such as cognitive behavior therapy, and particularly social skills training, will presumably be more comfortable with the skill-focused function of executive coaching than those who use more psychodynamically oriented approaches and interventions.

To reiterate, while executive coaching may be exclusively directed at a specific skill target, such as increased confidence in platform speaking, executive coaching for the most part involves developing or enhancing skills and competencies, improving performance in specific areas, and attending to overall personal, professional, and career development. Thus, it should be no surprise that effective and successful executive coaches should have training and experience in all three coaching functions. Chapter 7 deals with improving executive performance; chapter 8 addresses coaching involving personal, professional, and career development issues.

References

Benton, D. (1999). *Secrets of a CEO coach.* New York: McGraw-Hill.

Giordano, D., Everly, G., & Dusek, D. (2001). *Controlling stress and tension,* 6th ed. Needham Heights, MA: Allyn & Bacon.

Karasek, R. & Theorell, T. (1990). *Healthy work: Stress, productivity and the reconstruction of work life.* New York: Basic Books.

Katzenbach, J. & Smith, D. (1993). *The wisdom of teams: Creating the high performance organization.* Boston: Harvard Business School Press.

Kinlaw, D. (1999). *Coaching for commitment: Interpersonal strategies for obtaining superior performance from individuals and teams,* 2nd ed. San Francisco: Jossey-Bass.

Levinson, H. (1981). *Executive.* Cambridge, MA: Harvard University Press.

Loehr, J. & Schwartz, T. (2003). *The power of full engagement: Managing energy, not time, is the key to high performance and personal renewal.* New York: Free Press.

Macher, K. (1988). Empowerment and the bureaucracy. *Training and Development Journal, 42,* 212–215.

O'Malley, M. (2000). *Creating commitment: How to attract and retain talented employees by building relationships that last.* New York: John Wiley & Sons.

Parsons, P. (2001). *Beyond persuasion. The healthcare manager's guide to strategic communication.* Chicago: Health Administration Press,

Roebuck, C. (1999). *Effective delegation.* New York: AMACOM.

Rossi, E. (1991). *The 20-minute break.* Los Angeles: Tarcher.

Sperry, L. (2002). *Effective leadership: Strategies for maximizing executive productivity and health.* New York: Brunner-Routledge.

Sperry, L. (2003). *Becoming an effective health care manager: The essential skills of leadership.* Baltimore: Health Professions Press.

Tuckman, B. (1965). Developmental sequence in small groups. *Psychological Bulletin, 63,* 384–399.

Wells, S. (1998). *Choosing the future: The power of strategic thinking.* Boston: Butterworth-Heinemann.

Whetten, D. & Cameron, K. (2002). *Developing management skills,* 5th ed. Upper Saddle River, NJ: Prentice Hall.

Witherspoon, R. (2000). Starting smart: Clarifying coaching goals and roles. In M. Goldsmith, L. Lyons, & A. Freas (Eds.). *Coaching for leadership: How the world's greatest coaches help leaders learn.* San Francisco: Jossey-Bass/Pfeiffer, pp. 165–185.

7
Performance-Focused Coaching with Executives

In board rooms around the country, executive coaching has one primary meaning: coaching that increases performance and productivity. As long as corporations are steadfast in their resolve to increase productivity, performance coaching will be in vogue. Corporations increasingly expect managers to coach their employees, and presumably most of this is performance coaching. When performance coaching involves senior executives, it is called *performance-based executive coaching* and it is the subject of this chapter. We begin by defining and differentiating performance-focused coaching from skill-focused and developmental coaching, then review the core competencies of effective executives and the role of these competencies in performance-focused coaching. This chapter then describes the process of this type of executive coaching. The remainder of the chapter focuses on various approaches to performance-focused coaching. Three different modes of this coaching function are described and illustrated.

Skill-Focused, Performance-Focused, and Development-Focused Coaching

Three different types of executive coaching can be described: skill-focused coaching, development-focused coaching, and performance-focused coaching (Sperry, 2002). Unlike skill-focused and developmental coaching, performance-focused executive coaching is a process and method for increasing performance and job effectiveness. In the short term, its primary objective is to increase leadership performance in a specific area. In the long term, such coaching endeavors to increase an executive's overall leadership performance to enable him or her to consistently function as an effective executive. Table 7.1 lists and briefly describes the three types or functions of executive coaching.

Performance, Competencies, and Performance-Focused Coaching

Performance refers to an individual's competencies and personal styles as they positively or negatively impact work outcomes. As noted in chapter 2, a competency is an amalgam of skills, talents, and experience. Requisite competencies may or may not be specified in an executive's job description, functions, and performance standards. High level executive performance requires these basic competencies.

TABLE 7.1 Comparison of Three Types of Executive Coaching

Type/Function	Description	Goals
Skill-focused coaching	Process and method for learning or enhancing technical, operational, analytic, relational, strategic, or self-management skills	*Short term:* reversing skill deficit or enhancing specific leadership skill *Long term:* increasing leadership competencies
Performance-focused coaching	Process and method for increasing performance and job effectiveness	*Short term:* increasing leadership performance in specific area *Long term:* increasing overall leadership performance to achieve consistent functioning as an effective executive
Development-focused coaching	Process and method for fostering professional, career, and personal growth in executives and the employees they manage	*For the executive:* increasing personal and professional transformation *By the executive:* professional and career development of employees *For the organization:* developing leadership potential, skills and performance or potential of existing executives

Since all competencies involve skill components, there is some measure of overlap between skill-based coaching and performance-based coaching. Sometimes personal style interferes with and negatively impacts an executive's effectiveness.

What exactly is performance-based coaching? As a rule, coaching to correct performance involves interventions to remedy problems that interfere with an executive's job performance or risk derailing his or her career (Witherspoon, 2000). In short, the primary purpose of this type of coaching is to reduce or eliminate impediments to higher level executive performance. It is a strategy for increasing, correcting, or recalibrating overall performance and job effectiveness as a function of leadership competencies and personal style. As elaborated in the next section, performance and core competencies go hand in hand.

Competencies and Performance-Based Coaching

Core Competencies of Effective Executives

As noted in chapter 2, effective senior executives are characterized by a unique set of core competencies. This section briefly reviews the core competencies observed in effective and successful executives (Sperry, 2002). Optimally effective executives rather consistently embody all seven of the competencies in the high or optimal ranges of the Leadership Effectiveness Continuum. By contrast, minimally effective and moderately effective executives exhibit some but not all of these competencies, and always in the lower ranges of the Leadership Effectiveness Continuum.

It is interesting to note that the Level 5 leadership pattern (Collins, 2001) seems to fully personify the optimal ranges in all seven core competencies, while the Level 4 pattern seems to match the optimal ranges in nearly all the core competencies, except for acting with integrity, humility, and a sense of balance. For that competency, Level 4 executives are more likely to fall into the moderate or high ranges, primarily because keeping their egos in check is not perceived as important. Here are brief descriptions of the seven core competencies for senior executives.

1. **Possesses requisite job capabilities**—Highly effective leaders possess requisite job capabilities and keen understandings of customers, markets, operations, and emerging issues to accomplish the corporate vision. They make and accept decisions based on facts, experience, and warranted assumptions about changes in markets, resources, and regulations.
2. **Exhibits high energy, health status and passion**—Highly effective leaders manifest significant energy reserves to achieve short- and long-range goals despite arduous working conditions. They also maintain high levels of physical and psychological well-being despite adverse circumstances, demands, and emotional stress.
3. **Understands individual and organizational dynamics**—Highly effective leaders have the capacities to accurately "read" individuals, situations, and changing dynamics of organizations. As a result. they can utilize such information to make adjustments in personnel, structures, strategies, and their implementation.
4. **Acts with integrity, humility, and a sense of balance**—Highly effective leaders create a committed organization that acts with full unparalleled integrity, courage, humility, and authenticity. As a result, employees find the executives honest and trustworthy. Such leaders serve as role models by acting consistently and fairly. Being around leaders with this competency seems to make others want to be better workers and persons. Such leaders manifest high degrees of stability and balance of corporate, personal and family needs and demands. The presence of this competency distinguishes otherwise successful and highly effective executives from optimally effective (Level 5) executives (Collins, 2001).

5. **Builds relationships and mobilizes commitments**—Highly effective leaders develop trusting relationships with colleagues and reports and foster highly productive teams. They hire and maintain strong talent pools by continuously developing their reports, skills, knowledge, and capacities. Furthermore, they inspire and motivate individuals to achieve and remain loyal to the organization's strategy, vision, and goals.
6. **Communicates a compelling vision and acts strategically**—Highly effective leaders create and communicate a compelling vision of the future that reflects corporate values, resources, trends, and opportunities. They regularly solicit ideas, provide honest feedback, share information with staff and others, consistently practice effective listening, and manifest good verbal and written communication skills. The compelling vision and strategy are then brilliantly executed and implemented.
7. **Produces extraordinary results**—Highly effective leaders engender high productivity and high morale; workers feel that they are valued and can grow with the organization. All these outcomes are important markers of well-being and the end results of optimal leadership operating within the context of a corporate culture and structure of discipline, optimism, and consistency.

Table 7.2 illustrates these core competencies for each of the four ranges of leadership effectiveness.

TABLE 7.2 Core Competencies of Four Ranges of Leadership Effectiveness

Acts with Integrity, Humility and a Sense of Balance

Optimal: Consistently and genuinely lives with integrity and courage, keeps ego in check, leads by example, and maintains good balance of work, family, and own needs

High: Generally acts with integrity but seeks recognition and is inconsistent in acknowledging others' contributions; maintains some balance of work, family, and own needs

Moderate: Acts with integrity occasionally and expediency the rest of the time; self-promotion is a priority; little balance of work, family, and own needs

Minimal: Manages impression of honesty and caring but is expedient, places self-interest over corporate need; imbalance characterizes work and family life

Understands Individual and Organizational Dynamics

Optimal: Highly sensitive and responsive to others' needs, is very capable of modifying organizational dynamics to optimize individual–organization fit

TABLE 7.2 (*Continued*)

High: Reasonably sensitive to others' needs, has some capacity to modify organizational dynamics to optimize individual–organization fit

Moderate: While sensitive to others' needs, has little limited interest or capacity to modify organizational dynamics to optimize individual–organization fit

Minimal: Insensitive to others' needs, has limited understanding of organizational dynamics, lacks political skills and savvy to be responsive to fit issues

Exhibits High Energy, Health Status, and Passion

Optimal: Exudes consistently high levels of energy and physical and psychological health; passionate about the organization's vision and those who seek to achieve it

High: Shows high but inconsistent levels of energy and physical and psychological health, has occasional health concerns; passionate about the organization's vision, but not necessarily for those who seek to achieve it

Moderate: Shows moderate levels of energy and stamina, can sustain extensive travel and long hours but with some health problems; has moderate passion for job

Minimal: Displays low energy, is prone to acute and chronic health problems that limit involvement and enthusiasm for the organization's vision and its people

Possesses Requisite Job Capabilities

Optimal: Exhibits very high levels of attainment on all requisite competencies, has the experience and expertise to analyze and respond to any strategic initiative

High: Exhibits high levels of attainment on most but not all requisite competencies, has the experience and expertise to analyze and respond to most strategic initiatives

Moderate: Exhibits moderate levels of attainment on most requisite competencies and has the expertise to analyze and respond to many strategic initiatives

Minimal: Exhibits low levels of attainment on most requisite competencies, has insufficient expertise and experience to respond to most strategic initiatives

Builds Relationships and Mobilizes Commitments

Optimal: Proactively garners employee commitment by actively and consistently creating and maintaining a culture of trust, respect, and cooperation

High: Actively seeks to increase employee commitment and makes some effort to foster a culture of trust, respect, and cooperation

TABLE 7.2 (*Continued*)

Moderate: Exhibits some interest in and capacity for increasing employee commitment but makes minimal effort to create a culture of trust, respect, and cooperation

Minimal: Exhibits little interest in or ability for increasing employee commitment to the organization, does not seek to create a culture of trust, respect, and cooperation

Communicates a Compelling Vision and Acts Strategically

Optimal: Actively seeks input in developing and sharing a compelling corporate vision and realistic strategy, works tirelessly to achieve it by acting strategically

High: Actively promotes a compelling corporate vision and strategy developed by a few for the many, expects that it will be implemented

Moderate: Communicates a corporate vision that has limited input from others, is less concerned with consistent strategic action and implementation

Minimal: Communicates unclear or conflicting information regarding corporate vision and strategy, fails to include others in strategy development or acts nonstrategically

Produces Extraordinary Results

Optimal: Engenders high productivity amid a culture of productivity, health, and well-being wherein employees feel valued and can grow personally and professionally

High: Engenders a high level of productivity by focusing on employee commitment with some effort directed to employees' personal and professional growth

Moderate: Engenders a moderate to high level of productivity and employee commitment, with little effort directed to employees' personal and professional growth

Minimal: Seeks high productivity in the short run at the expense of employee commitment, health, and development, obviating the likelihood of sustained productivity levels

Core Competencies in Performance-Based Coaching

As noted in chapter 2, four of the core competencies are considered prerequisites for achieving the main competency: producing extraordinary results that include high performance, high productivity, and high job satisfaction levels. The core competencies required to achieve extraordinary results are (1) possessing the requisite job capabilities; (2) exhibiting high energy, health status, and passion; (3) understanding individual and organizational dynamics; and (4) acting with integrity, humility, and balance.

Two other core competencies are considered requisites for achieving high or optimal performance. I believe they are also necessary for achieving extraordinary results. The requisites are (1) building relationships and mobilizing commitments and (2) communicating vision and acting strategically. If one or more prerequisites are not fully present, it is unlikely an executive who may produce notable or even extraordinary results in the short term will be able to sustain such extraordinary results in the long term.

Thus, these core competencies are of inestimable value in performance-focused executive coaching. They can serve as useful criteria in assessing an executive's baseline, setting specific goals or outcomes, and monitoring progress toward achievement of the goals or outcomes. More specifically, coach and client can discuss the executive's current level of functioning in terms of the four ranges for each of the seven core competencies (see Table 7.2) as they consider the factors that foster or impede more productive functioning.

Process of Performance-Based Coaching

Typically, an executive will work collaboratively with a coach to achieve certain objectives. First, they assess the executive's overall competencies for his or her current position. Second, they clarify expectations—those of the executive and his or her superior—of current job performance. Third, they prioritize the executive's needs as they relate to current job performance. Fourth, they establish a plan for continuing improvement. Finally, they implement the plan and periodically evaluate outcomes. Coaching for performance improvement tends to be an ongoing process that typically spans several months or quarters.

The basic protocol for this form of performance coaching involves the same four phases of the coaching process described in chapter 5. The first phase is to develop a working collaborative relationship with the client. The second is to define and assess the nature of the performance problem. The third is to establish a goal and implementation strategy for increasing performance. The fourth step is to implement and evaluate the strategy and goal attainment. I have found the following general questioning sequence useful for understanding and then addressing performance issues.

What exactly is your concern about ______ (performance issue)?
What holds you (the team, the unit, etc.) back from achieving the result you need or want?
What specifically must be done to _______ (resolve the issue)?
What resources can you bring to bear on it?
What specifically do you need from ____ (yourself, the team, specific employees)?
What do you need to do to make it happen? (coach, set expectations, coordinate, motivate, oversee, delegate)?

Each of these general questions may be followed up with specific questions before moving on to the next step in the sequence. The idea is similar to the "working through" strategy in counseling and psychotherapy. The questioning sequence forms the basis for "working through" or resolving a performance issue.

Fournies (2000) provides a somewhat different approach to performance-focused coaching that emphasizes behavioral analysis. Behavioral analysis is a logical process of dissecting a problem and then addressing it in a systematic fashion. Detailed transcripts of performance coaching sessions included in this chapter make his approach appear tangible and practical.

Varieties of Performance-Focused Executive Coaching

The demand for high performance and productivity on the part of executives sustains the practice of executive coaching, particularly its performance-focused function. The remainder of this chapter sketches common ways in which performance-focused coaching is practiced. Chapter 5 cited three different modes: two-way coaching, three-way coaching, and coaching in a team context. These modes are described in more detail and illustrated to provide readers with a fuller appreciation for the many creative ways in which executive coaches work with their clients in order to achieve their stated goals and outcomes.

Two-Way Performance-Focused Executive Coaching

The most common mode of executive coaching involves a coach working in a collaborative relationship with an executive client. This is two-way coaching; it differs from three-way coaching wherein an executive and perhaps his or her superior is involved in the coaching process and from coaching in a team context (see chapter 5 for a full discussion of these modes of coaching).

Case Example: Increasing Commitment

Julian Krathwohl was briefly introduced in chapter 6. He is an associate vice president of customer services for a medium-size national insurance company that is attempting to implement a major change initiative by which it hopes to increase profitability and meet customers' increasing expectations for quality and service delivery needs. In order to achieve these two outcomes, the company must reduce high turnover rates by increasing employee commitment to the organization.

The culture of this century old insurance company is proud and staid. Tradition and consistency are valued over creativity and change. Like Julian, many executives and other employees have been with the company for several years and experienced previous change efforts, none of which were really achieved. As a result, employees learned to "play along" with change efforts, knowing that in time things would revert to the way they were. While many previous change efforts were interesting experiments and not vitally important, resolving the current situation was critical if the company was to survive. The board, CEO, and the rest of the top management were in agreement that performance-focused coaching with executives was the key strategy to achieve this overall initiative. Julian has met about six times with his coach on a biweekly basis and at least 20 more meetings are anticipated.

The transcript below starts in the middle of the seventh session as Julian continued to discuss the pressure from his boss related to turnover in Julian's units at the home office. In their previous session, Julian realized the initiative was not going to go away and, unlike past situations, his job was on the line. He knew he had to do something but was unclear about the direction to take. The transcript begins with a variant of the third question (J = Julian; EC = executive coach).

EC: Julian, what could you do to increase employee commitment to the company's vision?

J: Well, I suppose I could ask more of my staff to work as teams and expect them to develop action plans.

EC: What are some ways you can personally generate more support and commitment for the vision?

J: I suppose I could stop by all team meetings and make sure that everyone is doing what is expected. But with my schedule, I couldn't possible be at all meetings and monitor everybody's involvement.

EC: What are some strategies that could keep them involved in changing their attitudes and behaviors?

J: I don't know. But I do know that when we made changes in the past, it didn't take too long before employees to return to their old ways.

EC: Well, how did you and your colleagues attempt to personally influence employee commitment?

J: What do you mean by "influence commitment?"

EC: For instance, were employees recognized and rewarded for supporting those changes?

J: Are you suggesting that we would have to pay workers extra to get them to do their jobs?

EC: There has to be some incentive for people to change. For example, you consider changing the way performance is measured and feedback is given. Besides pay increases, are there other ways you can think of to prompt change?

J: Maybe we could identify those who are meeting and exceeding performance standards and find some way of recognizing them.

EC: What might you do personally for those workers?

J: I could make sure that the performance standards and reviews of my staff include specific actions involving mission and vision.

EC: What else could you do to impact the rest of the company?

J: [Silence] Nothing comes to mind right at this moment.

EC: Well, how often do you thank your people for a job well done?

J: They get performance awards at our annual employee recognition ceremony.

EC: Research as well as my experience suggests that recognition has its biggest impact the closer it follows the desired behavior you are trying to instill. Formally recognizing workers for performance only once a year is much too late. And, workers may not make the connection between the reward and performance related to achieving mission and vision.

J: Right now this corporation doesn't have other ways to recognize workers more often.

EC: What about yourself? Are there some ways that you yourself could provide such recognition?

J: Maybe I could hold some sort of semiannual or quarterly award ceremony.

EC: Could you just thank workers when you notice they are supporting the corporate vision?

J: That seems a bit unnatural to me. I've never done that in the past. [Silence] Probably because it would make me feel uncomfortable and ill at ease.

EC: What is it that makes you uncomfortable and ill at ease.

J: It would seem insincere to say thank you in the name of the organization.

EC: Is your appreciation for employees who support your leadership efforts sincere or insincere?

J: It's definitely sincere.

EC: So why not directly express your personal appreciation to them?

J: You mean say that I personally appreciate the job they are doing?

EC: If you really do appreciate their efforts, could you sincerely thank them?

J: I could if I talked to them individually and tied it directly to their performance.

EC: Wonderful! It will have a larger impact than you can imagine. Can you commit to giving that kind of recognition several times this week?

J: Yes, if I connect it directly to our current performance targets, I would thank the workers who were meeting those targets.

EC: What would be a reasonable number of times to give that recognition in the next 5 days?

J: Well, I'm willing to try it at least four times over the next week—maybe even shoot for once a day.

EC: So, you'll commit to offering recognition at least four times this coming week?

J: Yes.

EC: Can we talk about how it worked and the impact it had when we get together next week?

J: Definitely! Who knows, it could make a difference. I'm willing to try it.

Until this coaching session, Julian did not seem to be particularly involved in the coaching process. As noted earlier, the coach assessed the corporate culture as somewhat bureaucratic and skittish about change. He sensed that

Julian was not particularly adventurous when it came to implementing new initiatives. In this session, Julian's level of readiness for change seemed to have shifted from contemplation to preparation for action. The executive coach essentially followed the questioning sequence full circle. In the next session, Julian reported that giving recognition to employees directly was somewhat clumsy the first time but he was able to offer recognition on five occasions and was pleasantly surprised at the effect. Subsequent sessions dealt with other commitment enhancing strategies. See chapter 6 for more on methods for enhancing commitment.

Three-Way Performance-Focused Executive Coaching

Three-way executive coaching is a somewhat nontraditional form. The conventional mode of executive coaching is for a coach to work one-on-one with a client. Three-way coaching involves the coach, the executive, and a target employee. This mode of coaching is unique in terms of goal setting. Two sets of goals are established, one set for the executive and another for the employee. The coach's input and feedback are transmitted only to the client and not to the employee. The benefit is that three-way coaching can be incredibly effective and show results in a relatively short time. The downside is that it demands that the executive risk being quite vulnerable in the presence of the coach and employee and also requires that the executive have a high degree of trust in the coach and a moderate degree of self-esteem.

Case Study: Improving Performance Indirectly

Jillian Jefferson, a 42-year-old African American regional bank vice president was introduced in chapter 4. She was concerned with the mediocre performance and reactivity of Albert Jacqui, one of her branch managers. His performance was rated as mediocre primarily because of missing deadlines for branch reports and his apparent lack of proactivity, even though his branch's performance was consistently high and customer satisfaction was one of the highest in the region. Following her supervisor's suggestion, Jefferson asked the bank's psychological consultant to briefly evaluate Jacqui for his suitability for executive coaching. Jefferson was surprised to learn after a brief evaluation that the consulting psychologist suggested that her management style might be a factor in Jacqui's performance and suggested that further inquiry might be useful.

Jefferson had pursued executive coaching with a 40-year-old Caucasian female counseling psychologist for about a year. She mentioned the consultant's observation about her impact on Jacqui's performance to her coach the next time they met. This led to a discussion of Jefferson's concerns about Jacqui's underperforming and reactivity. While her concern about Jacqui was mentioned only in passing earlier in the course of coaching, Jefferson said she wanted to address the matter formally.

After further inquiry, the coach wondered aloud whether Jefferson's one-way communication style might have produced the unintended effect of discouraging Jacqui's proactivity and possibly provoking his underperformance in certain areas such as his failure to meet deadlines for reports. Jefferson laughed and commented that her previous success was attributed to her "monologues." When asked to clarify, she indicated that her verbal acuity had gotten her through college and given her an advantage over more soft-spoken candidates for promotion to branch manager.

After further discussion, the coach suggested a three-way meeting with Jacqui. Jefferson respected and trusted her coach and despite some initial reluctance agreed to three-way coaching. A two-fold goal for the meeting was agreed upon. Jefferson was to increase her two-way communication, and Jacqui would increase his proactivity and hopefully become more conscientious with regard to report deadlines.

The coaching plan and strategy were straightforward. The coach would meet with Jefferson and Jacqui. Jefferson would inform Jacqui of the purpose of the three-way meeting by saying something like, "I'll be getting some input from my coach," and secure Jacqui's permission. Jefferson and Jacqui would discuss an issue or concern. Jefferson's communication strategy in that meeting was to make short statements followed by specific questions. She agreed that this was a recipe for two-way communication and would effectively break her one-way monologue-like pattern with Jacqui. Both agreed it would be difficult.

The executive coach's role was straightforward: guide, prompt, and support Jefferson's effort to shift to a two-way style of communication. A brief meeting was scheduled for the next day.

At the start of the meeting, Jefferson outlined the goal for the meeting and the role of the coach. Without waiting for Jacqui's response to the agenda, she immediately launched into the new direction she envisioned for the region. She noted the expected outcomes for the region and, of course, for Jacqui and his employees. As her monologue continued, Jacqui slumped down in his chair.

After about 3 minutes, the coach interrupted and said Jefferson might try something beside telling and selling. Jefferson stopped abruptly. She raised her eyebrows and blinked her eyes (the so-called "recognition reflex") as she instantaneously recognized that she had shifted into her one-way monologue mode. Some nervous laughter followed. After a pause, she told Jacqui of the new direction in which she intended to refocus the region in the coming year. She said she expected him to be more proactive as a manager rather than the reactive crisis manager he had been for the past 2 years. Then she paused and asked for his ideas on how he would lead his branch in this new direction.

Silent at first, Jacqui then responded predictably by saying that he could talk to his staff and get their ideas. After that, he stopped and slouched back in his chair. In the past, innocuous one-liners like that would have sent Jefferson into one of her monologues, and Jacqui would have relaxed and waited for her to finish. However, this time she asked what good talking to his staff would do. Jacqui was silent and did not respond and, biting her lip, neither did Jefferson. Another minute or so passed, and Jacqui began to slowly list some of the activities his staff could do. Jefferson then asked him what he was willing to commit right now. After another pause, Jacqui listed three action priorities. Jefferson answered that this was the type of thinking she wanted from him. She spent the rest of the 20-minute meeting attempting to make short statements followed by questions to foster proactive responses from Jacqui. This was clearly a challenge for her, and she occasionally slipped back to the one-way style.

After the meeting was over and Jacqui had left the room, Jefferson and her coach debriefed. She recognized that Jacqui had interacted quite differently with her during this meeting compared to previous meetings, and she reported her awareness of the different ways she expressed herself in the one- versus two-way communication modes. She agreed to practice this new mode of communication in additional meetings. The coach met on three subsequent occasions with Jefferson and Jacqui and both met the goals set for them. Jefferson was pleased to report to her coach that Jacqui had met the deadlines for three quarterly reports.

Performance-Focused Executive Coaching in a Team Context

In certain situations, two-way coaching has some inherent limitations. Most often, the problem or demand facing the client involves some or all of his or her team members. In such situations, the goals of coaching may be better accomplished by directly involving the team. The following case study illustrates the application of performance-based coaching to reducing impediments and allow the client to increase her competency in effectively leading her team.

Case Study: Increasing Team Leadership Performance

Four months ago, Justine Lopez was promoted to vice president of customer services for a large retailer. Before that, she held an executive staff position for 4 years, and served as the manager of customer relations at one of the corporation's largest stores before that. She was enthusiastic, easy to get along with, and was well liked and regarded by those with whom she worked. One of her responsibilities was to lead team meetings. Because of her dissatisfaction with a number of recent team meetings, she sought coaching to improve her performance as a team leader. She had previous experience in leading meetings. Although she was not the most assertive person in the corporation, she always managed to get the job done, but she no longer got the results she expected from her new team. The executive coach suggested that it would helpful for her to sit in on one or two upcoming meetings and observe the process. Lopez agreed.

After the next team meeting, Lopez met with the coach and the coach described her assessment. They agreed that a considerable amount of lively, somewhat tangential interaction occurred but only four of the seven team members verbally participated. Furthermore, the group seemed to lack clarity in the areas of problem solving and decision making. Lopez and the coach contracted to work together to achieve three objectives: (1) to increase input from all team members, (2) to increase the focus of discussion, and (3) to improve team problem solving and decision making. Furthermore, they agreed that the coach would be involved in the next few meetings in the role of performance coach as well as observer.

At the start of the next meeting, Lopez announced the meeting agenda and mentioned the three objectives she wanted to accomplish. She indicated that the coach was there to help her achieve them. As agreed earlier, Lopez said that she expected the team to give her feedback whenever they noticed she was straying from the objectives. The purpose of this statement was to activate the team to take responsibility for the process and outcomes of the meeting.

Not surprisingly, in the next 30 minutes, Lopez and the team lost track of the discussion. Only some members participated, and there was considerable imprecision and lack of clarity surrounding the decision they were attempting to make. Lopez also seemed to have lost track of her role and her three objectives. The coach then intervened. Looking at and speaking directly to Lopez, she indicated that the discussion seemed to be disjointed and asked what Lopez wanted to focus on at that point. Lopez gracefully took the cue and focused the discussion. Fifteen minutes later, the coach intervened again. This time she asked whether Lopez was ready to move to the next point of the agenda or wanted to hear from some of those who had not yet spoken. Lopez took the cue and specifically asked two individuals for their comments. About 10 minutes before the meeting was scheduled to end, the coach said that even though a decision had just been made, it appeared to have little clarity among team members. She suggested that Lopez check out what the team members thought they were committing themselves to do.

At the end of that and the next two meetings, Lopez asked the team for feedback about her effectiveness in leading the meeting and to what extent she had achieved her three objectives. Each time the coach intervened, Lopez seemed to take the input and decide what she would do about it. Lopez's performance as meeting leader continued to improve in subsequent meetings. After the fourth meeting, with the active involvement of the coach, Lopez said she felt she met her objectives. Both agreed that the coach's in-meeting involvement was no longer needed.

Concluding Comment

This chapter described and illustrated the performance-focused function of executive coaching. In addition to describing the conventional mode of performance-focused coaching (coach and an executive working in a one-to-one format), we discussed two lesser known and utilized modes of executive coaching: three-way coaching and coaching within a team context. Finally, one of our objectives in writing this chapter was to suggest that the core competencies and the Leadership Effectiveness Continuum were theoretical models, but had immediate applicability in the executive coaching process. This is not to say that the core competencies are unique to performance-focused coaching and have no value in skill-focused or developmental coaching. However, these competencies, because they are performance-driven and effectiveness-oriented are natural subjects for performance-focused coaching.

References

Collins, J. (2001). Level 5 leadership: The triumph of humility and fierce resolve. *Harvard Business Review. 79*, 67–75.

Fournies, F. (2000). *Coaching for improved work performance.* Rev. ed. New York: McGraw Hill.

Sperry, L. (2002). *Effective leadership: Strategies for maximizing executive productivity and health.* New York: Brunner-Routledge.

Witherspoon, R. (2000). Starting smart: Clarifying coaching goals and roles. In M. Goldsmith, L. Lyons, & A. Freas (Eds.). *Coaching for leadership: How the world's greatest coaches help leaders learn.* San Francisco: Jossey-Bass/Pfeiffer.

8
Development-Focused Coaching with Executives

Increasing numbers of otherwise effective executives are seeking help to improve the quality of their personal, relational, or professional performance—in other words, to become more fully functioning. Executive coaching that addresses these concerns is called variously growth-oriented coaching, developmental coaching, or development-focused coaching.

While the goal of performance-focused coaching is for executives to function in the high effectiveness range of leadership, the goal of development-focused coaching is to increase an executive's capacity to function more in the optimal range of leadership effectiveness as well as in the optimal range of his or her personality style. While executive coaching with a developmental focus has some similarities to personal or life coaching, they nevertheless have some important differences. This chapter introduces development-focused coaching and distinguishes it from personal and life coaching as well as skill-focused and performance-focused executive coaching. Two types of development-focused coaching (coach–executive and executive–employee) are then described. Finally, various ways of practicing development-focused coaching are illustrated with case materials.

Skill-Focused, Performance-Focused, and Development-Focused Coaching

Table 8.1 lists and briefly distinguishes the three types or functions. Development-focused coaching is a process and method for fostering professional, career, and personal growth of executives and the employees they manage. The goals and outcomes of this kind of coaching vary, depending on the target. Typically, the expected outcome for executives is to increase their own personal and professional transformations. Because executives are expected to assume coaching functions, another goal is to foster professional and career development in the employees they lead. The expected outcome of development-focused coaching for the organization is promoting leadership potential by means of developing or enhancing skills and performance of its executives.

TABLE 8.1 Three Types of Executive Coaching

Type/Function	Description	Goals
Skill-focused coaching	Process and method for learning or enhancing technical, operational, analytic, relational, strategic, or self-management skills	*Short term*: reversing skill deficit or enhancing specific leadership skill *Long term:* increasing leadership competencies
Performance-focused coaching	Process and method for increasing performance and job effectiveness	*Short term*: increasing leadership performance in specific area *Long term:* increasing overall leadership performance; fostering consistent functioning as an effective executive
Development-focused coaching	Process and method for fostering professional, career, and personal growth in executives and the employees they manage	*For the executive*: increasing personal and professional transformation *By the executive*: professional and career development of employees *For the organization:* developing leadership potential, skills, and performance in potential or existing executives

Executive Development-Focused Coaching versus Personal Coaching

The question is often asked: "Is not what you're calling development-focused coaching with executives really the same as personal coaching and life coaching?" The answer is a qualified no. In chapter 1, personal coaching, also called life coaching, was described as a process that "involves helping generally well functioning people create and achieve goals, maximize personal development, and navigate transitions on the path to realizing their ideal vision for current and emerging chapters of their lives" (Auerbach, 2001, p. 10). While personal coaching focuses on an individual's overall development, that is, "all aspects of their lives" (Williams & Davis, 2002, p. xv), we distinguished executive coaching as focusing on development within the context of an individual's job and organization. As noted earlier, to be effective, executive coaches must be mindful of the corporate context and organizational dynamics in aiding their clients in planning and achieving developmental goals. Generally speaking, personal and life coaches are less mindful of such organizational dynamics.

Consider again the examples of two acquaintances who have similar training and background in marketing. One is a freelance marketing consultant who has "no stomach for the corporate world" and enjoys the entrepreneurial life. This individual might find personal coaching beneficial in achieving personal and career goals. The other individual is a marketing director working for a *Fortune* 100 company who has been immersed in corporate life for 14 years. She would most likely be better served working with an executive coach with expertise in organizational dynamics to achieve both her performance goals and her personal and professional development goals.

Developmental Processes and Development-Focused Coaching

Chapter 2 described two key dimensions of executive leadership: leadership effectiveness and personality style. Development-focused coaching challenges executive coaches to conceptualize these two dimensions of performance and well-being simultaneously. The first dimension involves overall leadership while the second dimension involves the executive's unique personality style and the way it influences and is influenced by the demands of the job and the organization.

The notion of "developmental lines" (Sperry, 2002b) can be helpful in conceptualizing these two related dimensions. Chapter 2 described such developmental lines for the six personality styles commonly observed in executives and the developmental line of leadership effectiveness. The developmental line of leadership extends from the minimal to the moderate to the high to the optimal range of leadership functioning or effectiveness. The developmental line of personality style extends from the minimal to the moderate to the optimal range of personality style functioning.

We noted that the two dimensions were integrally related in a continuous and interdependent fashion. We also suggested that individuals who function in the adequate range of leadership effectiveness were rather likely to function in the adequate range of personality style—their particular personality styles would uniquely flavor their leadership effectiveness. If you were to observe six executives who function in the moderate range of effectiveness and manifest six different personality styles functioning in the adequate range, you would note six characteristically different ways each executive would think, act, and relate to others.

It is useful to recall that Collins (2001) found that Level 4 executives reflecting the high range of leadership effectiveness were successful in the short run but almost never in the long run, in large part due to their self-focused strivings, and were rarely able to maintain reputations of respect and trustworthiness over the long run. On the other hand, Level 5 leaders reflecting optimal effectiveness as well as optimal levels of personality functioning were successful in achieving results in the short and long terms, largely due to their focus on the organization and its employees rather than upon themselves. Figure 8.1 illustrates the relationship of leadership effectiveness and personality style in terms of the Continuum of Leadership Effectiveness and the Continuum of Personality Style Functioning.

LEADERSHIP EFFECTIVENESS

PERSONALITY STYLE FUNCTIONING

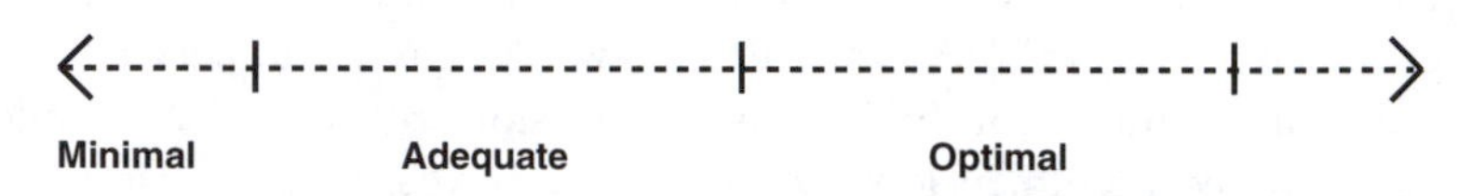

Fig. 8.1. Relationship of Leadership Effcetiveness and Personality Style Functioning

Optimal Leadership Effectiveness and Personality Functioning as Goals

These two developmental lines can provide useful guides for setting developmental goals and implementing coaching strategies. From this developmental lines perspective, overall coaching goals can be conceptualized as moving in the direction of the optimal range of functioning in either leadership effectiveness or personality style functioning or both.

While it is unlikely that an executive in the minimal range of effectiveness would be kept around long enough to be offered executive coaching, most executives involved in coaching function somewhere in the moderate range (Levels 1 to 3 on Collins' leadership scale). A reasonable developmental goal is to move into the high range.

Likewise, a sizeable number of executives who seek coaching who are in the high range of leadership effectiveness. Individuals in this range, including those designated as Level 4 leaders, who desire to move closer to the optimal range of leadership and personality functioning represent what some consider the primary realm of development-focused coaching. Why is this? It is because these individuals are already highly productive managers and have little if any need for performance-focused coaching. To the extent these individuals want to become better leaders by becoming better persons or finding their "true selves," they seek development-focused coaching.

Collins' 5-year study of major corporations showed convincingly that Level 5 leadership was essential for corporate transformation. It was noted while executives at the other four levels in the hierarchy can and did produce high degrees of success, their efforts were not sufficient to elevate their organizations from mediocrity to sustained excellence. The Level 5 leader builds enduring greatness through a paradoxical combination of personal humility plus professional will. These Level 5 executives require the capabilities of all the lower leadership levels plus the special characteristics that apply only to Level 5 (Collins, 2001). Interestingly, wise corporate boards of directors intuitively realize that long range success reflects corporate transformation and that it only emerges when a company has a critical mass of optimally functioning or transformed executives, and thus these boards are likely to support development-focused coaching.

Discrepancies between Leadership Effectiveness and Personality Functioning

We have so far focused almost entirely on the range of leadership effectiveness. While it is true that most often, the range of leadership effectiveness matches the range of personality functioning, a discrepancy can exist between an executive's ranges of leadership and personality functioning. Executive coaches occasionally work with executives who are assessed as functioning primarily in the high range of leadership effectiveness and lower range of personality functioning.

Such executives tend to be quite successful in motivating employees and achieving results in the short run. However, they are unlikely to be able to sustain such results over the long run, in part because of high staff turnover. Further investigation may indicate a lower range of personality style functioning. For example, if an executive's personality style is a blend of the confident and conscientious styles but he or she functions at the lower end of the moderate range of personality functioning, it would not be surprising if the executive came across as self-centered and hard driving and was not perceived as caring or empathic by his or her direct reports. Accordingly, the goal of development-focused coaching might be to foster the kinds of behaviors and attitudes characteristic of both personality styles at the higher end of the high range and perhaps even into the optimal range. Presumably, growth in this dimension can have a bearing on growth in the leadership effectiveness dimension.

In short, executive coaches doing development-focused coaching would do well to conceptualize a client's overall performance and well-being in terms of a continuum ranging from minimal to optimal functioning within the context of the developmental lines of personality style and leadership effectiveness. The next step would be to collaboratively set developmental goals reflective of a higher range of functioning at either or both leadership effectiveness and personality functioning.

Varieties of Executive Development-Focused Coaching

The developmental function of executive coaching is conceptualized and implemented in a variety of ways. The remainder of this chapter sketches some of the more common ways that development-focused coaching is practiced. Most of these approaches illustrate both personal and professional development, and all are mindful of organizational dynamics. With the exception of the last approach, all involve development-focused coaching provided by an executive coach to an executive client. The last approach illustrates how executives who have benefited from development-focused coaching can provide development-focused coaching to their direct reports.

Dynamically Oriented Development-focused Coaching

Like others who provide development-focused coaching, KRW International operates from the basic premise that job performance is inseparable from personal history or life outside the executive suite. Headquartered in Minneapolis and founded by Fred Kiel, a counseling psychologist by training, KRW is somewhat unique in that it employs highly skilled clinicians, including those with Ph.D.s and clinical and counseling psychologists to provide executive coaching and consultation with senior executives. The typical executive client referred to KRW is a highly promising, technically skilled candidate who needs help developing requisite leadership skills for advancement to senior management positions. KRW requires corporate clients to commit to its process for at least 18 months.

KRW's development-focused coaching process consists of four stages. The first step is assessment. Based on the premise that personal history impacts job performance, a key consideration in the assessment is an analysis of the origins of the executive's personality style and patterns and its impact on his or her functioning in the workplace. The adaptiveness of this style and patterns is evaluated and assuming it is in some way problematic, any change efforts the executive must undertake are identified. The executive's key strengths and the extent to which he uses them to their best effect are then identified.

The alignment of the executive's work style with his or her deepest values and the organization's mission is assessed. Considerable data are collected via interviews with the executive client, the client's superiors, colleagues, and direct reports, and also from his or her spouse, children, and close friends. Several intensive and extensive interviews are conducted. Workplace colleagues are asked about the client's integrity, emotional competence, stress management, motivation, leadership, and technical proficiency. Family members are asked about marriage, parenting, friendships, early family history, values, and defining experiences. The results of these interviews are compiled into a report that may be as long as 300 pages. Confidentiality is safeguarded and the client decides whether and how the data might be shared with others.

The second stage is an extended feedback process called the insight session that takes place over 2 days. In an off-site setting, the client and two KRW consultants review interviewee feedback without identifying sources. Feedback involves three areas: effectiveness in professional life, effectiveness in personal life, and family history. Based on the theory that improving performance depends not only on identifying and addressing shortcomings but also on leveraging strengths, the feedback blends strengths and shortcomings.

While criticism predictably captures most of their attention, positive feedback most surprises clients. Clients are asked to explore the underlying motivations that drive them and to look at the impacts of their behaviors on the key people in their lives. Not surprisingly, resistance to change is common. Accordingly, interview data feedback is useful in breaking through an executive's denial and eventually reaching self-understanding and transformation. Getting others' feedback in their own words, unlike feedback obtained via psychological testing, makes what others have to say harder to deny, yet at the same time easier to accept because the feedback involves a relational context.

The third stage of the process requires clients to consolidate and internalize what they learned. Awareness is a powerful catalyst for change. Fortunately, because clients are so achievement-oriented, they can be very effective when they finally decide to change and invest energy into their personal development. One indicator of this emerging self-awareness is recognition of the impacts they have on others' lives, including the enormous amount of stress they can trigger in others.

During this stage, each client is required to create a values mission statement. The goal is for the executive to focus on what is important to him or her and indicate how he or she will put the values in practice. When the client and coach review the statement, the emphasis is on congruency between value and action. For instance, if an executive states that family is important, but he seldom spends time with his children, the coach points out the disparity. Based on the mission statement, the executive is encouraged to draft a development plan targeting his or her specific shortcomings and strengths.

In the fourth stage, based on the development plan, other coaching specialists are brought in to focus on a client's specific areas of weakness. For example, one specialist may address time management, another may focus on interpersonal and communication skills, and a third may emphasize delegation and team building. The primary executive coach continues to follow up with the client regularly. In the early months, follow-up is at least weekly. It is not uncommon for the primary coach to "shadow" a client at work or even reinterview key individuals in the client's life in order to monitor progress.

Case Example In an interview with Tony Schwartz (2000), Jim Berrien, who is now president of Forbes, described his experience of development-focused coaching at KRW. In 1993, while he was working as a senior vice president and group publisher at American Express, he began development-focused coaching. After his insight session, he describes meeting individually with each of the 34 people including family members who had been interviewed.

"It was very difficult," he says of the experience, "but it was also the beginning of a major fix. The next step was to get a percentage of those people to point out whenever I slipped back into old behaviors." One of his key challenges was to become a more supportive and empathic leader. "I have a very strong personality and a need to achieve," he says. "I used to believe that there was only one model that worked—to be a type-A, hard-charging, extroverted killer. Now I'm wholeheartedly convinced of the fallacy of that model. What makes a high-performing team is the ability to create a climate of support."

The fourth stage of his coaching began with some simple behavioral changes. For example, he had a habit of drumming his fingers on the table and staring at people intently during meetings. Through feedback, he learned that the finger drumming he viewed as merely a by-product of high energy was read by others as evidence of boredom and impatience. The staring he attributed to concentrated focus was experienced by others as intimidating. "I still have a reputation for demanding high performance," Berrien says, "but I've been able to channel my energy so that it's more motivating to people, whereas they used to feel threatened by it. It took concentration on my part, and ongoing feedback from my troops and my family, but I think that the people around me would agree that there has been a huge change in my behavior" (Schwartz, 2000, p. 264).

Data-Based Development-Focused Coaching

Some executive coaches find that collecting formal assessment data can be useful in the coaching process. In fact, one way of practicing development-focused coaching is to center it on data that will serve as the basis for planning coaching goals and targets and for monitoring progress from session to session and evaluating overall outcomes. Currently, 360-degree evaluations and various inventories that provide feedback on an executive's style and functioning, including measures of emotional intelligence, are in vogue. Of course, psychologically trained coaches have access to a greater number of psychological inventories than other coaches. The following case example includes a transcript of one of the early sessions in which data feedback was first given.

Case Example Cindy Kim was introduced in chapter 4. She is a 31-year-old director of development for a national arthritis foundation. She has been in her present position for nearly 2 years and significantly increased the foundation's endowment. Her dream is to launch and lead her own public relations firm. She reports directly to Ronald Davison, the executive director. During her annual performance appraisal meeting with Davison, they discussed her performance which included marginal ratings in team leadership. Cindy admitted that her staff meetings were not well focused and productive. She recognized that becoming a more proficient team leader was important not only for her present job but also for her long term career plans. She agreed to work with an executive coach on team leadership and related areas.

She met with her executive coach on two occasions, and in the interim, the coach observed her meeting with her staff of seven volunteer coordinators.

Thereafter. she was given a series of assessment inventories, including a 360-degree evaluation. Following is a transcript that involves feedback on the results of the assessment.

EC: Cindy, the results of the self-assessment inventories you took recently suggest that you have a high need to please and to be accepted by others. Individuals with these scores in this range tend to seek approval from others. Also, since these individuals find conflictual situations uncomfortable they tend to avoid them. One way of doing this is to avoid making necessary comments or decisions so as not to risk losing the approval of others. Another way is to keep conflict from arising through diversion or by neutralizing it. We started talking about this pattern already before you took the assessments. I'd like your feedback on this. Do you believe that these scores accurately reflect you?

C: I'm a little embarrassed to admit it, but it seems like they do. [Silence] When it comes to confronting others, sometimes I guess I wait too long or don't do it at all.

EC: The results of the 360-degree evaluation also suggest that others recognize that your need for approval and acceptance seems to influence your decision making.

C: Ron is always saying that I'm a nice person. At my last performance appraisal, he said it again and added parenthetically, "You know that nice persons finish last."

EC: What was he trying to say to you?

C: I'm not really sure. He didn't really say. But, I have to admit, I didn't ask for particulars and he didn't give any.

EC: Last week when I was observing you during your meeting with your staff, I noticed that when a remark was made that seemed critical of one of your staff, you quickly made a comment that seemed to justify or neutralize the remark. Some people call that rescuing behavior. Do you recognize your response as a form of rescuing?

C: I guess, I really hadn't thought about it.

EC: For instance, last week when Marty was giving Julie feedback about how irritable and blunt she can come across to others, you said something to the effect that Julie only talks like that when she's in her role as manager, but otherwise doesn't come across in that way.

C: I do remember saying that. You're right. I guess I did try to take the edge off of things. I admit I don't really like conflict all that much. I wonder if that's what Ron meant by me being a nice person.

EC: There's a second observation that is suggested by the assessment inventories. That is that you seem to be reluctant to allow others to make mistakes. Specifically, that you delegate responsibility to others, but later take it right back if they aren't doing the job the way you think it should be done.

C: That's pretty accurate because I'm a perfectionist and I want the work that this unit does to be done right. I don't want this unit to be criticized or second-guessed in any way.

EC: What's your sense of the things that we've talked about so far?

C: Well we've talked about my need for approval, my rescuing people and problems with delegation. I suppose I should be dealing with situations rather than avoiding conflict and be giving people constructive feedback instead. I guess I may be unnecessarily oversensitive about others criticizing my program. Maybe it's more oversensitivity to loss of approval than perfectionism.

EC: Why do you say that about the oversensitivity?

C: Well, because as far back as I can remember now, neither my boss nor peers has complained about the program and what it does.

EC: Then what might you do about the matter of delegating responsibility to others?

C: I should stop taking responsibility from people I gave it to in the first place.

EC: I think you're right about that, Cindy. Giving and taking away responsibility can lead others to feel they are powerless or incompetent. I have two recent articles on delegation that address these very points. I can get them to you and hopefully they'll be useful in helping you decide what to, when to, to whom, and how to delegate. Next time we can review your recent efforts at delegation.

C: Great.

EC: With regard to the first matter—approval seeking and avoiding conflict and tendency to rescue others—what steps might you take to change that avoidance and rescuing pattern?

C: First of all, I need to be more aware of what I'm doing. I think it's a lot clearer to me now as we've talked. Second, I need to remind myself that I don't have to rescue others. They're big people, they can take care of themselves. Also, I have to bite my tongue when a potential conflict situation arises. That probably will be the hard part.

EC: I agree it probably will. Can I offer you a suggestion?

C: By all means.

EC: Here's a simple but effective strategy that really works. First, take two slow, deep breaths. Second, ask yourself: What am I thinking and fearing will happen if things proceed? Do I really need to rescue anybody? Third, take another deep calming breath and say nothing—at least not right away. This strategy can short-circuit the urge.

C: I'll try it. Thanks for the suggestion.

EC: You're welcome. Is there someone in your unit that you can trust to give you feedback on this rescuing pattern?

C: Yeah. There are two gals who I'm sure will give me feedback if I ask for it.
EC: That's very encouraging. Well, we've already got our meeting scheduled for next week. I'll see you then, Cindy.

This coaching relationship continued for the next 10 months during which Cindy made considerable progress in leading her team. Team meetings became more focused and productive.

Collaborative Performance Coaching

This case involves all three modes of executive coaching. In addition to two-way coaching, three-way coaching involves collaborative meetings involving the coach, client, and client's supervisor. Unlike the case example in chapter 7, the third party (client's supervisor) is only involved in selected meetings related to goal setting and reviews of progress. Team-based coaching occurs later in the process.

Case Example Yesterday marked Harold Whitney's first year as vice president of product development and his first meeting with his executive coach. Whitney was introduced in chapter 4. He quickly established a reputation as a steady performer with a no-nonsense style, and met or exceeded quarterly quotas, something his predecessor had been unable to accomplish consistently. The CEO hoped that Whitney might succeed the current COO who was set to retire in a year or so. Unfortunately, while productivity was up, the CEO was concerned about Whitney's style and its apparent impact on turnover and morale as well as the large number of sick and personal days Whitney took. At their first personal appraisal review meeting, the CEO expressed these concerns and Whitney responded to the concerns about turnover and morale by saying that he expected everyone to give 100% if they wanted to keep their jobs. To the concern about time away from work, Whitney said, "It's the price for being a Type A personality." Nevertheless, Whitney agreed that these concerns were legitimate.

The CEO liked Whitney and appreciated his spunk and candor, but he also knew that Whitney had some rough edges that had to be attended to before he could be seriously considered for the COO position. When the CEO proposed that Whitney consider executive coaching, Whitney surprised him by saying he thought it was a good idea and thought it might help.

In their first meeting, the coach spent time becoming acquainted with his new client, getting an initial understanding of Whitney's concerns and expectations, and describing the coaching process. Whitney and the coach agreed that working collaboratively on establishing goals and strategies was important and would characterize their work together. Whitney was asked to think about goals and targets of coaching to be discussed at their next meeting. They agreed that the coach would prepare a draft version of a coaching plan. A three-way meeting to include Whitney's CEO would then be held and a development-focused coaching plan would be formalized. Table 8.2 is the agreed-upon coaching plan.

TABLE 8.2 Development-Focused Coaching Plan for Harold Whitney

Developmental Goals

In a three-way coaching meeting of Whitney, his CEO, and the coach, the following developmental goals were collaboratively established:

1. Reduce unit turnover and improve morale
2. Improve health and reduce number of sick days taken
3. Assess and foster promotability to COO and/or career development

Developmental Targets

Subsequently, Whitney and his coach specified the following developmental targets re: goals #1 and 2 for three months re: targets #a–d.

Improve listening and communication skills (#1)
Improve relational sensitivity, particularly with engineers in his unit: (#1)
Increase self-awareness and management of his perceived insensitivity and arrogance (#1)
Increase health status and stamina (#2)
Involvement in the corporate Leadership Development Program (LDP) with performance-based coaching (#3)

Coaching Strategy and Approach

The coach's strategy included:

Weekly two-way coaching meetings of 90 minutes each in Whitney's office
Assessment: MBTI, Emotional Competency Inventory (ECI), 360-degree feedback
Team-based coaching to foster improved unit functioning
Referral for executive health evaluation and recommendations
Intermeeting (homework) assignments

Key Interventions

The following interventions were implemented

1. **Listening and Relational Skills:** Focused on listening and communication skills and empathy training to increase responsiveness to his employees' needs
2. **Team and Unit Relations:** Feedback from coach's observations on his relations unit members and 360-degree inventories helped Whitney come to terms with his insensitivity and arrogance. He became more accessible and better able to hold up high performance expectations in a more humane fashion.
3. **Self-Management:** Worked on the intrapersonal skills of emotional self-awareness and flexibility to more realistically set and adjust his personal and professional expectations regarding performance; worked on improving health status and stress tolerance through health promotion activities including a tailored nutrition, exercise and stress management plan based on health evaluation
4. **Career Development:** Waited to pursue target #e after sufficient progress was achieved on the first set of targets; then, simultaneously with the LDP, coaching would become more performance-based

The coaching plan contained both short-term goals (reducing turnover and personal and sick days off) and long-term goals (improving promotability via involvement in the LDP). During a three-way coaching meeting at the 3-month mark, Whitney had made progress on increasing his health status and decreasing days off. He and the CEO concurred that morale had improved. Initially, the team-based coaching was somewhat uncomfortable for Whitney as he faced employee feedback about his driven style, but it made a difference He recently joined the LDP program which was to continue for another 18 months. Progress in the coaching process was deemed on track. Whitney and his coach agreed to meet biweekly and another three-way session was scheduled in 3 months. The CEO was more confident that in time Whitney could assume the COO role.

Integrative Development-focused Coaching

The capacity for exhibiting high and sustained levels of energy and passion is considered an essential competency for executives to function in the high and optimal ranges of leadership effectiveness (Sperry, 2002a; Collins, 2001; Loehr & Schwartz, 2003). The performance pyramid described and illustrated in chapter 2 emphasizes energy, health, and passion as prerequisite competencies of leadership effectiveness. Low energy, vulnerability to influenza and common colds, symptoms of burnout, and absences due to illness are incompatible with high levels of productivity and wellness. Too often executive coaching focuses only on organizational, intellectual, and psychological factors and ignores physical factors such as energy level and heath status.

This approach to development-focused coaching integrates strategies for increasing energy and optimizing health with traditional coaching strategies (Sperry, 2002a; Sperry, 2003). It includes a focused assessment of individual and organizational factors that impact health and well-being, health status profiling, and resource enhancement, i.e., interventions in which a client's health and well-being are increased (Tenant & Sperry, 2003).

Case Example: Enhancing Energy Level and Healthiness This case illustrates the process of executive coaching focused on energy and health enhancement. Sidney Welkert has been a senior vice president of engineering for 4 years and was the inside favorite for the corporation's top position when the current president and CEO was set to retire in 18 months. Welkert is 51, has been married for 24 years, and has one married daughter. For the past 3 years, he has collaborated with an executive coach, meeting for a half day each month.

Most of the concerns discussed with the coach dealt with personnel issues, usually involving problems with prototype development and project management. In the past 2 years his division met or exceeded its productivity and profit projections, turnover was less than 3%, and his employees rated him highly as an effective and trustworthy manager. In terms of overall leadership effectiveness, he would be rated as functioning in the highly effective range. Were it not for some chronic health concerns that last year accounted for 11 sick days, declining energy levels, and occasional periods of moodiness and irritability, he might easily be considered a peak performer.

Three months ago, feeling confident that his division was on target, he thought it was time to focus on his health concerns as they related to job performance. He revealed his misgivings and apprehension about his candidacy for president because of his health concerns. He imagined that the job of president would be more stressful and require even more air travel than his current job. He also knew that younger, presumably more healthy appearing candidates, were under consideration. He asked the coach to be frank and forthcoming with feedback and advice. Should he save face, bow out of the competition, and continue to do his best in the current position?

Focusing on such health concerns was not new for this executive coach. He made a personal commitment several years earlier to achieve and maintain optimal level health. Seven years earlier, he earned a Ph.D. with dual majors in organizational psychology and behavioral medicine, and launched an executive coaching and consultation practice with a focus on health. Over the years, he developed a resource network of various medical specialists such as cardiologists and gastroenterologists, as well as nutritionists and exercise physiologists who specialized in health promotion. While he occasionally referred his executive clients to these specialists, he was reasonably comfortable working within a scope of practice that included health and work issues.

In their first meeting, the executive coach performed a global assessment of Welkert's energy, stress response, body type and weight gain, personality, and relational patterns. Through focused questioning, the coach learned that Welkert's diet consistently mostly of complex carbohydrates, no red meat, and only occasional fish and chicken. Welkert said he was embarrassed to admit that he craved snack foods such as chocolate-covered nuts, donuts, and chocolate chip cookies, but added that he also snacked on apples, grapes, and bananas. Except for an occasional glass of wine, he never touched alcohol or other recreational drugs and quit smoking 10 years ago. He took a number of nutritional supplements including vitamins and minerals "just to be safe" but no prescription medicines in the past year or so. Welkert indicated he adopted the Zone Diet—a high carbohydrate, low fat nutrition plan—about 16 months ago at the suggestion of his wife who followed it and reached her ideal weight for the first time since the birth of their daughter. Although she lost weight on this nutrition plan, it seemed ironic that Welkert, who was previously only 10 pounds above his ideal weight, gained 15 additional pounds despite 4 hours of exercise a week. He had been jogging for 20 years even though his knee joints were becoming increasingly painful and arthritic. He admitted that his energy level was inconsistent throughout the day, that he craved sweets and starchy foods, and that he had been more irritable and impatient for the past year or so and wondered whether that was diet related. Lately, the only time he seemed energized and exhilarated was when initiating new projects. He was usually overstressed and moody when finishing projects or when engaging in work that was repetitive, detailed, and tedious.

Welkert was referred for a complete executive medical evaluation. It had been more than two years since his last comprehensive medical evaluation. The current evaluation included extensive lab testing and, because of a family history of heart disease, a cardiac stress test. The report indicated that Welkert was approximately 22 pounds above optimal weight for someone of his age and level of conditioning. His cardiac stress test was in the normal range and exhibited a level of exercise conditioning usually seen in amateur athletes. He was noted to have chronic sinusitis and mild to moderate levels of osteoarthritis in both knees and the right hip. Two treatment recommendations were provided. To reduce sinus symptoms, the recommendation was to reduce sugar and eliminate dairy products from his diet. In addition, a 12-week trial of glucosamine sulfate, a surprisingly effective natural remedy commonly prescribed by alternative medicine physicians, was suggested, with referral to a joint specialist if the trial was not successful. Insulin dependence, which the examining physician said was the first stage of adult-onset or type II diabetes, was diagnosed and the recommendation was made for an initial trial of either weight loss or medication. Overall, Welkert's health was assessed as average to above average for his age and gender.

A profile of Welkert's health concerns, health status, health behaviors, personality patterns, and body type was prepared and shared with him. The coach noted that Welkert's energy level was inconsistent throughout the day, that he craved sweets and starchy foods, that he was creative, impatient, irritable, and easily angered, and that he appeared to carry most of his weight around his waist and hips, i.e., "love handles." Psychosocially, Welkert had a variety of friends and colleagues and was most attracted to individuals who were original thinkers and stimulating conversationalists. He seemed energized and exhilarated when initiating new projects and most stressed when finishing projects and engaging in work that was repetitive, detailed, and tedious. He was particularly intrigued by the interrelation of his work style, energy cycles, and stress patterns.

Welkert and his coach talked about Welkert's health patterns and they discussed ways to optimize his diet to reduce his food cravings and achieve weight loss. It appeared that the high carbohydrate diet was a poor choice. A better nutritional strategy was a higher protein diet that emphasized eggs, poultry, fish, and some complex carbohydrates and limited nonstarchy vegetables.

With regard to the peaks and troughs of his energy cycle, Welkert agreed to take 10- to 20-minute stress–rejuvenation breaks twice daily, just before his energy and mood approached low points, at 10:30 A.M. and 3:00 P.M. Instead of reaching for caffeine and sugary snacks, he would instead mentally disconnect from the task at hand and take a walk or do deep breathing or centering exercises to revitalize his energy reserves (Rossi, 1991; Loehr & Schwartz, 2003).

Welkert's exercise plan needed some fine tuning. A more optimal exercise strategy would emphasize strength training with some aerobic conditioning. He expressed interest in working with a personal trainer who could design and monitor a strength training program. Because of his joint pain and damage, the trainer urged Welkert to replace jogging with lap swimming.

Another key part of the recommendations involved stress reduction and management. Because Welkert was overly stressed by job functions that required extensive involvement in detail-oriented oversight of construction sites, the coach asked whether it was possible to shift much of this activity to one of his employees. Welkert indicated that oversight was actually one of his foreman's duties. While it was not one of Welkert's stated job functions, he believed he needed to roll up his sleeves and show his employees his personal commitment. It became clear that he was a "big picture" person rather than a "detail" person. Delegation of oversight tasks to the foreman increased Welkert's job fit considerably. He and the coach agreed that he would follow these recommendation for 4 months and they would evaluate the outcomes.

Four months later, Welkert indicated he was feeling considerably better. The stress–rejuvenation breaks resulted in higher and more consistent energy patterns throughout the day. Welkert could not recall when he last felt so energetic and productive. He felt less pressured and irritable after he delegated all his daily oversight responsibilities. Now he simply monitored progress weekly. Using his creativity to conceptualize and plan new projects was not only immensely gratifying for him, but also more energizing and less stressful. Furthermore, the new diet plan seemed to work. He was within 5 pounds of his ideal weight, and his sinus and joint symptoms considerably lessened. His physician indicated that lab tests revealed no indications of diabetes or insulin resistance.

At 6 months Welkert continued to do well. For the first time since college, he was at his ideal weight. He enjoyed lap swimming and strength training workouts with his trainer. He was able to exercise without joint pain and the removal of dairy products from his diet had nearly eliminated sinus congestion. He had taken only one sick day in 10 months and jet lag was no longer a problem for him. Finally, he felt more confident as he embarked on interviews for the job of president and CEO.

Development-Focused Coaching in Leadership Development Programs

Research shows that nearly 80% of leadership development training occurs on the job, typically through interactions with coaches (Thach & Heinselman, 2000, p. 222). Formal leadership development programs have been around for years, but only in the past decade have progressive corporations placed a higher priority on leadership development. Interestingly, as these corporations increased their investments in these formal programs, some have emphasized coaching as a core component. Thach and Heinselman (2000) noted that organizations that espouse the philosophy of continuous improvement can easily incorporate a coaching model as the basis for leadership development. They describe a four-phase model for a corporate leadership development program. The phases are assessment, developmental plan, public announcement, and implementation.

The first phase is assessment and its goal is to evaluate current leadership skills. Using a variety of assessment devices such as interviews and 360-degree feedback data, a benchmark of current leadership competency is established. The next phase is the creation of a developmental plan or contract. Each leader selects one or two high impact areas on which to focus, and then specifies a plan for achieving improvement.

The third phase is public announcement—informing others of the leader's developmental goal. This action purportedly raises the leader's own commitment to the announced course of action and lays the foundation for periodic follow-up conversations with observers to assess progress toward the goal. The implementation phase is perhaps the most tangible and important. It involves both formal developmental activities and informal follow-ups with feedback participants. The leader meets with the coach, typically in regularly scheduled monthly meetings as well as following up by e-mail and phone. Follow-up with feedback participants occurs every 60 days. This process does not stop when the leader's goal is reached, but rather the leader begins the cycle again with an updated development plan.

Several major corporations established leadership development programs based on executive coaching or incorporating it as a component of their programs. Ford Motor Company and Alabama Power Company implemented leadership programs based on executive coaching models. Both corporations experienced downsizing and reengineering programs in the 1970s and 1980s. As a result, both faced potential shortages of senior managers. Executive coaching was instituted to increase the leadership pool and transform their cultures. A further objective of the Ford leadership program was for each executive to be trained to act as a coach to his or her managers and staff. (Freas, 2000). Bose Corporation and Securities Industry Automation Corporation exemplify corporations that incorporated executive coaching as a key component of their leadership development programs.

Case Study: Coaching in a Leadership Development Program

MathWorks is a global leader in developing and supplying technical computer software to universities, government research laboratories, financial institutions, and the technology sector. Privately held and profitable every year since its inception in 1994, MathWorks has 500 employees. Despite its innovative software products and profitability, the corporation had some major concerns, particularly with one unit.

Top management's concerns were shared by employees as well. In an employee survey in which they were asked to identify the corporation's biggest internal problem, employees overwhelmingly named the operations division. This division had the reputation of being consistently behind in fulfilling orders and engendering increasing customer complaints. Because of low productivity, poor customer satisfaction, and a culture that accepted poor performance as a norm, the vice present of operations' proposal to institute a leadership development program was approved by the president. The vice president, aided by outside consultants, took the lead in planning and implementing the program.

At the outset of the program, a detailed analysis of the division's work flow and process was undertaken. It indicated the work process was so fragmented and circuitous that any hope for a sense of ownership and pride in workmanship was unlikely. Lack of leadership ability within work teams further compounded matters. What was needed was a new work structure and effective leadership that would transform the division's culture to one of teamwork, ownership, and pride. The program was to be a 2-year experiment in transformation; coaching was one of three critical components. Team development and training team leaders were the other two components.

The hope was to establish cross-functional teamwork that would "force a more mature level of interaction and empowerment. The newly formed culture—now filled with leaders—would be the key to better business results. Each person would see themselves as part of this interconnected business unit, responsible for its success or failure" (Slobodnik, Slobodnik, & Haight, 2000, p. 283). The coaching component was to be the keystone to accomplishing this transformation. Only the coaching component is described here.

Because of turnover and other factors, many employees in this division were inexperienced and were overly dependent on their managers for direction. At the same time, these employees resented being told what to do. Thus, the new leadership style to emerge had to provide them with the experience and support they would need to grow and mature in their work patterns. It was to be a collaborative form of leadership. Performance-based coaching is, of course, an excellent approach to redirecting employee work patterns. "Using managers as a triage team proved to be an excellent mechanism for providing that support initially and was probably the most important reinforcement of the new way of working .... Managers were able to observe the old patterns as they happened and redirect the behavior" (p. 283).

Because senior executives framed the transformation as a systemic change for the division rather than as a leadership problem, they met minimal resistance and division managers adopted maximal ownership of the process. Senior management also gave its full support and indicated its expectation that division managers would function as coaches and role models of the collaboration. Thus, managers did not simply talk about teamwork and collaboration, they practiced them. Not surprisingly, these managers began to communicate and interact differently, and employees responded by becoming more participative and proactive. Managers spent considerable time coaching and teaching employees how to manage their emotions, foster effective two-way communications, and resolve conflicts. "Managers benefitted from the parallel process of coaching each other, the team leaders, and anyone who came knocking. They read a lot on current management thinking and attended conferences .... They learned from daily experiences about the competencies they needed in this new web-like system .... They started to view themselves not as managers, but as change agents, coaches and internal consultants" (p. 286). Interestingly, the managers developed a 360-degree review process for evaluating themselves.

An early success of the coaching initiation was "open-door Fridays" that provided employees weekly opportunities to "contribute new ideas or vent their emotions in a safe, receptive forum. Managers also used it to introduce some basic tools and analytical problem-solving skills to get team members through some difficult roadblock early in the process" (p. 286). As the new culture stabilized, managers who were resistant or incapable of functioning as coaches were eventually counseled to move on.

The 2-year leadership development experiment at MathWorks succeeded. The culture of the operations division was permanently transformed and remains in place. Productivity, quality, and customer satisfaction have continually exceeded expectations and turnover has been minimal.

Development-Focused Coaching: Executive–Employee

We have described various ways in which development-focused coaching can be utilized to foster development in executives. Should development-focused coaching be reserved only for executives? An increasing number of corporations would say that it should not. Until recently, corporations that espoused values such as "employees are our most important resources," "a primary responsibility of our managers is to develop employee potential," and "we can only grow if our employees grow too" were often at a loss as how to operationalize such values. Development-focused coaching between executives and employees is a tangible way of operationalizing them.

Development-focused coaching is an effective method for dealing with an employee's future job responsibilities or career changes. While managers readily agree that employees are their most important resources, some managers insist that career issues are the responsibilities of human resources specialists. Managers may believe they have insufficient skills or they may be wary about raising expectations that they cannot meet, particularly those involving promotions or raises. Other managers who agree that an employee's development needs are the managers' responsibility likely to postpone dealing with the developmental needs and career issues of their employees in favor of more pressing matters. They might want to meet with employees and discuss their futures in the corporation or overall careers for an hour or two, but they point to having too many employees and too little time. The result is that the average employee receives very little development-focused coaching and even less career counseling over the course of his or her lifetime.

Is development-focused coaching much different from career counseling? Yes. Career counseling is an area of professional expertise that requires formal training and experience. It is a process that typically involves scheduled sessions, a formal assessment of vocational interests, abilities, and personality needs, and focused discussion and inquiry for the purpose of maximizing person–career fit. Development-focused coaching requires only limited training, and can easily be handled by most managers whenever they have contacts with employees. Kaye (2000) contends that managers need only take advantage of "coachable moments"—short, informal, spontaneous opportunities for career development that occur throughout the course of a typical work day.

The three steps to this approach to development-focused coaching are recognize, verbalize, and mobilize (Kaye, 2000). The manager first recognizes a coachable moment by picking up cues from an employee whose actions or words suggest openness to developmental feedback. Next, the manager talks to the employee in a way that helps the employee focus on developmental options. Finally, the manager must immediately mobilize or suggest specific steps the employee can take to develop his or her career.

This approach to development-focused coaching is a skill that is easily learned and utilized. Developing a sensitivity to coachable moments is more likely to occur in organizations that actually embody the corporate value that employees are their major human resources and where coaching is formally specified as an executive's job standard. Whether this coaching skill becomes second nature to an executive is a function of both the desire to develop personnel and the effort to practice the skill. The following case example illustrates this straightforward method.

Case Study: Executive's Development-Focused Coaching of Employee

Warren Williams, vice president of sales for a technology company, has worked for a corporation that believes that development of employee potential is a key management role. Three years ago, the company began an executive coaching program that emphasized both performance-focused and development-focused coaching. In the course of his own coaching, the CEO learned how to provide development-focused coaching to those who directly reported to him. The results were such that he decided that all executives should be expected to provide development-focused coaching to their direct reports. Managers were provided training in recognizing and responding to coachable moments. Then, last year, development-focused coaching became a written performance standard for managers at all levels of the organization.

Two occasions arose for Williams to do some development-focused coaching. First he learned that Jill Garcia, one of his regional managers, was under fire from several of her account managers because of late postings and recording errors made by her administrative staff. Following a meeting of regional managers, Williams pulled Garcia aside to discuss those concerns. Garcia responded: "Yah, I can understand their complaints. There have been some errors. The only way to avoid them is to monitor my staff very closely. But it's not my job, and I don't really want to do it." Williams recalled that when he talked to Garcia about taking regional manager position a year ago, Garcia reluctantly agreed, saying that her strengths were more in research rather than in line management. At the time, Williams needed someone to take that region and Garcia was a loyal, steady player, but it was becoming clear that this regional manager was experiencing poor job fit. Williams said, "Jill, you've really helped me out this past year. I know you have some valuable modeling and forecasting skills, but this job is not allowing you to use those skills and your interests as much as you probably could. Maybe there's a way to apply those skills more directly to our marketing efforts. Would you be willing to draft up a proposal along those lines?"

When Williams returned from lunch, Sandra Smith, one of the word processing personnel, handed him a set of visuals she produced on her computer. They were as professional as anything the corporate graphic design department produced. She said, "I was getting this mock-up ready to send to graphics, but I thought I'd try out what I learned in the computer imaging course I'm taking at the university. That new color laser printer we just got does everything." Williams recognized and acknowledged Smith's new skill and interest and added, "You might want to ask Raymond in graphic design if they have some new computer imaging programs that you might want to learn."

When a manager picks up cues that an otherwise conscientious employee is not performing adequately or consistently, the cues may reflect poor job fit, as with Garcia. Similarly, if a manager picks up cues about an employee's new skill or interest, it means the employee may be engaged in self-assessment about his or her career. While the new skill may not result in a different job or new career, it reflects self-directedness, a broadening of skills, and increased job satisfaction, as in the Smith example. In both situations, coachable moments are at hand.

Concluding Comment

It has been said that, above all other characteristics, the hallmark of the truly exceptional executive is the capacity to recognize *and* develop talent in others. Notice that both recognition and development, not one or the other, are the hallmarks. While talent recognition seems to be a talent in and of itself, developing another's talents and capacities is a learned skill. Thus, for those executives who can recognize talent and abilities in others but who are not skilled in developing them, development-focused coaching can be incredibly valuable.

This chapter has described several approaches using development-focused coaching with executives. We believe quite strongly that development-focused coaching is not only valuable for executives. The case example of Warren Williams who utilized development-focused coaching with two employees during the course of single day illustrates the importance and value of executive–employee development-focused coaching. Thus for the executive coach, the ultimate goal of development-focused coaching with an executive client should be that the executive can and does engage in development-focused coaching with his or her own employees.

References

Auerbach, J. (2001). *Personal and executive coaching: The complete guide for mental health professionals.* Ventura, CA: Executive College Press.

Collins, J. (2001). Level 5 leadership: The triumph of humility and fierce resolve. *Harvard Business Review, 79,* 67–75.

Freas, A. (2000). Coaching executives for business results. In M. Goldsmith, L. Lyons, & A. Freas (Eds.). *Coaching for leadership: How the world's greatest coaches help leaders learn.* San Francisco: Jossey-Bass/Pfeiffer, pp. 27–41.

Kaye, B. (2000). Career development: Anywhere, anyplace. In M. Goldsmith, L. Lyons, & A. Freas (Eds.). *Coaching for leadership: How the world's greatest coaches help leaders learn.* San Francisco: Jossey-Bass/Pfeiffer, pp. 235–243.

Loehr, J. & Schwartz, T. (2003). *The power of full engagement: Managing energy, not time, is the key to high performance and personal renewal.* New York: Free Press.

Rossi, E. (1991). *The 20-minute break.* Los Angeles: Tarcher.

Schwartz, T. (2000). It takes a strong stomach to listen to how other people see you. *Fast Company, 32,* 264–265.

Slobodnik, D., Slobodnik, A., & Haight, E. (2000). MathWorks. In D. Giber, L. Carter, & M. Goldsmith (Eds.). *Linkages Inc.'s best practices in leadership development handbook.* San Francisco: Jossey-Bass, pp. 277–297.

Sperry, L. (2002a). *Effective leadership: Strategies for maximizing executive productivity and health.* New York: Brunner-Routledge.

Sperry, L. (2002b). From psychopathology to transformation: Retrieving the developmental focus in psychotherapy. *Journal of Individual Psychology, 58,* 398–421.

Sperry, L. (2003). Biopsychosocial issues: Psychotherapy and the quest for optimal physical and psychological health. *Journal of Individual Psychology, 59,* 94–103.

Tenant, G. & Sperry, L. (2003). Work-family balance: Counseling strategies to optimize health. *The Family Journal, Counseling and Therapy for Couples and Families, 11,* 404–408.

Thach, L. & Heinselman, T. (2000). Continuous improvement in place of training. In M. Goldsmith, L. Lyons, & A. Freas (Eds.). *Coaching for leadership: How the world's greatest coaches help leaders learn.* San Francisco: Jossey-Bass/Pfeiffer, pp. 219–230.

Williams, P. & Davis, D. (2002). *Therapist as life coach: Transforming your practice.* New York: Norton.

9
Executive Consultation and Executive Psychotherapy

Executive coaching, as we have suggested in earlier chapters, can be a potent and effective intervention. Nevertheless, it is hardly a panacea. In chapter 4, we noted that while many executives are good candidates for executive coaching, others are not. There are a number of reasons why executives do not profit from coaching, which include organizational dynamics as well as insufficient motivation, psychopathology, and character issues. In such circumstances, other interventions such as executive consultation and executive psychotherapy may serve as useful and necessary adjuncts to executive coaching.

This chapter begins by describing executive consultation and executive psychotherapy as distinct from executive coaching. It then distinguishes the two main types of executive consultation. A subsequent section describes and illustrates two forms of psychotherapy with executives.

Executive Consultation and Psychotherapy as Distinct from Executive Coaching

Although executive psychotherapy, consultation and coaching exhibit similarities, they also have differences. This section provides a capsule summary of executive psychotherapy and executive consultation in contrast to executive coaching. Table 9.1 highlights their distinctive features.

Executive Consultation

Essentially, executive consultation is one type or form of organizational consultation in which the consultant *can function in a number of roles which include* sounding board, expert adviser, and evaluator. Executive consultation is most effective when the consultant forms a collaborative relationship with an individual executive in order to address and process a broad range of professional and personal issues of concern to the executive. Compared to executive coaching and executive psychotherapy, the process of executive consultation can vary widely. While some consultations are brief and can consist of a single encounter, executive consultation can also be an ongoing process extending over several years' duration. In such instances, the executive consultant may be on a retainer which is renewed annually.

TABLE 9.1 Comparison of Executive Consultation, Coaching, and Psychotherapy

Strategy	Distinctive Features
Executive consultation	Form of organizational consultation in which a consultant functioning as a sounding board, expert adviser, and/or evaluator, forms a collaborative relationship with an individual executive to address a broad range of professional and personal issues of concern to the executive; while the consultation process can be very brief, it tends to be ongoing and long term.
Executive coaching	Form of executive consultation in which a coach works collaboratively with an executive to improve that individual's skill and effectiveness in communicating corporate vision and goals and facilitating team performance, organizational productivity, or personal development; the process is typically of short duration, although when part of an leadership development program may be ongoing for 1 or 2 years.
Executive psychotherapy	Process in which a therapist and executive establish a close, collaborative relationship and utilize psychotherapeutic methods to achieve greater self-understanding and resolution of work-related problems and/or symptoms; usually briefer, less intense, and more focused on work-related issues than traditional psychotherapy; typically involves weekly meetings of short to medium duration.

Unlike organizational consultation where the focus is the team or entire organization, executive consultation focuses primarily on the individual executive. In my experience, executive consultation requires considerably more knowledge, skill, and experience than executive coaching or executive psychotherapy. Accordingly, those who consult with executives "must have detailed knowledge about the executive's work as well as of the organizational setting. Above all, they have to know how people stay well at least as much as how they get sick" (Greiff & Munter, 1980 p.195).

Advisement in Executive Consultation

Executive consultation is a broad type of intervention ranging from evaluating executives and candidates for executive positions to advising executives or corporations on policies regarding executives. Commonly, two types of executive consultation are evaluation and advisement. Two roles are involved in executive consultation focused on advisement: the sounding board role and an expert advising role. In the sounding board role, the consultant actively listens to the executive's ideas or concerns and objectively poses pertinent questions to assist the executive in developing perspective on the issue or concern. This process can greatly clarify the executive's impressions and validate the reasonableness of his or her conclusions. While listening, the consultant monitors for mistakes and is especially alert to patterns of errors that the executive might not recognize. In the expert role, the executive consultant provides specific suggestions bearing on a decision whether related to a personnel matter or a personal concern.

This section discusses advisement on corporate leadership issues. Readers who are interested in advising executives on career and family issues or personal and health issues are referred to chapters 10 and 11 of *Effective Leadership: Strategies for Maximizing Executive Productivity and Health* (Sperry, 2002). While a psychologically trained executive consultant could conceivably function as an advisor of issues of a therapeutic nature, such advisement is best avoided because of potential conflicts of interest and complex confidentiality issues it poses in favor of a referral for psychotherapy.

Personal advisement is much less formalized and structured than executive evaluation. While some executive consultants specialize in executive evaluation, most consultants prefer the personal advisement type of consultation. Personal advisement typically involves an ongoing relationship between a consultant and an executive. This relationship may extend for years and the relationship may continue even when the executive changes corporate affiliations.

Unlike the kind of trusting relationship that develops in psychotherapy and limits behavior inside and outside the therapeutic setting, the trusting relationship in executive consultation has fewer boundaries. For example, consultants and executives might get together for lunch or dinner, play golf or tennis together, or speak by telephone whenever necessary. They can establish a close, personal friendship, exchange gifts, and attend events such as family weddings, bar mitzvahs, and funerals. Not surprisingly, executives who deal regularly with high stress and myriad top level decisions view personal advisement as a key factor in achieving and maintaining high level executive performance.

Executive consultants are typically external consultants—they hold no positions within the executive's organization. As outsiders, they are not encumbered by loyalty to any member of the organization and this affords them the capacity to be objective. Above all, such a consultant can provide the executive with support during lonely and worrisome times. The executive may have discussed corporate matters with a significant other, trusted staff member, colleague, or friend. However, close personal relationships can sour, and the executive faces the possibility that the former listener will be indiscreet with privileged information that has been shared. Executive consultants uphold strict confidentiality and also provide insulation from flatterers and opportunists. A consultant is free to question and confront the executive on major decisions—a path not open to those on staff without fear of repercussions. The chances of an executive making a gross error are minimal when backed by this kind of relationship.

As the executive–consultant relationship develops, the consultant may become involved in the executive's social life and activities and may be asked to play tennis or golf, have dinner at a club, or spend a weekend at the family's summer home. The consultant may find himself or herself in situations where it would seem very natural to disclose personal information such as one would exchange with a close friend. However, there is a difference between a friendly client and a close friend.

Furthermore, issues of transference to which the consultant must be sensitive can easily arise (Tobias, 1990). While this can be new territory for those without formal clinical training, it is familiar ground for coaches and consultants with mental health backgrounds.

Strategy for Executive Advisement Executive consultation usually involves directed discussions initiated by the executive who sets the agenda. Talks may focus on immediate concerns involving people problems such as staff conflict, an employee grievance, or a hiring or firing decision. It may involve nagging concerns such as office relocation, morale of a subsidiary, personal health or fitness, or a family concern. Discussions may involve extremely sensitive considerations such as possible mergers, executive–board relations, succession, or retirement concerns. Whatever the issue or concern, this type of executive consultation typically occurs in the executive's office and may last a short time or a whole day.

Executive consultants often deal with executives whose characterological style may preclude sensitivity and empathy to others. However unlike psychotherapy, the consultant must work obliquely around characterological issues, so the adaptive effort of the executive and the client organization may be supported (Levinson, 1991). Also unlike the 50-minute psychotherapy hour, the consultation may last 10 minutes or 10 straight hours. Extended consultations allow the consultant to directly observe a variety of encounters between the executive and others that provide first-hand data as well as the opportunity for feedback to the executive.

Advisement on Leadership and Corporate Issues Typically, discussions of leadership and corporate issues are initiated by the executive, and are most likely to take place in his or her office. The agenda is set by the executive and typically consists of here-and-now issues. An executive tends to hold certain expectations of the consultant. First, the executive believes the consultant will be able to increase his or her effectiveness as a leader and as a person. A second expectation is that the consultant will help integrate information, providing not only perspectives and objectivity, but also a keen insight into problems with people.

While senior executives expect that their staffs will provide them with briefings, financial reports, feasibility studies, and projections in advance of major decisions, they cannot expect these insiders who tend to be very close to these decisions to provide objectivity and perspective. This is why the consultant's skills in serving as a sounding board and expert are so appreciated. Third, executives expect that it will be safe to share their deepest concerns and even immature thoughts in the belief that the consultant will help them grow personally and become more effective in meeting the scrutiny of more critical audiences.

During the course of their meetings, the consultant guides the executive to think through the presenting concern by asking key questions, helping the executive formulate the problem, generate and consider various courses of action, and anticipate the consequences of the options. Accordingly, helping an executive formulate the right questions and make informed judgements is a critical task of the executive consultant.

Finally, the consultant must also be available to advise the executive because the executive may not be able to act wisely without specific information that provides a reasonable rationale for appropriate action. Through all these activities, relationships that develop with executives must remain professional—friendly relationships rather than friendships—not the type of therapeutic relationship that develops in an executive psychotherapy program.

Case Study: Advisement Sylvia Steiner is the CEO of an information technology firm that she began 2 years ago. The corporation has nearly 100 employees in two west coast metropolitan areas. Steiner previously worked her way up through the ranks to become vice president of information technology at a major banking corporation. During her 3 years as vice president, she was the company's top performer. However, when it became clear she was unlikely to crack the "glass ceiling," she moved on and began her own firm. Last year, Steiner was recognized as Executive of the Year by a regional business council. She is bright, entrepreneurial, and well regarded by her employees and competitors.

Steiner worked with an executive consultant at the corporate headquarters of the banking corporation and had found the advisement and mentoring relationship with this female consultant extremely useful and supportive. Steiner was the first woman to occupy a vice president position and found her male peers to be competitive and distrustful.

When she left to begin her own corporation, she did not believe her corporate budget would permit her to continue the consultation and the relationship was terminated. During the beginning of the second year of her corporation's meteoric growth, she felt she needed to resume the consulting relationship. It was an exhilarating time to be in on the ground floor of health information technology, yet she was becoming overwhelmed with the number and gravity of decisions facing her. A year earlier, she started the company with 6 employees including herself, and now she had 34. A recent market analysis indicated that expansion would require her to add at least more 50 employees within 6 months.

One option was to stay with the original software development mission and the other was to expand the mission to include product distribution and service. While the financials made the decision seem a "no-brainer" and her board of directors would approve the expanded mission, her intuition was that the expansion was fraught with danger. She also was concerned about her vice president of product development who, while brilliant and incredibly productive, was eccentric, moody, and engendered turmoil in her unit. In addition, corporate turnover seemed awfully high, about 18% the first year. Her board believed that such a turnover rate was the norm for a high tech company. They also reminded her that the company was a start-up and not a mature organization. Neither explanation comforted Steiner. She had carefully chosen her staff at her corporation and she nurtured their career development. Not surprisingly, they were grateful, committed, and extraordinarily productive, just as her executive consultant predicted. Steiner recognized that the consultant kept her on target and provided valuable advice.

Meeting again with her consultant was most heartening. Before turning to the matter of the corporate mission and "squeaky wheel" concerns such as the difficult vice president, the consultant suggested that Steiner review her own job function and responsibilities.

Steiner quickly realized that she focused too much of her time and effort on operations to the detriment of key CEO functions. Her executive vice president had the title of chief operating officer, but Steiner performed some of his duties because he failed to do so. Steiner felt too stretched and stressed to coach him, and and continued to handle his responsibilities. It quickly became evident that she had relinquished many of her cherished leadership principles and practices. Specifically, she had not taken sufficient time to hire the best "fit" people for her top management team and had not spent sufficient time developing them.

Steiner met with her executive consultant for one full day every week. By the end of the third meeting, she was more confident that her intuition was correct. It would be a mistake to expand and double the number of employees. The expansion would probably capture a bigger part of the market, but would the cost be worth it? Would she be satisfied with the quality of her product and the culture of her corporation? Would she remain true to her values? When she answered no to all three questions, she knew what she needed to do and was again confident that executive consultation had made a difference.

Executive Psychotherapy

Cynthia Walker was introduced in a case study in chapter 4. She was fearful of termination from her managerial position and sought executive coaching despite the nagging sense that she might need psychotherapy. She believed her problems managing the division and its difficult employees stemmed from her passive nature and domineering mother. The executive coach suggested framing the problem as one of skill deficits in assertive communication and negotiation, and said psychotherapy might well be indicated if the coaching effort was not sufficiently helpful. Developing more effective assertiveness and negotiation skills was sufficient to make a difference for Walker. However, it is conceivable that the skill focus, however necessary, might not have been sufficient in her case.

It should not be surprising that many executives prefer to work on difficult issues and personal concerns in the context of executive coaching because of the stigma still associated with professional counseling and psychotherapy. However, the indications for and the methods of executive coaching and psychotherapy are different from those related to executive coaching. When indicated, executive counseling and psychotherapy may be the executive development strategies of choice.

What are some of the indications for executive psychotherapy? Executive psychotherapy is particularly well suited for dealing with personal problems or organizational changes that impact an executive's motivation, job performance, or personal well-being. Concerns such as fear of failure, relationship issues, career dilemmas, symptoms or impairments related to depression and anxiety, substance abuse, and work addiction can be addressed by this form of psychotherapy. A provider of executive coaching is expected to have formal training and certification—and perhaps licensure—to practice psychotherapy. Unlike "employee psychotherapy" wherein a supervisor or manager attempts to correct a job-related problem, a workplace conflict, or a substance abuse issue, executive coaching is a professional undertaking usually pursued outside the workplace. It involves a much higher degree of confidentiality than either executive consultation or executive coaching.

This section describes and illustrates executive psychotherapy as an effective strategy for maximizing professional and personal performance and well-being. It begins by situating executive psychotherapy amid two somewhat related strategies: executive consultation and executive coaching. Then it describes two forms of executive psychotherapy that I utilize regularly. The first is dual career couples therapy, and the second is what I have come to call "work-focused psychotherapy." Both types of executive psychotherapy are described in considerable detail and case studies illustrate their applications.

Executive Psychotherapy with Dual Career Couples

The number of dual career couples is increasing dramatically. When both spouses hold jobs outside the home, they have a "dual earner" marital relationship. If both spouses hold professional or executive level positions, their relationship is referred to as "dual career." The workplace implications of conflicts among dual career couples are profound and therapists who can effectively engage these couples therapeutically can greatly impact their lives. This intervention is different enough from individual psychotherapy and traditional marital therapy to be considered an area of subspecialization (Rice, 1979). The obvious implication is that clinical consultants can greatly enhance the functioning of dual career couples. Stoltz-Loike (1992) notes six underlying themes related to effective dual career couple functioning:

1. Couples must establish boundaries between themselves and others.
2. Spouses must be able to express emotional and physical supportiveness to each other.
3. Effective couple relations depend on mastering and using basic communication skills.
4. Effective couple relations depend on mastery and using conflict resolution skills.
5. Dysfunctional couple patterns can be framed as problems in need of solutions.
6. Effective couple relations involve processes of change that couples tend to fear and resist.

Depending on the level and severity of conflict, treatment can range from simple psychoeducational intervention to focused systemic intervention or to more in-depth psychodynamic intervention. While psychoeducational and systemic strategies aim to teach relational and coping skills or achieve adaptive solutions, these approaches tend to be of limited use in helping dual career couples work through resistance to change or the developmental blocks that lead to relational and therapeutic impasses. Therapeutically confronting these resistances and impasses may require exploring issues from early childhood in each spouse's development. Confronting and resolving such unfinished developmental business on the part of one or both spouses is often a step in the process of developing a mature dual career couple.

Developmental issues underlie the six common conflict areas for dual career couples (Glickhauf-Hughes, Hughes, & Wells, 1986). Three of these (power conflicts, competition, and commitment) will be briefly described.

Power conflicts often reflect childhood experiences that indicate others cannot be counted on to meet their needs. As adults, individuals who had such experiences are likely to develop a look-out-for-number-one attitude. In addition, when parents are insensitive to their children's needs and frustration levels, the children will likely become adults who have difficulty tolerating the frustration caused by unmet needs. Thus, compromise with a spouse may be both difficult and painful because it is associated with loss rather than mutual gain.

Equity is often proposed as a solution for resolving power conflicts or struggles, but the solution requires several things. First, the spouses must keep each others needs in mind. Second, each spouse must develop the ability to tolerate the frustration of not having his or her needs met immediately. The third requirement is the ability to view a spouse's requests as legitimate and not as attempts to control or dominate. In terms of Erikson's stages of psychosocial development, (Erikson, 1994) the resolution of power conflicts by equity is difficult if either or both spouses have insufficiently mastered the developmental tasks of trust and autonomy.

Another common conflict of dual career couples is competition. The opposite of competition is cooperation or collaboration. Collaboration requires the capacity to separate one's own feelings from the spouse's feelings and behavior, the ability to sustain and augment self-esteem via encouragement, and the acceptance of competitive feelings of oneself and one's spouse. The developmental obstacle that can impede resolution of a couple's conflicts about competition arises from insufficient mastery of the tasks of autonomy and initiative by one or both spouses.

A third common conflict involves commitment. Since many dual career spouses value success, achievement, and independence, and respond more to external rather than internal validation, they find it easy to "hedge their bets" about relationships and thus place a higher priority on personal attainment and satisfaction. To commit oneself to another requires the ability to be intimate, to develop an internal reward system, and to make the spousal relationship a priority. The developmental tasks that must be mastered involve industry and intimacy.

Essentially, psychodynamic intervention strategies are necessary when problem solving and communication training are not working or are only partially effective because of resistances and impasses secondary to more basic developmental issues (Rice, 1979).

Case Study: Psychotherapy Involving Dual Career Couple Davis and Cynthia Bernstein have been married 7 years and have a 4-year-old son. They presented for therapy after a particularly hostile argument during which Davis had slapped Cynthia in the face. Although this was the first such incident, both were shaken sufficiently to seek professional help.

Davis, 43, is chief financial officer for a manufacturing corporation. Cynthia is 45 and a partner in a major law firm. She had worked full time for the law firm for 6 years before her son was born. She then took a 3-month maternity leave and returned to work on a 20-hour-a-week basis. She hoped to be made a full partner in the firm 6 months earlier, but was told she would not even be considered until she returned to full-time status. This greatly distressed her as she felt strongly about spending "enough" time with her son, at least until he began first grade. She felt some guilt about working during her son's "most formative years" as her mother continued to remind her.

Both Cynthia and Davis come from traditional families. Their mothers were full-time homemakers and fathers were the sole breadwinners. They were also the first generations of their respective families to attend college. Both began careers immediately and were quite successful. They met about 2 years before they married and discussed their desire to balance a family while continuing their careers. Things never quite worked that way after the baby was born. Cynthia ended up assuming nearly total responsibility for childcare. When the child was 2 years old, they agreed the child would attend daycare full time so that Cynthia could return to her career full time. Davis never seemed to be free to transport the child to or from daycare and was always too tired to help with household chores or spend time alone with Cynthia. For 3 weeks she attempted to juggle her work and home responsibilities before dropping back to 20 hours a week, much to the consternation of the senior partners and Davis, but to the delight of her mother. Davis insisted that they needed a full-time income from her to meet their increasing expenses since they had recently purchased a ski lodge condominium.

These events served to fuel an already incendiary relationship marked by periods of sharp verbal exchange followed by the same "cold shoulder" treatment or "stonewalling" (Gottman, 1994) they noted in their parents' relationships. Although they never seriously considered separation or divorce because of their religion, they noted a decline in sexual relations since the baby was born to a point in the past year when Davis complained that he had "lost all interest, because I'm too tired and stressed out."

Davis's corporation was recently involved in a hostile takeover and he has spent considerable time and effort making the merger work. Work has become very stressful for him because of increasing travel demands and the fact that he has much less time to play golf and ski with his friends.

Since Cynthia moved when Davis was transferred right after they were married, she left behind a support network she formed in college. Except for one unmarried woman in the firm, Cynthia has not had or taken the time to develop other friendships.

After two sessions of comprehensive assessment had been completed, issues of inequality of power, gender stereotyping, and inhibited sexual desire were prominent. Results of a formal evaluation confirmed the therapist's impression of low marital cohesion and adaptability with unclear boundaries. The negative impact of Cynthia's mother was obvious to the couple. Psychological testing suggested Davis had narcissistic and obsessive-compulsive personality traits and Cynthia displayed prominent histrionic personality traits.

Although both were quite successful in their careers, skills of communication, negotiation, encouragement, conflict resolution, and time management were not evident in their relationship, although their time management skills seemed adequate. While Davis's support network was adequate, Cynthia's was not. Cynthia experienced considerable couple and career asynchronisms as moderate stressors. Because of the chronicity of their presenting concerns, the couple met criteria for Level 3 marital discord. Blaming and projection were common and reflected both their hostility and increasing hopelessness.

Their different personality styles, lack of relational skills, and power, boundary, and intimacy issues led to their ongoing conflict and inability to resolve their differences. Given their relatively strong motivation to make changes and commitment to stay together, their prognosis appeared favorable. Relevant goals were mutually negotiated to increase the likelihood the couple would assume ownership and be more motivated and adherent to the treatment process. The treatment goals were to: (1) reduce the present level of conflict and distress: (2) establish clearer boundaries regarding careers and their families of origin; (3) establish a more equitable relationship and gender sensitivity; (4) develop more effective relationship skills of communication, conflict resolution, negotiation, empathy, encouragement, and time management; (5) increase their understanding of individual and couple dynamics; and (6) assist Cynthia in better understanding and resolving her career and family asynchronism.

These six goals were stated in the developmental order in which they would be addressed therapeutically, that is, symptom relief and boundary restructuring would be prerequisites for working on equity and gender sensitivity along with skill building, which would be followed by insight and awareness. Based on the assessment of the situation, severity, systems, skills, and support network, three therapeutic strategies were matched. The interpersonal systems strategy would be employed to achieve the first three goals. A psychoeducational strategy was planned for the fourth goal, while a psychodynamic strategy was envisioned for the fifth and sixth goals. Since the couple had a sufficient level of readiness for change, commitment to the marriage, and motivation for treatment, it was anticipated that a collaborative therapeutic relationship could be achieved and that an active, albeit supportive, therapist style would be well tolerated.

Considerable in-session modeling of effective communication, conflict resolution, and negotiation skills was needed based on the couple's incendiary style, family history, and limited success in this area. For this reason, the use of a cotherapist was indicated. Both therapists modeled and enacted potentially conflictual situations for the couple to observe, discuss, and then role play. Similarly, because both spouses reflected cultural gender stereotyping in which histrionic behavior in females was considered feminine while obsessive–compulsive behavior in males tended to be rewarded professionally, more androgynous cotherapist interaction could greatly enhance efforts to increase gender sensitivity.

Because of Davis's empathic deficits reflective of his narcissistic personality style, the therapist would utilize mirroring along with empathy training. However, the therapist's use of encouragement through reframing and stroking would be necessary for both spouses given their narcissistic and histrionic styles.

As anticipated, the treatment process eventually became a collaborative endeavor, but not until they were able to reduce their hurtful incendiary communications and establish reasonable boundaries involving job and family demands. Surprisingly, they responded quickly to skill building tasks and other psychoeducational interventions. By the eighth session, they had met the first four treatment goals and stabilized their relational system. The next twelve sessions focused primarily on individual and family-of-origin dynamics that the couple brought to their marriage. Relapse prevention strategies were introduced. The last session reviewed their progress and current levels of functioning. Both agreed they were less stressed and much happier about their relationship and careers. Davis recognized the need for additional work on issues of entitlement and blame. Subsequently, he continued for six additional individual sessions with the couples therapist.

Work-Focused Psychotherapy

Psychotherapy can be directed toward general treatment goals or more focused goals. Today, because of both economic and clinical advances, increasing emphasis is placed on focused treatment. Furthermore, because executives have strong biases toward problem solving and pragmatic issues, they tend to find long-term dynamically oriented psychotherapy foreign and tedious. Production of fantasy material and disclosure of affects may be resisted initially. Similarly, the slow pace of progress and changes in long-term therapy may be significant sources of frustration for them. Not surprisingly, executives tend to prefer time-limited and focused approaches in line with their natural inclinations toward actions and outcomes. Accordingly, work-focused psychotherapy was developed to meet these expectations (Sperry, 1996; 2002).

Lowman (1993) noted the need for psychotherapy to specifically address work and work dysfunction. He defines work dysfunction as any persistent difficulty or failure at the work site associated with psychological characteristics of the individual. Dysfunctions can be independent or interactive with the nature of the worker's job or the organizational context in which the work takes place. Lowman proposes a classification of work dysfunction, and differentiates psychopathology and work dysfunction with the understanding that both problems can coexist. The clinician's first task is to assess the presence of psychopathology and its relation if any, to work functioning while also assessing the presence of work dysfunction and its impact on psychopathology.

As therapeutic goals of treatment have become more delimited, work problems have emerged as areas in which clinicians can make important contributions to individual well-being. Furthermore, such therapeutic goals can often be accomplished without a major restructuring of personality and in a relatively time-efficient manner.

Lowman (1993) contends that for most individuals, issues involving work and the workplace are resolved in a relatively non-conflictual manner. Individuals typically find careers or jobs that are to some degree satisfying and fulfilling and they function reasonable well in work settings. Work dysfunctions include the failure to find, implement, or sustain a satisfactory work role and changes in a person or the work situation that create psychological difficulties. Clinicians are consulted by executives and corporate officials regarding individuals for whom the usual development process has proven in some way dysfunctional. The clinician's role is to assist such individuals in understanding and changing dysfunctional aspects of their personalities, work, or the work environment.

Lowman (1993) developed a classification or taxonomy of work-related dysfunctions that I have found useful in both clinical and organizational consultation situations. The taxonomy describes patterns of under-commitment (underachievement, procrastination, organizational and/or occupational misfit, fear of success, and fear of failure); patterns of over-commitment (workaholism, type A behavior patterns, and job and occupational burnout); work-related anxiety and depression (performance anxiety, generalized anxiety, and work-related depression); personality dysfunctional patterns, (problems with authority, and personality-disordered work behavior); life role conflicts (including work–family conflicts); transient situational stress; and perceptual inaccuracies. A final category of the taxonomy is dysfunctional working conditions (defective job design, defective supervision, and dysfunctional interpersonal relationships).

A central theme of Lowman's approach is that characteristics of individuals that combine to create work difficulties do not exist separate from those of organizations and occupations. In providing psychotherapy to executives who present with work-related concerns, the clinician must evaluate the executive's workplace, even if evaluation must occur outside the actual work context. In treating work-related issues, the clinician must caution against allowing a psychological view to mask from consideration other factors that may be germane. Ignoring features of the work itself or the work context that may be the primary source of the executive's difficulties is a common error of clinicians beginning to treat work-related issues.

Determining whether work difficulties exist independently of, in combination with, or secondarily to psychopathology is an important diagnostic consideration. The clinician, if not the executive, needs to be clear on the plan for addressing work-related difficulties and, when appropriate, psychological difficulties unrelated to work. In cases in which both psychopathology and work difficulties are present, it is useful to have some sense of which situation is primary and how the one relates to the other. For instance, an executive who is recently divorced, clinically depressed, and about to be laid off may need help in determining which is the most pressing issue and which will be the initial focus of the therapy. On the other hand, executives whose work difficulties are much broader and involve overarching conflictual life themes such as procrastination or fear of success may benefit from working on the central theme or focal issue, addressing both work and nonwork concerns. Among executives, common themes and focal issues are particularly noted in seven areas: (1) over- and under-commitment, (2) loss, (3) interpersonal conflict, (4) developmental dysynchrony, (5) characterological issues, (6) life role conflicts, and (7) symptoms.

The clinician does well to keep these central dynamics firmly in mind and then interpret or reframe behavior—whether work-related or not—in light of the central theme. However, in manifesting resistance, the executive may attempt to shift the treatment focus among significant life concerns or undermine genuine progress made in one area by lamenting lack of progress in another.

In work-focused psychotherapy (Sperry, 1996; 2002), the quality of the therapeutic relationship depends to an extent on the executive's perception that the clinician is on his or her side, and in many treatment approaches, self-discovery is the goal. Thus, assuming the validity, or at least the perceived validity, of the executive's understanding of the work situation may be a better stance than unnecessarily or prematurely bringing in outside parties. However, the clinician can still raise questions or interpretations, particularly when he or she has reason to doubt the reality of the executive's presentation of a work concern and can do so in the context of a private relationship between two parties attempting to understand and work through issues at hand. Besides, if the executive's life style dynamics are the sources of the work-related problems, it is very likely that they will present themselves in the therapeutic relationship or in a pattern of reactions that will become apparent with time.

Furthermore, the clinician must guard against over-analyzing and over-interpreting work issues except when clear and compelling evidence indicates that such factors are the driving forces. For example, an executive presenting with depression and complaints of job burnout may be manifesting clinical depression or may simply be exhibiting common symptoms of burnout. Accordingly, the clinician could intervene with various strategies. Suggesting a job or career change, at least on a temporary basis, is one practical, perhaps well founded way to proceed. Recommending physical exercise and vigorous nonwork activities as antidotes to the emotional exhaustion associated with the job might also be appropriate, or the clinician might assist the executive in exploring reasons for the career choice or the tendency to become overly involved with high-flown goals that result in depression when personal efforts are ineffective. These strategies might be pursued over the course of therapy, particularly issues related to family-of-origin or family constellation dynamics are also present.

Short-term, behaviorally-focused interventions seem to be particularly effective in treating many work dysfunctions provided that more complicated psychopathologies and severe personality disorders are not present or, at the least, that the broader, contextual issues are kept in mind (Sperry, 2003). Lowman (1993) suggests that metaphorical approaches that encapsulate central dynamics of the person through the presenting work concerns are also effective. Kopp (1995) describes a number of strategies for utilizing metaphors in a psychotherapeutic context that is particularly valuable in working with executives in short-term psychotherapy.

The clinician may need to "work around" life-long characterological issues when working with individuals experiencing both personality disorders and work dysfunctions. Whether in executive consultation or in work-focused psychotherapy, it is quite useful to distinguish between "working through" and "working around." The process of "working through" usually involves extensive and repeated utilization of interpretation, confrontation, or cognitive restructuring to effect changes in personality structure. In contrast, the process of "working around" is not directed at the arduous task of changing or modifying personality structure, but rather involves psychologically side-stepping the facet of the individual's personality structure that is operative in a given situation.

Accordingly, reframing, redirection, distraction, minimization, and paradox are the specified intervention strategies. For example, a clinician or consultant working with an executive who reports experiencing a narcissistic injury could be told: "I know you're upset. But when you look at the bigger picture, you really have a lot going for you, so why sweat the small stuff" (minimization); or, "Letting him get to you like this is really giving him a lot of power over you. Do you want that?" (redirection).

Practical career counseling and career management can also be useful with some executives, particularly those with relatively pervasive personality disorders. For instance, stern warnings about the real-life work consequences of continued aberrant work behavior may be as instructive and influential in working with certain personality disorders as long-term psychotherapy. Such executives may be much more motivated to be compliant if they face job loss or restriction.

Finally, marital and family issues are common among hard working, hard driving executives who travel frequently and spend long hours away from home. Not surprisingly, communication difficulties, role conflicts, and sexual problems are common. Family therapy can provide more functional interaction and improved conflict resolution and communication. Similarly, couples therapy can be quite useful for relational and sexual issues, particularly when the executive is involved in a dual career marriage. In short, adjunctive family or couples therapy might complement work-focused individual psychotherapy with the executive.

Case Example: Psychotherapy of a Female Executive Ellie Costansa is a 32-year-old single white female who is the chief information officer for an up-and-coming biotechnology firm that develops cutting-edge pharmaceutical products. She was referred by the vice president of human resources because of anxiety and memory problems. The initial evaluation involved an assessment of her current and past levels of functioning, strengths, personality style, capacity to develop therapeutic relationships, readiness for treatment, and her presenting concerns: memory lapses and anxiety.

Although she indicated that "memory problems" were constant throughout her life, they had worsened in the past 2 months. She also reported engaging in fantasies and daydreaming, particularly when authority figures like her superior gave her tasks with deadlines. The fantasies were largely about men and sex. She indicated a single incident of fondling by her older brother when she was 10 years old of which she was frightened and confused and reportedly had only recently recalled. However, she remembered instances of "memory lapse" that occurred much earlier in her life and usually involved her parents. She had considerable difficulty establishing and maintaining intimate relationships with eligible men over the past 5 years. Prior to that, she indicated that she seldom dated even though she was quite attractive, interesting, and available. The four men she had become intensely attracted to were "womanizers" who flaunted the other women with whom they were involved in front of Costansa. Her response was to become "insanely jealous" of the women, and "promise to do anything" to hold onto the men. Occasional binge drinking—particularly on weekends—was also reported.

She denied prior psychotherapy and psychiatric treatment. Her family consists of both parents who are alive and well and still residing in the home where Costansa was reared. Costansa is the youngest of three siblings and the only female. Her mother is described as emotionally distant, demanding, and "unconcerned" with Costansa's feminine needs. Costansa seldom wore dresses, used make up, or adopted "feminine manners" until she started college. Her mother had a "breakdown" (presumably a depressive episode) after Costansa left home for college. Her father was described as caring and concerned but he made little effort to shield his daughter from her mother's demands. He apparently was grieved over his wife's expectation that Ellie should "dress and act like a boy" but did not voice his concern—at least publicly. Her brothers were described as "jocks" who were extremely competitive. Costansa described herself as a "tomboy" in grade school and "boy crazy with hormones" throughout high school.

An investigation of her current life functioning showed that she has a stable network of female friends, some difficulty relating to her parents, and an unsatisfying and distressing relationship with her current boyfriend. However, she described moderate impairment at work, particularly the confusing and distressing relationship with her female superior. She earned high evaluations for her job performance from subordinates and from her superior's boss, but not from her immediate superior. Her mental status exam was unremarkable. Based on these findings, her DSM-IV diagnosis was V62.2 occupational problem, anxiety disorder NOS, with histrionic, passive–aggressive and self-defeating traits.

Although Costansa was quite anxious at the beginning of the initial session, she was easily calmed and showed other indications that she could and probably would be able to form an effective collaborative therapeutic relationship. Because she had been quite successful in meeting personal goals she set (losing about 18 pounds and maintaining the weight loss for 3 years and giving up smoking a year earlier), she seemed to have sufficient capacity and readiness for change in therapy. A contract for five sessions was agreed upon and subsequently authorized by her insurance carrier. The focus of the sessions was to be reduction of her anxiety and memory loss. Accordingly, five weekly sessions were scheduled.

During the last of our planned formal sessions, therapeutic progress was reviewed and plans for follow-up sessions, should they be needed, were discussed. My progress note for the session stated: "This is last of 5 planned sessions. While the original referral was to evaluate and treat a dissociative disorder, an atypical anxiety disorder was diagnosed and individual psychotherapeutic treatment involving systemic, psychodynamic, and cognitive-behavioral strategies was employed. The client collaborated fully and effectively in the treatment process and several positive changes were noted. While she occasionally drank, she denied binging or intoxication."

Approximately 18 months after our last formal session, Costansa called to report that she was engaged to be married in 4 months and requested premarital counseling, indicating, "I don't want to repeat my parent's experience." Three conjoint sessions were scheduled. They focused on helping Costansa and her fiancé understand their families of origin and relational expectations and patterns. It was heartening to note that Costansa maintained all the therapeutic gains achieved during formal therapy, and it appeared that her fiancé would show her the respect, caring, and companionship she sought from a partner.

Concluding Note

Hopefully, these discussions and case studies clarify the similarities and differences among executive coaching, executive consultation, and executive psychotherapy. The indications for and the methods of executive consultation and executive psychotherapy are different from those of executive coaching.

Those who practice executive coaching need to know the theoretical and professional boundaries of all three specialties and know when to refer an individual for executive consultation or executive psychotherapy. One ongoing concern is the matter of those who are basically psychotherapy providers who offer to help executives under the guise of providing executive coaching or executive consultation, and actually provide psychotherapy instead. It is not uncommon for me to hear psychotherapists who admit to having no formal training or experience in executive coaching take pride in saying they started psychotherapy with an executive who approached them about coaching. This is misrepresentation that has, as noted in chapter 10, ethical ramifications.

References

Erikson, E. (1994) *Identity and the lifecycle.* New York: Norton.

Glickhauf-Hughes, C., Hughes, G., & Wells, M. (1986). A developmental approach to treating dual-career couples. *American Journal of Family Therapy, 14,* 254–263.

Gottman, J. (1994). *Why marriages succeed or fail.* New York: Fireside.

Greiff, B. & Munter, P. (1980). *Tradeoffs: Executive, family and organizational life.* New York: New American Library.

Kopp, R. (1995). *Metaphor therapy: Using client-generated metaphors in psychotherapy.* New York: Brunner/Mazel.

Levinson, H. (1991). Counseling with top management. *Consulting Psychology Bulletin, 43,* 10–15.

Lowman, R. (1993). *Counseling and psychotherapy of work dysfunctions.* Washington, D.C.: American Psychological Association.

Rice, D. (1979). *Dual-career marriage: Conflict and treatment.* New York: Free Press.

Sperry, L. (1996). Work-focused psychotherapy with executives. *Individual Psychology, 52,* 48–57.

Sperry, L. (2002). *Effective leadership: Strategies for maximizing executive productivity and health.* New York: Brunner-Routledge.

Sperry, L. (2003). *Handbook of diagnosis and treatment of the DSM-IV-TR personality disorders.* 2nd ed. New York: Brunner-Routledge.

Stoltz-Loike, M. (1992). *Dual-career couples: New perspectives in counseling.* Alexandria, VA: American Counseling Association Books.

Tobias, L. (1990). *Psychological consulting to management: A clinician's perspective.* New York: Brunner/Mazel.

10
The Practice of Executive Coaching

Increasing numbers of mental health professionals have already gravitated into coaching, and even more are expected to enter this exciting and challenging area of practice in the near future for the many reasons noted in chapter 1. Mental health professionals who aspire to practice executive coaching will parlay their clinical skills and apply them to various leadership and organizational challenges and aid executives and their work teams to become more productive and effective. Many will find this experience gratifying and rewarding as they discover how to apply their clinical sensitivity to the corporate world; others will find this experience frustrating as they discover the many ways in which coaching is different from clinical practice and the legal and ethical ambiguities that they must confront (Campbell, 2001).

This chapter addresses the process of becoming an executive coach. It describes various practice styles, common legal and ethical issues, and the process of transitioning into and building a coaching practice. While previous chapters focused on the knowledge and skills necessary to function as an effective coach, this chapter focuses on transitioning into an executive coaching practice.

Learning More about the Practice of Executive Coaching

The previous chapters have provided a rather detailed picture of the process and practice of executive coaching. Reading a book like this can be quite useful for acquiring background knowledge and assessment and intervention strategies, but it is no substitute for the requisite experience needed to actually practice such coaching. While a book cannot provide such experience, it can suggest specific strategies and tactics for gaining that experience. This section provides a few approaches that may be helpful for mental health professionals who are ready to become more involved with the practice of executive coaching.

Making the decision to expand your practice or switch fields is a weighty one that has financial and legal consequences and should not be undertaken lightly. An informed decision requires becoming as knowledgeable as you can about available resources and opportunities for preparing to do executive coaching. These include obtaining training and supervised experience and the specifics of making the transition from practicing therapy to practicing executive coaching. Following are seven suggestions.

1. Begin to acquire a working knowledge of executive life and the corporate world by perusing one of the many textbooks on organizational behavior or a recent edition of the classic text, *Leadership in Organizations* by Yukl. You might find it helpful to read some of the better best sellers about leadership and highly effective organizations. Some recent examples include *Hidden Value: How Great Companies Achieve Extraordinary Results with Ordinary People* by Reilly and Pfeffer; *Results-Based Leadership: How Leaders Build the Business and Improve the Bottom Line*, by Ulrich, Zenger, and Smallwood; *From Good to Great* by Collins; *First Break All the Rules: What the World's Greatest Managers Do Differently* by Buckingham and Coffman; and an older classic, *Leaders: The Strategies for Taking Charge* by Bennis and Nanus. Skim the daily *Wall Street Journal* or business section of your local paper; subscribe to one of the weekly business magazines like *Business Week* or *Nation's Business.* Carefully read the *Harvard Business Review, Fast Company*, and *Fortune.*
2. After getting acquainted and more comfortable with the corporate world and the lives of executives, you can start looking for books on executive coaching. There are many such books, perhaps too many, and that makes finding really good and useful ones difficult. I suggest that you start with books specifically directed at mental health professionals who are considering expanding their practices to executive coaching. Three good choices are *The New Private Practice: Therapist-Coaches Share Stories, Strategies and Advice* edited by Grodzki (2002), *Personal and Executive Coaching: The Complete Guide for Mental Health Professionals* by Auerbach (2001), and *Therapist as Life Coach: Transforming Your Practice* by Williams and Davis (2002). All three describe personal coaching and life coaching as well as executive coaching. The distinction between executive coaching and life or personal coaching is important in many respects, not the least of which relates to career planning. More specifically, it is much easier for individuals who are psychologically trained and have experience with psychotherapy to transition into personal coaching and life coaching than into executive coaching. Executive coaching requires a good working knowledge of organizational dynamics and some experience, hopefully supervised, in working with executives in corporate contexts.
3. Take formal course work, workshops, and seminars on coaching, organizations, organizational behavior, organizational diagnosis, etc., as indicated later in this chapter in a section titled "Thinking Like a Coach." While formal training in coaching is not yet common in schools of business or in graduate programs in organizational psychology, educational institutions almost certainly provide training in organizational

behavior and consulting is available. Attend courses and workshops on organizational consulting offered at annual meetings of professional organizations such as the American Psychological Association.

4. We suggest you learn about organizational behavior and leadership *before* securing training in coaching. Because of the complexities of organizational dynamics and corporate contexts, executive coaching is very different from life and personal coaching. Those looking to transition into executive coaching need to fully understand the differences before making informed decisions. Look into formal training and certification in coaching from a reputable seminar-based or on-line training institute. The International Coach Federation, is an advocacy organization promoting standards of training and practice as well as certification of coaches. It is a good source of information about the field and a clearinghouse of sorts. Be aware that some coach training programs unfortunately downplay the differences between executive coaching and life or personal coaching.
5. Seek out and talk with mental health professionals who practice executive coaching in your area. Find out how they became interested in the field, how they managed the transition or expanded the scopes of their practices, and what challenges they faced. Ask how they acquired their knowledge and experience bases. Inquire about their experience, formal supervision, and how they deal with consultation matters. Ask them about the professional coaching organizations and training programs and about practice opportunities in your community. Note which of these individuals you might potentially become affiliated with in the future.
6. Because executive coaching increasingly involves working with project teams and management teams, use every opportunity to study group dynamics and group processes in your clinical practice. Become acquainted with or more skilled in family therapy and group therapy. If you have little training or experience in these modalities during your graduate training, volunteer to co-lead therapy groups in your clinic or practice with an experienced group therapist. If functioning as a group co-therapist is not possible, supervision—particularly supervision of group and family therapy—can be gained by videotaping your sessions and meetings and reviewing your work weekly or biweekly with an experienced colleague.
7. Look for a mentor or supervisor to review your work. Regular contacts can be in person or by phone. This person need not have a background in mental health. Base your choice on the mentor's experience, reputation, and your perceived ease in working with him or her. A fee is typically involved for formal supervision as well as with formal consultations.

Three Practice Styles of Executive Coaching

Often you will read about or hear mental health professionals discuss expanding their practices. This usually means they are adding a new or different clientele to their existing clinical practices. For example, a mental health professional in an independent psychotherapy practice who typically works with relatively stable and successful self-paying adult professionals may open his or her practice to brief therapy sessions based on referrals from an employee assistance program (EAP) or from a capitated health plan. He or she might also consider consulting on mental health issues of older adolescents at a university counseling center or under contract with the Social Security Administration to perform stress disability evaluations. All these expanded services are within the realm of therapeutic practice.

Another possibility is moving outside the realm of therapeutic practice. Executive coaching—or executive consultation as noted in the previous chapter—is considered a type of practice outside the therapeutic realm. Expanding a practice to include coaching may be described as adopting a dual-focused practice or integrated practice style because it involves an addition to the core practice of therapy. Constricting a practice is the opposite of expanding it. In this section, *constricting* a practice refers to the single-focused practice style. Each of these practice styles is described here and compared to the "traditional" style of practice.

Single-Focused Practice

In this form, the mental health professional serves as a full-time executive coach. He or she no longer functions as therapist and uses only the executive coach title. In addition to relinquishing their mental health licensures, these individuals relinquish their previous identities as therapists and mental health professionals.

Dual-Focused Practice

This mental health professional establishes and maintains two parallel professional practices: one in executive coaching and the other in therapy. These individuals may opt to have two separate offices to reduce confusion among the people who seek their professional services and personnel who work for them. If they are unable to maintain two separate offices, it is absolutely essential to establish and maintain separate billing systems and use separate business cards, stationery, and forms in order to distinguish both practices. A dual-focused practice requires the professional to have the consummate ability to shift roles and effectively articulate the two distinct services. Of the three practice styles, this one presents the most potential for ethical and legal difficulties.

Integrated Practice

In this form of practice, the mental health professional utilizes his or her coaching skills as an additional skill set in order to provide an expanded set

TABLE 10.1 Factors Differentiating Three Different Practice Styles

Factor	Coach (Single-Focused)	Therapist (Traditional Practice)	Coach-Therapist (Dual-Focused and Integrated)
Mindset	Proactive, practical optimistic, strategic; nonpsychologically minded	Supportive, interpretive, serious, reparative; directly and intentionally psychologically minded	Facilitative, able to listen without interpretation, strategic; indirectly psychologically minded
Training	No prescribed background; no prescribed coaching training	Graduate degree and supervised experience in psychotherapy discipline	Prescribed graduate degree and supervised experience *plus* some coaching training or experience (no consensus on type or amount of training or experience)
Licensure require-ment	No	Yes	Yes for dual-focused and integrated practice styles
Liability	Limited	Specified	Complex for dual-focused practice style

of therapy services for a broader population. These practitioners can assist clients who have progressed beyond illness symptoms and returned to baseline functioning and want to continue growing and learning to achieve wellness and peak performance. Those who adopt this practice style are referred to as therapist coaches (Grodzki, 2002). Certain legal implications are associated with this practice style, particularly with regard to licensure and liability.

Traditional Practice

Traditional mental health professionals practice as they were trained—to provide counseling and psychotherapy services. Traditional practice is well regulated by licensure requirements and state and federal statutes and is governed by professional codes and standards of ethical practice.

Table 10.1 compares certain aspects of these four practice styles. Some of these factors are discussed later in this chapter.

Process of Transitioning into Executive Coaching

Becoming a coach involves a socialization process wherein the mental health professional begins to think in terms of organizational dynamics and act from that perspective. This is not to suggest that psychologically trained executive coaches must necessarily relinquish their identities as mental health professionals, but rather they extend their roles, knowledge, and skill repertoires to include both personal and organizational dynamics. In other words, an effective executive coach who is psychologically trained will retain his or her clinical acumen while at the same time exhibiting organizational acumen. The result is that he or she is sensitive to all dimensions when working with executives.

Thinking Like a Coach

In a sense, the worlds of the therapist and the coach are quite different. Learning to think like a coach means considering both organizational dynamics and roles and tasks in therapy and coaching. The coach's role can be viewed as a continuum ranging from directive to nondirective (Lippitt & Lippitt, 1978). In a directive role, the coach acts primarily as an expert whereas in nondirective roles, he or she is primarily a process coach (Schein, 1987) who facilitates the client's expertise.

It is not uncommon for nonpsychologically trained coaches to adopt the expert or technical advisor role (Gallessich, 1982). Here the client needs knowledge, advice, or service the coach can provide upon request. As noted in chapter 1, coaching and therapy have similarities; they also have differences.

A comparison clarifies the roles and task differences of a therapist and a coach. In most forms of therapy, the therapist functions more in a process-oriented and nondirective role. While the coach may assume a variety of roles such as expert, advocate, trainer, fact finder, and sounding board during the course of a single consultation, the therapist's range of roles tends to be limited. Nevis (1987) uses the metaphor of "working by sitting down" to describe the work of a therapist and "working by standing up" to describe a coach's work. The therapist tends to perform his or her service on his or her own turf where the usual supports and rules prevail. A coach usually works on a client's turf, usually without the usual supports.

Unlike the therapist, the coach usually must negotiate the "rules of the game." Therapy involves private events where the therapist has low public visibility. In coaching, public events prevail, they are evaluated by many people, and the coach may be highly visible. In therapy, the client's values are generally close to those of the therapist, while in coaching, the client who hires the coach may be the only one in his or her system who has values similar to the coach's.

In therapy, the client is seen as owning a problem, even if he or she is confused about its nature. It is often unclear in an organizational context what the problem is and who owns it. While therapy emphasizes intensive, interpersonal contacts between therapist and client, coaching usually involves contacts with various parts of a system, usually with less intense interpersonal content. Finally, Nevis (1987) notes that clients expand considerable effort in proving themselves to therapists, while in coaching clients expect coaches to prove themselves. In short, coaching tends to be a process that is less formal, less scheduled, and more complex due to the variety of agendas and the multiplicities of roles.

Becoming Accepted as a Coach

Coaching has made and will continue to make valuable contributions to the workplace. Its value is a function of its recognition and utilization. While some corporations have time-honored traditions of psychiatric involvement, others have not, largely because of a lack of awareness or misconceptions about the role of coaching in the workplace. For coaches to become involved in coaching, they must be viewed and accepted as valuable resources. Several strategies exist for becoming accepted and valued. Essentially, a coach must be sufficiently flexible and be willing to adapt his or her approach to a corporate environment that is considerably different from the customary therapist–client relationship.

First, the coach must recognize and accept that life in the executive suite differs from a therapy wherein the therapist can make decisions and exert considerable influence over the lives of those in treatment. In the executive suite, coaches are seldom involved in decision making and function primarily as advisors.

Next, coaches must be able to alter their traditional psychotherapeutic perspectives focusing on intrapsychic and interpersonal dynamics of a single client to an organizational perspective focusing on the nature of work, productivity and profit, and the multidimensional dynamics of executives, management teams, and divisions of the organization. A coach must be able to adapt to the customs and styles of a corporation related to personal attire, security procedures, or the system of reporting relationships. Honoring the corporation's structure and culture is expected. Similarly, the coach must be able to clearly define and accept his or her role as a coach rather than as a decision maker. This is particularly important when corporate decisions conflict with a coach's recommendation. Accepting such decisions and their outcomes while continuing to offer further recommendations may prove discomforting initially, but represents the reality of corporate life.

Finally, a coach must be prepared to negotiate difficult and complex ethical issues such as those related to informed consent and confidentiality. A subsequent section overviews these and other ethical issues a coach must regularly contend with. Only a coach who is willing and able to adapt to the unique challenge posed by the workplace, its power structure, culture, and customs is likely to be accepted in that role and experience some degree of fulfillment in a workplace function.

Unfortunately, little training in coaching in mental health training programs is available at the present time. This means that most coaches will acquire knowledge bases and skills through actual experience with little opportunity for formal training, reflection, or the kind of close supervision available in clinical training programs. Given the range of conceptual knowledge and skills that must be acquired, translated, extended, and unlearned in order for a coach to function effectively in a workplace (Sperry, 1993), it is not unreasonable to suggest that the coach seek opportunities to formally learn and reflect about the transition from therapist to coach.

There is a difference, as noted earlier, between knowledge and skill acquired through experience without time to reflect or be supervised and experience-based learning that has these components. Whether coaching involves ethical concerns about scope of practice is a consideration for an increasing number of professional organizations and state licensing boards. However, the issue of competence to practice remains a major professional issue.

When can a person claim he or she has sufficient training and expertise to practice executive coaching? The opinion of this writer is that minimal training in executive coaching involves a basic reading knowledge of the field and some supervised experience. There is always the possibility of arranging ongoing case supervision with an experienced coach. Ideally, this would involve meetings, but could also be conducted via regular telephone conferences if distance is a factor.

Acting Like a Coach

Just as a mental health professional thinks somewhat differently from an executive coach about formulating professional issues and concerns, a coach also acts differently. The usual expectations and demeanor for a clinical psychiatrist involve limiting contacts with clients to the office or clinical setting and acting in a fairly prescribed therapeutically detached manner. The executive coach, on the other hand, is expected to have extensive contact with his client in both professional and social contexts. Dinner at an executives' private club, tennis or golf during an exercise break at a seminar, or a weekend visit to a CEO's country home are not uncommon social contexts for executive coaches.

While a therapist may observe strict rules about personal disclosures to therapy clients, the issue is more complex in a corporate social setting. It is often inappropriate not to share some of one's nonprofessional self in such contexts, but doing so without constraint could ultimately be a disservice to a client. A coach must maintain awareness of his or her boundaries and the client's need for those boundaries to be maintained because the power of transference often leads a client to want more informal, social, and personal contact with a coach (Tobias, 1990).

An effective executive coach manifests certain attributes not usually expected of a clinical psychiatrist, particularly one in private practice. A coach should be able to mix comfortably with a wide variety of individuals from factory workers and clerk typists to CEOs. He or she should be able to tolerate back-to-back meetings and conferences, and be comfortable and effective in giving lectures and presentations. Executive coaching can involve both formal presentations and formal and informal teaching or lecturing. Also, coaches should be comfortable around executives who make quick decisions and whose styles tend to be active and pragmatic. This style contrasts with the more reflective, passive, and theoretical styles of many therapists. Finally, a coach should have the interest and capacity to quickly assess individuals, groups, and situations since he or she may not have the luxury of conducting one or more evaluation sessions as would be common in a therapy practice.

Common Legal and Ethical Issues Associated with Executive Coaching

Since coaching is a new and developing area of professional practice, growing pains are to be expected. Many of these growing pains are most obvious in circumstances involving legal and ethical considerations. As of this writing, no graduate degree programs in coaching exist. No state or national licensing is required of coaches and, as a result, no universally accepted ethical or practice standards are available.

Some confusion exists in the area of ethics and licensure for mental health professionals seeking to incorporate executive coaching into their practices. To remain compliant with legal statutes and limit the possibilities of liability and malpractice actions, mental health professionals must be aware of both the ethical standards imposed by their professions and under legal statutes in addition to ethical and legal considerations unique to the practice of executive coaching by mental health professionals. In this section, we briefly address issues of confidentiality, boundaries, liability and malpractice, informed consent, competency, and scope of practice. Interested readers are referred to a chapter titled "Ethics in Coaching" in Peltier's book (2001) for a fuller discussion of legal and ethical issues.

Confidentiality

The executive coach must explain verbally and in writing his or her intention to maintain confidentiality in the coaching relationship while clearly indicating that there are exceptions to confidentiality. The usual exception involves the executive's superior to whom an accounting of progress in coaching is commonly expected. Generally speaking, an executive coach can provide general feedback on the nature of progress, but cannot reveal specifics unless he or she is directed to do so or makes an agreement with the client to reveal specifics.

Mental health professionals who practice coaching are urged to clearly explain in writing that the concept of *privileged* communication that applies to therapy typically does not apply to coaching. This means that although a coach has an ethical responsibility to maintain the confidentiality of coaching conversations, such conversations are not legally privileged and thus the coach can be compelled to disclose them without a court order.

With regard to the matter of mandated reporting, executive coaches who hold mental health licensure are still required to meet state statutes regarding abuse and neglect, even if they are in their "coaching only" modes and do not consider their licensure to be operative when they obtained the information required to be reported. The fact that a license is currently held is all that matters regarding the mandate to report.

Practice Boundaries

The first significant issue to address is the decision about practice style. As noted earlier in this chapter, the basic practice question is whether executive coaching activity should be viewed as a part of an existing mental health practice or as a separate entity of practice. What problems could accompany either approach? For example, what are the ethical and legal issues for licensed counselors or therapists who wish to add coaching to their existing practices? Therapists should not attempt to coach and they should refuse requests for coaching from their therapy clients. It is best to keep therapy and coaching practices separate. The point is to establish boundaries between the two different practices by devising different business names, using different business cards, and maintaining separate accounts and billing for the two practices.

Liability and Malpractice

Another area at issue is malpractice liability and insurance coverage under existing insurance policies. What is a coach's liability? Counseling clients can sue. Can coaching clients also sue? Based on recent court rulings, a person who holds licensure in one of the mental health professions (counselor, psychologist, marriage and family therapist, or social worker) can be sued under that license. Liability concerns lessen when mental health professionals engage in executive coaching as long as they maintain separate coaching practices. Some indicate that you can further liability-proof your practice by referring to your coaching clientele as "coachees" rather than as patients or clients.

Informed Consent

We previously suggested that mental health professionals who plan to practice executive coaching carefully review printed materials related to their practices including business cards, informed consent forms, contracts, brochures and all other forms of advertising. While the matter of informed consent is important in mental health practice, it is absolutely critical for those who opt for the dual practice of coaching *and* therapy. In any materials related to their coaching practices, mental health professionals should state specifically that coaching is not psychotherapy, and that they practice in that area as coaches rather than as therapists. It is essential that a written contract for coaching be presented to, discussed with, and signed by each executive client. The contract should contain a description of services to be provided, the coach's credentials, and terms of payment and fee information. It should also specify procedural steps for clients to provide feedback and resolve problems.

Competency and Scope of Practice

Mental health professionals who decide to pursue an integrated practice style, that is, to use coaching skills as an additional skill set in their therapeutic practices, have the responsibility of meeting competency standards and staying within scope-of-practice boundaries or face legal and professional sanctions. This means that one cannot advertise or use executive coaching models or techniques without having the requisite training and experience. Before such coaching services are offered to clients, licensure and other statutes and ethical codes and standards require that licensed mental health professionals obtain specific training and achieve competency in coaching techniques, just as they must in all areas of mental health practice. Accordingly, if one has no training in performing 360-degree evaluations or using scaling methods and related solution-focused techniques, additional training would be required.

Toward a Code of Ethics for Coaching

The International Coach Federation has adopted a code of ethics for the practice of coaching. This code, while considerably shorter and less detailed than mental health professional ethical codes, is a beginning in an otherwise unregulated area of professional practice. It can be accessed at *www.coachfederation.org*. It may be some time before the field of coaching develops into a recognized profession with a consensus on minimal training and experience requirements and it is unlikely that a consensus on ethical standards will emerge soon. In the meantime, those who retain their identities, licensures, and professional memberships in national mental health organizations will be accountable for complying with applicable ethical standards and legal statutes.

In this section we have briefly addressed some of the more common ethical and legal considerations that arise at the nexus of executive coaching and mental health practice. However, all mental health professionals should seek guidance on these and other ethical and legal issues from their licensure boards, professional organizations, insurance carriers, and attorneys.

Marketing Your New Practice Option

In addition to thinking organizationally, you must consider how you can sell yourself and how your developing consultative skills can fill needs that exist in your community. The term *marketing* may sound somewhat alien to a therapist, but it essentially refers to understanding the needs of potential clients, evaluating and developing your capabilities to meet those needs, and utilizing a variety of methods to bring potential customers (clients) in contact with the supplier (or coach). It is essential to develop a marketing plan.

Your marketing plan should be well thought out. Biech's *The Business of Consulting* (1999) is a readable and useful resource for developing an effective marketing plan involving both direct and indirect strategies. Your marketing plan may specify that you spend 4 to 6 hours a week soliciting new business or clients. This may mean writing an occasional article or arranging to have your practice highlighted in a short article in the local business newspaper. It may mean offering to talk at meetings of business executives or speaking to local chapters of the Young Presidents' Organization (YPO). It may mean writing a manuscript for submission to a national business magazine or journal or your local business newspaper. If your work is published, you can give reprints to potential clients to further validate your expertise. Another strategy is developing a coaching group composed of other full- and part-time executive coaches who are available to provide services to larger corporations or provide specialty coaching, for example, coaching executives to handle media interviews. Having a marketing plan also means that you may narrow or expand the focus of your practice.

Being an Executive Coach

As this last chapter draws to an end, our thoughts turn philosophical. In mental health practice, the typical goal of treatment is to help symptomatic and troubled individuals whose functioning has become disordered to return to a relatively normal or adequate baseline level of functioning and well-being. By implication, clients expect therapists to function at relatively normal or adequate baseline levels of functioning and well-being. In executive coaching, however, the goal is typically to assist executives increase their levels of functioning and well-being *beyond* their baselines. It is not unreasonable then to expect that executive coaches would or should function beyond normal or adequate baselines.

In many ways, executive coaching is more than a job or even a career. It can become a way of life and a journey of personal and professional growth and development. Executive coaches encounter many of the same concerns of finding integrity and value in their work as their other professional colleagues, particularly the need to balance work with family and find and nurture their true selves. It is ironic that the same coaches who challenge and assist their executive clients to become optimally effective executives with good fits and balances in their lives may lead rather unbalanced lives.

An even weightier challenge for an executive coach is to move beyond "becoming" to actually "being" his or her true self. Writing about his personal and professional experience in moving from becoming to being, Bellman (1990) notes: "Being a consultant is more comfortable than playing one. Even if I play the consultant role well, it is still an act. It is still not me. When the costume and the script differ dramatically from what I am thinking, feeling, or being, I am clearly acting and not being myself. Coaching must provide me the opportunity to be myself often if it is to be fulfilling ... Successful work is more solid when it comes directly from me, rather than through a role" (p.19). I think the same can be said of coaching.

Concluding Comment

Throughout this book we have emphasized the distinction between life or personal coaching and executive coaching. While others seem to emphasize their similarities, we believe the main difference (recognition and capacity to deal with the organizational dynamics impacting executive performance and well-being) cannot be downplayed or dismissed. Like the proverbial elephant in the living room, the distinction is there and cannot be ignored because it poses potentially grave consequences!

Today, increasing numbers of mental health professionals are considering changing their practice styles to include executive coaching to one degree or another. As we noted in this chapter, the decision to become involved in the practice executive coaching is a weighty one that has many professional, legal, and ethical consequences. Becoming an effective executive coach requires some knowledge and experience of organizations and executives. It provides an unparalleled opportunity to work closely with some of the most intelligent, creative, and extraordinarily interesting individuals you may ever meet. What's more, helping these individuals optimize their performance and potential can prompt the executive coach's own personal and professional development in a way that the traditional practice of therapy seldom does.

References

Auerbach, J. (2001). *Personal and executive coaching: The complete guide for mental health professionals.* Ventura, CA: Executive College Press.

Biech, E. (1999). *The business of consulting: The basics and beyond.* San Francisco: Jossey-Bass.

Bellman, G. (1990). *The consultant's calling.* San Francisco: Jossey-Bass.

Bennis, W. & Nanus, B. (1985). *Leaders: The strategies for taking charge.* New York: Harper and Row.

Buckingham, M. & Coffman, C. (1999). *First break all the rules: What the world's greatest managers do differently.* New York: Simon and Schuster.

Campbell, J. (2001). Coaching: a new field for counselors? *Counseling and Human Development, 34,* 1–14.

Collins, J. (2001). *From good to great: Why some companies make the leap and others don't.* New York: HarperCollins.

Gallessich, J. (1982). *The profession and practice of consultation.* San Francisco: Jossey-Bass.

Grodzki, L. (Ed.). (2002). *The new private practice: Therapist–coaches share stories, strategies and advice.* New York: Norton.

Lippitt, G. & Lippitt, R. (1978). *The consulting process in action.* San Diego: University Associates.

Nevis, E. (1987). *Consulting in organizations: A gestalt approach.* Cleveland, OH: Gestalt Institute of Cleveland Press.

Peltier, B. (2001). *Psychology of coaching: Theory and application.* New York: Brunner-Routledge.

Reilly, C. & Pfeffer, J. (2000). *Hidden value: How great companies achieve extraordinary results with ordinary people.* Boston: Harvard Business School Press.

Schein, E. (1987). *Process consultation. Volume II: Lessons for managers and consultants.* Reading, MA: Addison Wesley.

Sperry, L. (1993). *Psychiatric consultation in the workplace.* Washington, D.C.: American Psychiatric Press.

Tobias, L. (1990). *Psychological consulting to management: A clinician's perspective.* New York: Brunner/Mazel.

Ulrich, D., Zenger, J., & Smallwood, N. (1999). *Results-based leadership: How leaders build the business and improve the bottom line.* Boston: Harvard Business School Press.

Williams, P. & Davis, D. (2002). *Therapist as life coach: Transforming your practice.* New York: Norton.

Yukl, G. (2001). *Leadership in organizations,* 5th ed. Englewood Cliffs, NJ: Prentice Hall.

Index

- Masterful Coaching (MARTIN)
- Handbook of Coaching (HUDSON)
- Life Coaching Handbook (MARTIN)
- Therapist as Life Coach (Williams & Davis)
- From Coach to Corporation (MARTIN)
- The Heart of Coaching (CRANE)
- The Portable Coach (LEONARD)